EDUCATIONAL RESEARCH UNDONE

KEY TEXT
REFERENCE

EDUCATIONAL RESEARCH UNDONE
THE POSTMODERN EMBRACE

Ian Stronach and **Maggie MacLure**

Open University Press
Buckingham · Philadelphia

Open University Press
Celtic Court
22 Ballmoor
Buckingham
MK18 1XW

and
1900 Frost Road, Suite 101
Bristol, PA 19007, USA

First Published 1997

A catalogue record of this book is available from the British Library

ISBN   0 335 19433 8 (pb)   0 335 19434 6 (hb)

Library of Congress Cataloging-in-Publication Data

Stronach Ian.
    Un/doing educational research: engagements with the postmodern/
Ian Stronach and Maggie MacLure.
        p.   cm.
    Includes bibliographical references and index.
    ISBN 0-335-19434-6 (hc) – ISBN 0-335-19433-8 (pbk.)
    1. Education – Research – Philosophy.   2. Postmodernism and education.
    3. Deconstruction.   I. MacLure, Maggie.   II. Title.
LB1028.S8455   1997
370.72–dc21   96-48465
                                                                                                              CIP

Typeset by Type Study, Scarborough, North Yorkshire
Printed in Great Britain by St Edmundsbury Press Ltd, Bury St Edmunds, Suffolk

I neither thought the Sun,
Nor Moon, nor Stars, nor People, <u>mine</u>,
Tho' they did round about me shine;
And therefore was I quite undone.

Traherne, 1637–1674

Contents

Acknowledgements

The authors would like to thank the following journals, publishers and co-writers for agreement, permission or encouragement to draw on, and develop, previously published work. These comprise: Jack in two boxes: a postmodern perspective on the transformation of persons into portraits, *Interchange* (Canada), 24(4), 1993 (M. MacLure and I. Stronach); Polemical notes on 'policy hysteria' and the rise of 'conformative' evaluation, *Evaluation and Research in Education*, 8(1/2), 1994 (I. Stronach and B. Morris); The future of evaluation: a retrospective, *Cambridge Journal of Education*, 25(3), 1995 (I. Stronach and H. Torrance); Mobilizing meaning, demobilizing critique? Dilemmas in the deconstruction of educational discourse, *Cultural Studies* (USA), 1, 1996 (I. Stronach and M. MacLure); Can the mothers of invention make virtue out of necessity? An optimistic deconstruction of research compromises in contract research and evaluation, *British Educational Research Journal*, 22(4), 1996 (I. Stronach, J. Allan and B. Morris); Fashioning postmodernism, finishing modernism: tales from the fitting room, *British Educational Research Journal*, 22(3), 1996 (I. Stronach); Telling transitions: boundary work in narratives of becoming an action researcher, *British Educational Research Journal*, 22(3), 1996 (M. MacLure); The mourning after the knight before (Pt 1), *Chreods*, 10, 1996, and *Cultural Studies*, 3, 1997 (I. Stronach). In addition, versions of Chapters 2, 3 and 5 first saw the light of day at American Educational Research Association conferences; 'Eccentric subject, impossible object' (San Francisco, 1995) (M. MacLure and I. Stronach); 'Deconstructing the notion of "policy hysteria": five readings, some unprincipled coupling and no happy endings' (New Orleans, 1994) (I. Stronach and M. MacLure); 'Jack in two boxes' (San Francisco, 1992) (M. MacLure and I. Stronach). Chapter 4 was co-authored with Liz Jones and began as a seminar contribution at the Manchester Metropolitan University (I. Stronach and L. Jones, 1995).

We'd also like to thank a number of people more personally. Singly and/or jointly, we wish to acknowledge particular debts to: Tony Brown, Andy Convery, Richard Davies, Ivor Goodson, David Hamilton, Dave Hustler, Liz Jones, Saville Kushner, Charles Sarland, Lou Smith, Kate Stronach, Laura Tickner, Harry Torrance, Barbara Walker and Rob Walker. Ian Stronach is also indebted to the critical support of former colleagues at Stirling, Brian Morris and especially Julie Allan, who was a critical first reader of some sections of the book, and to a former member of the Centre for Applied Research in Education (CARE), Tom Fox, who always wanted to go further, though probably not in this direction. Both authors owe a lasting debt of gratitude to members of CARE, especially John Elliott, Nigel Norris and Barry MacDonald, for maintaining an intellectual and conversational space where educational research is taken both seriously and playfully. In addition, we would like to thank students at CARE, at Stirling, and the Teaching and Learning Enquiry Group at The Manchester Metropolitan University for their critical contributions. Needless to say, they are not responsible for the shortcomings of what follows.

We are also grateful to the Master and Fellows of Trinity College, Cambridge, for permission to publish the photographs from the Munby Collection which are included in Chapter 3.

'. . . Opening . . .'

> Deconstruction, if such a thing exists, should open up.
>
> (Derrida, 1987: 261)

I

Think of the title at the top of this page as a *picture*. An opening, a beginning, that is also not one, because insinuated into something else. A crack? Or perhaps a violent opening such as a rupture or an incision. Perhaps a danger-ous opening in some ground or structure: an abyss. Or perhaps the opening marks the space where some of the dots in the line that stretches before and after it have been rubbed out. An erasure. Or it might even be blocking a space where something else might have emerged. Then again, maybe the opening is holding something together rather than dividing it. A suture or a scar, then. But perhaps the opening is not really a breach in the line at all, but just a kind of complication of it. A sort of fold or pocket. Now forget about the title being a picture, and think of it again as *writing*.

II

Introductions are always tricky. But for books that deal with postmodernism, poststructuralism or deconstruction, introductions are doomed to disappoint in two ways that are unavoidable, and quite distinct from the infinite number of more chancy ways that any introduction to any kind of book can dis-appoint. They disappoint if they try to state clearly what postmodernism etc. 'is', and to position readers securely within the framework of the book-to-come; and they disappoint if they resist doing that. If we could be architects of our own disappointment, we would choose the second. If this chapter is an opening, it is not intended to be an opening like the foyer of a well built struc-ture, or the departure lounge for an intellectual journey which will be neatly finished off in the conclusions. We wanted to open without making the kinds of promises that often accompany introductions – for instance, that in this space readers will find definitions of terms; or a digest of the book's contents; or a map of the route that the book's arguments will follow. Indeed we prefer to think of 'openings' – plural – to invite a reading of *all* the chapters in the book as a collection of reiterated openings on the question of how one could engage educational research and postmodernism, rather than as a coherent progression towards the closure of a definitive answer, either in the form of a dénouement or as a kind of precipitate of the book as a whole.

The successive chapters don't learn from their predecessors, or build on one another in an accumulative sense. They are not divided into theoretical followed by empirical sections, or into substantive and methodological issues. We have resisted the impulse to impose a smooth trajectory that would write them towards a final closure. We move rather promiscuously, for instance, in different chapters, between the three big words that haunt this text – poststructuralism, deconstruction and postmodernism – without providing watertight definitions, and without attaching ourselves unilaterally to one or other of them. We will return to that problem of defining postmodernism, poststructuralism and deconstruction below, and simply point out for the moment that if these terms did have something in common, it would be that each problematizes the very notion of definition. Each blocks the escape route to a place outside language, or into metalanguage, from which its essential characteristics could be named – as if there were an essence of postmodernism, or a reality of poststructuralism, or an identity of deconstruction, to which the words 'postmodernism', 'poststructuralism' and 'deconstruction' correspond.

If there is an organizing principle or unifying thread in the book, it would reside in a kind of persistent practicality: a desire to put deconstruction etc. to work, or at least to bring it to bear, in the mundane business of doing educational research; and to represent to other educational researchers and research students one view, or set of views, of what an engagement with postmodernism can look like. When we first began to get interested in the prospects of postmodernism for educational research, existing work within education which shared similar interests tended to be rather programmatic or promissory. There were relatively few 'worked examples'.[1] As practising educational researchers, we wanted to explore ways of putting our emerging, and shifting, understandings to work in the contexts of the specific research projects and enquiries on which we were engaged.

As a result, the topics that we address in the chapters to follow reflect the foci of the particular research projects in which we have been involved. These range over a number of educational domains: the vocational curriculum, action research, recent English and Scottish education policy, the changing contexts of externally sponsored research and evaluation, teachers' lives and careers. Similarly, the methodological preoccupations that recur throughout the book would be familiar topics in any textbook on qualitative research in education: for example, the nature and uses of portrayal; the validity of research instruments; policy and curriculum analysis; the potential of life history and biography as research methods; the status of first person journals and reflective writing; the relation between researcher and researched; the construction of identity.

However, now that we have grounded the book before it has taken off, in an appeal to the familiar and the practical, it is important to state that it is not intended as a methodological primer on how to do postmodernist educational research. While our aim was to offer some 'examples', the very idea of examples is problematic, since it implies the pre-existence of general principles which the examples merely execute. The chapters to follow might better be considered as examples in the sense of simulacra – copies without originals; or examples which have had to invent their originals in order to pose themselves *as* examples. To the extent that this book communicates a sense of what a postmodernist practice of educational research could be, we would expect, and hope, that its effects would be something like Geertz's description of understanding across cultures: 'more like grasping a proverb, catching an illusion, seeing a joke' (Geertz, 1983: 70).

We are not concerned with making deconstruction *familiar* – which would be the usual aim of a methods textbook. This would be to reduce it to the predictability of a technology or a useful set of analytic tools (see below, III). We are more interested in the potential of deconstruction to make educational research *un*familiar. We look for unfamiliar places from which to look 'back' at educational issues. So, for example, we open the question of autobiographical writing and personal 'voice' in educational research through a reading of the diaries of a Victorian maidservant (Chapter 3). We take Halloween as an occasion to explore the ways in which events get translated into curriculum (Chapter 4). Our approach is intentionally eccentric – off-centre – both in the sense of giving more attention than seems warranted to unlikely or marginal instances, and in the sense of trying to establish a certain *distance* from the core assumptions and canonical texts of educational research. Many of the chapters approach their educational topics via detours and departures from the site of education, into anthropology, literary theory, fiction, postcolonialism.

Derrida has argued the necessity of the 'departure' as part of the deconstructive act. Using another 'off-centre' term, he writes of deconstruction as 'exorbitant' – as an attempt to get out of the orbit, to 'reach the point of a certain exteriority' in relation to the space that is protected, closed off, by disciplinary institutions (Derrida, 1976: 162). It is only by attempting such a departure that it is possible to question the assumptions which a discipline or field takes to be self-evident. Derrida's own work over the years, which could be seen as a prolonged interrogation of philosophy, has been characterized by such departures into seemingly non-philosophical sites – such as literature, the visual arts, psychoanalysis, speech act theory – in order to gain 'the necessary free space from which to interrogate philosophy anew' (quoted in Wigley, 1993: 186). More recently, Derrida has written of the positive effects of the development of literary theory over the past thirty years or so, as just such an 'opening of a space' where it has been possible to ask of philosophy, linguistics and psychology, as well as literary study, questions which they have been unable to ask of themselves, from within their own disciplinary boundaries (Derrida, 1990: 82). Literary theory, in refusing to respect the disciplinary boundaries which separate the literary from the philosophical or the scientific, has produced a positive 'mutation which no area of the institutional discipline [concerned] had been able to perform' (*ibid.*: 83).

It is precisely the *im*purity of literary theory – its resistance to containment within its 'own' disciplinary field, and its infidelity to the fences erected around others – that, for Derrida, constitutes its power to question the axiomatics and foundational principles of disciplines. It is a creature, and creator, of miscegenations, transplants and parasitic relations among elements that like to think themselves separate and self-contained. So, in describing literary theory as 'the opening of a space' – a phrase that recurs in Derrida's work as a figure for deconstruction[2] – Derrida is intentionally naming a paradox: the 'space' that is opened is actually, or also, a dislocation, a *denial* of the spaces that insulate disciplines and fields from one another. We want to try, in this book, to practise this kind of infidelity to educational research, in the hope of opening up connections and questions that are hard to see from within the space that marks its usual territories.

If, as Lather (1996: 2) suggests, most methodological texts offer problem-solving advice, on the assumption that 'better' methodology will produce better accounts, clearer formulations of problems and more efficient solutions, this one hopes to be problem-generating. It could be located within an emerging body of educational, feminist, postcolonial and anthropological research which recognizes, and tries to work within, the necessary *failure* of methodology's hope for certainty, and its dream of finding an innocent language in which to represent, without exploiting or distorting, the voices and ways of knowing of its subaltern 'subjects'. Such work, which we will return to throughout the book, tries to practise what could be called a methodology, and a politics, of disappointment – not (or not just) as a state of resignation about the impossibility of escape from the 'crisis of representation', but as a strategic act of interruption of the methodological will to certainty and clarity of vision.

In these different domains, researchers have been reclaiming words which, from the viewpoint of 'Enlightenment' reason, would have no productive or generative force. Thus Lather (1994) recommends the thinking of educational research as a 'ruin', and feminist ethnography as the 'practice of failure', urging researchers to abandon the 'drive to innocent knowing' that, despite its good intentions and person-centred methods (indeed because of them), never succeeds in its mission to rescue the researched from epistemic violence (Lather, 1996: 2). Britzman (reported in Lather, 1996: 2) argues that educational research should 'become unintelligible to itself'. Postcolonial writers such as Trinh (1989), Spivak (1993) and Bhabha (1994) make similar calls to abandon (the myths of) representational clarity and total accessibility to the subject. Even when done in the name of emancipation and the renunciation of colonial authority, such writers argue, the demand that the 'other' should be rendered fully comprehensible in the terms – i.e. the language – of the researcher inevitably amounts to a reimposition of cultural authority in the guise of an innocent and universal 'plain' language (see also St Pierre, 1996). Haraway (1992) and Viswasnaran (1994) both argue, from within feminism, for 'trickster' methodologies which would render research radically uncertain about the success or failure of its own interventions, and thus disable the oscillation between unproductive guilt and uncritical optimism about truth and authenticity that has recurred in humanistic versions of feminism. Similar attempts to address the 'leaky' nature of roles such as 'anthropologist' and 'native' have led to a reworking of researcher identity in anthropology (Strathern, 1991: 1995).

For all these writers, disappointment – of certainty, clarity, illumination, generality – is both a choice and an inevitability; something to be both resigned and committed to. Confronting the binary oppositions that have traditionally promised the comforts of certainty to philosophical thinking – between reality and appearance, reason and superstition, causes and effects, meaning and language, identity and imposture, local and universal etc. – they choose *not* to choose between them, nor to work to transcend them, nor, importantly, to ignore them, but instead to complicate the relations *between* them. Or rather, to open up the complications that have been smoothed over by the 'violent hierarchies', as Derrida calls them, that such oppositions establish, in which one term gets the 'upper hand' by dismissing its opposite as secondary, improper, marginal, false or frivolous (Derrida, 1976: 41). Haraway's 'eccentric' figures of/for postmodernism, for example – jokers, shape-changers, tricksters and cyborgs (see Chapter 6 and '. . . The mourning . . .') – are intended to frustrate the legislative and discriminative programme of humanism. They disorganize the distinctions between truth and fiction, nature and culture, authenticity and pretence which produce the rational, autonomous, universal human subject – a procedure that always counts some people out of full membership in the act of trying to count everyone in. Although often interpreted as a total abandonment of the Enlightenment project of emancipation and the rational autonomy of the human subject, such work actually stands both outside and deeply within its logics, trying to force a space for new questions about identity, humanity, agency.

The kind of opening which such work attempts is that of the *rupture* – of interruption and disruption – in the (uncertain) hope that this will generate possibilities for things to happen that are closed off by the epistemologies of certainty. Johnson refers to deconstruction as 'opening up meaning as a question, as a non-given, as a *bafflement*' (Johnson, 1994: 39, our emphasis). These are uncanny openings, then. They rupture things, not in order to let the light pour in, but to make it harder to see clearly. They open spaces which turn out not to be spaces, but knots, complications, folds and partial connections. It is impossible even to tell for sure whether they are openings or closings, since they are also blocking manoeuvres, which would prevent escape routes to happy endings, such as a Hegelian transcendence of contradictions, or a politics of identity which is securely grounded in the possibility of self-realization, or a resting point where meanings can be securely identified behind words.[3] We try to practise this kind of strategic uncertainty throughout, and within this book. Our aim is to mobilize meaning (see Chapter 5) rather than to fix it.

We would argue for such practices of uncertainty on political as well as methodological grounds. This may seem an unwise move at a time when, in the UK at least, many researchers and educationalists feel that they have already suffered a serious loss of authority in the public sphere, and a discrediting of their voices in the policy arena, during a decade of the most thorough restructuring of the education system for fifty years (Dadds, 1992; Alexander *et al.*, 1993). Whether or not educational research ever did enjoy a time when its findings were used to inform policy in a more direct and constructive way, and its theories were more respected by politicians and reformers, the argument developed in this book runs counter to moves which would attempt to claim authority for educational research by 'getting our message across' more clearly to policy-makers, press and public; or by imposing a un-animity of voice; or by offering simple solutions to intractable problems such as 'school effectiveness'. At a time when the English educational research com-munity is contemplating setting up a charter to enhance its status by polic-ing its membership, standards and practices (Deem, 1996), and issuing admonitions to researchers who fail to 'write in a readily understood language' (Bassey, 1993: 21), it seems to us that a better strategy for educational research might be to see how far it can get by failing to deliver simple truths. Such calls to 'clarity' (see also Ranson, 1996) fail to address the possibility that some forms of plain speaking amount to a surrender to populist rhetorics about edu-cation.

III

The idea of 'opening' as the name of this introductory space appeals, then. Indeed, it could almost stand as a slogan for postmodernism, poststructural-ism or deconstruction. If there was a 'metanarrative' that united these terms in a common cause, it might be entitled 'The resistance to closure'. Whatever their differences, which we address without resolving below, each of these words is often understood to carry a promise to *open* in a productive or gen-erative sense – to force or find an opening in discourses, regimes, policies, theories or practices which tend to the inertia of closure and certainty. Opening in its various positive modalities inhabits work (including this one) that announces itself as postmodernist: opening as *transgression* or *breaching* of the boundaries that mark and protect the territories of elite or expert know-ledge; as the *taking apart* of master discourses and policy texts to expose their ruses of power/knowledge; as the release of *possibility* from the dead certain-ties of Enlightenment reason; as the *fracturing* of the malign dualisms of identity that marginalize the 'other' (white/black, researcher/researched, man/woman; straight/gay); as the opening up to *interrogation* of the insti-tutional discourses that define the limits of the speaking subject before she or he ever speaks.

That sense of the productive potential of postmodernism as 'opening' can be seen, for instance, in this statement, almost a manifesto of Opening:

> If postmodernism means putting the Word in its place ... if it means opening up to critical discourse the lines of enquiry which were formerly prohibited, of evidence which was previously inadmissable so that new and different questions can be asked and new and other voices can begin asking them; if it means the opening up of institutional and discursive spaces within which more fluid and plural social and sexual identities may develop; if it means the erosion of triangular formations of power and knowledge with the expert at the apex and the 'masses' at the base, if, in a word, it enhances our collective (and democratic) sense of possibility, then I for one am a postmodernist.
>
> (Hebdige, 1989: 226)

Hebdige's declaration is interesting, however, not only for its reiterated openings, but also for the 'ifs' to which each is attached – a liaison which makes
his manifesto simultaneously lion-hearted and faint-hearted. This ambivalent
commitment points to a pervasive anxiety that has accompanied the dissemination of postmodernism through the disciplines, that the openings it
promises are also dangerous openings, that might cut away the grounds of its
own arguments, or remove any platform for critical or political agency.

The openings offered by postmodernism, therefore, can be seen as both
desirable and dangerous. The most extreme expressions of its perceived
dangers come from those quarters, in every discipline which postmodernism
has entered, which would want to reject it utterly. As Butler (1992: 3) notes,
rejections often start from a 'fearful conditional' drawn from some presumed
proposition of postmodernism or deconstruction, such as 'if everything is a
text', or 'if the subject is dead', before going on to outline the 'dangerous consequences [that] will surely follow'. Or else, she argues, they take the form of
a 'paternalistic disdain toward that which is youthful or irrational'. De Man
argues that both kinds of responses are manifestations of the same anxiety:

> It is a recurrent strategy of any anxiety to defuse what it considers threat-
> ening by magnification or minimization, by attributing to it claims to
> power of which it is bound to fall short. If a cat is called a tiger it can
> easily be dismissed as a paper tiger; the question remains however why
> one was so scared of the cat in the first place. The same tactic works in
> reverse: calling the cat a mouse and then deriding it for its pretense to be
> mighty.
>
> (De Man, 1982: 5)

The cartoon in Figure 1 neatly encapsulates the tenor of such objections.

Chapter 1 documents many of these objections to postmodernism – which
would include nihilism, triviality, relativism, self-promotionalism, obscuran-
tism, sexism, frivolity, superficiality, apoliticism, fascism, fetishism and elitism
– and explores the question of what might count as a postmodernist engagement with these. For the moment, we want to signal that the anxiety which
has produced a multidisciplinary catalogue of accusations is also to be found
within postmodernist writings, in various more or less explicit forms.
Hebdige's hopeful conditionals (which are themselves the intertextual traces
of an argument with the 'fearful conditionals' mentioned above) are just one
manifestation of an inescapable dynamic of closure that is impelled to try to
rescue, even when it resists doing that, some ground or principle or platform
of action from the dangerous openings of postmodernism, poststructuralism
or deconstruction.

Educational engagements with postmodernism exhibit the same kind of
anxiety, and the same kinds of attempts to contain or circumscribe its dangers,
that have recurred in every other field or discipline that has courted its
embrace. On the one hand, poststructuralism and deconstruction offer valu-
able resources for exposing the complicity of language in the workings of
reality, society, power, knowledge and identity. Foucault's exposure of the
regulatory force of such innocent linguistic acts as naming and categorization,
and his identification of the 'technologies of power' exercised in discursive

From In These Times, *the weekly newspaper.*

Figure 1

practices such as examination and instruction, have given a powerful edge to critical and emancipatory theories. Deconstruction has been put to use in the critique of educational policy texts and public discourses (Stronach, 1992, 1994). On the other hand, educational writings display the same kinds of 'fearful conditionals', the same uncertainty as to whether it is a poison or a remedy, that are found in other fields.[4]

Perhaps the most obvious strategy of containment is to reduce poststructuralism or postmodernism to the status of some additional insights, tools or strategies that would allow educational researchers to critique the false truths

of institutional discourses without preventing them from going about whatever is their usual disciplinary or methodological business. Paechter and
Weiner (1996: 268), for instance, recommend them as 'useful tools for analysis'. Hargreaves (1994: 39–40) advises against postmodernism as a 'theoretical
position', on the grounds of its supposed relativism, but allows that there are
'methodological advantages in adopting aspects of a postmodern stance *for a
while* during one's research, as an intellectual strategy.' A related move is to
appeal to some broader sociopolitical or historical frame that would somehow
contain, without denying the validity or multiplicity of voices, identities,
meanings and narratives opened up by postmodernism. Some writers name
an order of precedence of allegiances – for example, feminist first, postmodernist second – which would again subordinate postmodernism to the
sovereignty of a ruling paradigm or theory.[5] Another strategy of containment
is to make ethical discriminations that seek to separate the 'good' from the
'bad' postmodernism, or to extract the best and discard the rest: the democratic, progressive, critical or emancipatory from the reactionary, fascistic,
acquiescent, or nihilistic; the feminist from the patriarchal; the serious from
the frivolous (see Lather, 1991; and Chapter 8). Such is the anxiety about
certain versions of postmodernism that allegiances are occasionally formulated in advance of, and indeed stated as proscriptions against, even reading
certain dangerous texts. Paechter and Weiner (1996: 271), for instance, report
a seminar attended by UK educational researchers at which some participants
'expressed their unwillingness to read known sexist writing, however apparently important to the paradigm.'[6]

All of these engagements (a word about which we will have more to say
shortly) with postmodernism attempt to use its productive possibilities for
opening, while fending off its dangerous ones – the ones which might open
(on to) the abyss. If we are to maintain the kind of uncertainty that we committed ourselves to in II above, we will need to court the dangers as well as
the benefits of opening; to resist looking for the escape routes to the ground
of certainty. But it is inevitable that we will repeat something of those 'rescue'
gestures, born of the desire for closure that we have enumerated here as if they
were the correctable errors of others. There will always be appeals to some tacit
ground of value, politics or effectivity. For example, we will find ourselves elevating 'transgression' to the status of a 'heroic myth' (Mann, 1995: 9) of
emancipation in Chapter 5; and on the other hand deploying it as a technique
for subverting the culture of research exchanges via questionnaire and formative reporting (Chapter 6). We are always at risk of presenting our 'postmodern' reading of any issue as a 'better' one (even in the sense of a better
failure) than whatever interpretation we have placed on the 'other' side of the
argument. We will make discriminations, while denying them, between (for
us) the good or proper versions of postmodernism and the supposedly er-
roneous ones. Indeed, we already have. We try in many of the chapters to
address this dynamic, trying to look back on our own texts in order to deconstruct *their* pretexts (see especially Chapters 5 and 8). Chapter 8 and especially
'Mourning' are extended explorations of the (im)possibilities of the self-
deconstructing text – the latter so self-conscious about avoiding closure that
its 'real' title is withheld until somewhere around its middle.

But for all this, the most concealed closures that the book, and this chapter, effects will have been invisible to us, and necessarily so. As Spivak reminds us, the thought of a final escape from the 'closure' of metaphysics is a fantasy:

> We must know that we are within the clôture [closure] of metaphysics even as we attempt to undo it. It would be an historicist mistake to represent this 'closure' of metaphysics as simply the temporal finishing-point of metaphysics. It is also the metaphysical desire to make the end coincide with the means, create an *en*closure, make the definition coincide with the defined . . . within the logic of identity to balance the equation, close the circle. Our language reflects this desire. And so it is from within this language that we must attempt an 'opening'.
>
> (Spivak, 1976: xx)

IV

What kind of engagement of educational research and postmodernism do we envisage? Engagement is a doubled kind of opening – it can be a commencement of war, or an announcement of marriage. The engagements or embraces of educational research and postmodernism that we referred to in III above fall into one or other of these definitions. We want to resist choosing one rather than the other. We do not want to stage a war between the two, in which postmodernism will triumph over the supposedly 'modernist' delusions of educational research; or, alternatively, in which educational research will get the upper hand over postmodernism, reducing it to the status of an analytic tool or an occasional pursuit.

The adoption of a warlike posture that would try to defend the ground of postmodernism either against or on behalf of a critical, marxist, liberal or feminist 'opposition', or internally divide the field into the good and the bad postmodernisms in order to wage a similar contest, is a problematic move within deconstruction. Indeed, it is the pre-emptive gesture of 'closure' par excellence, since it repeats precisely the binary oppositions that deconstruction seeks to de-stabilize and dis-locate, as we argued in our second 'opening' above. But if we want to avoid a warlike engagement, so too do we want to avoid the aggressive frivolity of a refusal to engage at all with the objections to postmodernism. Soper sketches this caricature of the frozen tableau of banal antagonism between the left-political metaphysicians of modernism and the ludic jesters of postmodernism:

> on the one side [stand] the dogged metaphysicians, a fierce and burly crew, stalwartly defending various bedrocks and foundations by means of an assortment of trusty but clankingly mechanical concepts such as 'class', 'materialism', 'humanism', 'literary merit', 'transcendence' and so forth. Obsolete as these weapons are, they have the distinct advantage that in all the dust thrown up by their being flailed around, their wielders do not realize how seldom they connect with their opponents. On the other side stands the opposition, the feline ironists and revellers in relativism, dancing lightheartedly on the waters of *différance*, deflecting all

foundationalist blows with an adroitly directed ludic laser beam. Masters of situationist strategy, they sidestep the heavy military engagement by refusing to do anything but play.

(Soper, 1991: 122)

So, while we want to avoid the heroics of epistemological triumph, we also want to avoid the inverted heroics of renunciation and celebratory self-immolation, in which the denial of textual authority is always liable, as Connor (1992: 147) notes, to re-present itself as that characteristically modernist narrative of 'a heroically bracing encounter of the self with extremity'. Both forms of heroics are instances of the 'epistemology of fission' (Denüvo, 1992: 47) that preserve the agonistic stance of classic philosophical opposition, and therefore close off any real possibility of intervening in the field. Equally, however, we do not want to propose an epistemology of fusion, which would defuse the anxieties of postmodernism in a narrative of resolution and reconciliation.

What kind of engagement will the book enact? What would an engagement look like that was not either a commencement of battle or an announcement of marriage, and which did not carry within it the prospect of its own closure, whether of victory or consummation? We propose to stick with the verb in its intransitive form, and simply to 'engage'. To take part, without knowing in advance how things will turn out, or what have been the terms on which the engagement has been struck, or even who stands on what ground. Derrida (1994: 89) suggests that such an engaging, which affirms or promises (and 'promise' is one of the definitions given in the dictionary for 'engage') without knowing exactly what it commits itself to, is a necessary starting point for deconstruction – 'a certain emancipatory and messianic affirmation'.

The attempt to discriminate among theories and positions, to provide definitions and mark off territories prior to engagement, is bound to disappoint, first, because it so blatantly oversimplifies what Derrida (1990) calls the 'taxonomic disorder' of contemporary theory, in which paradigms and positions compete in a kind of feeding frenzy, each trying to consume and encompass the knowledge claims of competitors, while trying to keep themselves free of the contamination that comes from eating something that doesn't agree with you. Even the most cursory reading will show that there is an uncontrollable profusion of meanings associated with the words postmodernism, deconstruction and poststructuralism, rather than any kind of consensus over what each means and how it differs, or doesn't, from the others (see Chapter 1).

The space opened out and fought over by the words postmodernism, poststructuralism or deconstruction is therefore an unstable and very unclearly bounded territory, crossed and divided in turn by other theories and discourses, which similarly coalesce and fragment in uneasy alliances and disputes over territory – feminism, psychoanalysis, marxism, postcolonialism, cultural studies. So, to return to our theme of the disappointments of certainty, texts that open with definitions, frames and positioning statements disappoint by pre-emptively closing off large areas of the space in which they might play. The problem is not just that the space is too big, and the competing theoretical and paradigmatic options too different from one another to be susceptible to the carving out of one from the herd and elevating it to the status of the example that stands for the whole (Butler, 1992). The space is in principle un-closable, and un-boundable, because each time it opens itself up, it already carries 'inside' itself the contaminations of whatever it also ejects on to the other side of its definitional frame. The relation among the competing theories and paradigms never finally resolves itself, says Derrida, into the stable hierarchy of a biological table where each species is distinct from, and therefore secure in its relationship to (or dominion over), all the others.

We do not want to try to arbitrate among postmodernism, poststructuralism and deconstruction, then – though the refusal to do so is in some ways no less problematic. To treat them as interchangeable would be to suggest that they all 'amount' to the same thing, as if they were all manifestations of some underlying principle, or available to be 'lifted up', in a Hegelian transcendental move, to a higher plane where their contradictions would be resolved. On the contrary, in a parasitic relationship, things *both* differ and are connected and contaminated with/by one another.

We will maintain our resistance (or try to – see Chapters 5 and 8, where we note our failure), similarly, to defining educational research, and discriminating between postmodernist and modernist versions. From within this space of partial connections, there is no absolute 'free space', no 'point of exteriority' (see II above) on which to stand in order to tell the difference and assign positions. Whatever space this book opens up, it is also located *within* a pre-existing, highly complicated space. It cannot be a question of stepping outside; but rather an operation of 'spacing', which forces a space within. Our last injunction, therefore, would be to embrace the book, not as a space, but as a fold. We take our lead from this description:

> Rather than stepping outside, breaking the law by breaking the line, [deconstruction] is a question of 'opening' a space within the old one, where opening is not understood as a new space that can be occupied, but as an opening in the very idea of space, a loophole that is precisely not a hole within its own borders, but a kind of pocket secreted within the old sense of border.
>
> (Wigley, 1993: 195)

Notes

1 This is less true today, especially of work emanating from North America and Australia. Patti Lather, one of the pioneers of work in this area, was able to announce the contributors to a session at the 1996 Annual Meeting of the American Educational Research Association as exponents of a 'second wave' of poststructuralist research. In the UK, by contrast, a special issue of the *British Educational Research Journal* on postmodernism and poststructuralism, published in the summer of 1996, announced that these had 'finally hit education' (Paechter and Weiner, 1996: 267). We don't want to suggest that any of these periodizing statements, however, should be taken as definitive. The 'untimeliness' of these phenomena – as always just around the corner/already passé/just a passing phase/an all-too-present orthodoxy – is one of their 'uncanny' aspects.

2 See, for instance, Derrida (1981), where deconstruction is described as the 'opening of a space through a principle of dislocation'.

3 See, for example, Derrida's (1981: 40) account of the significance of '*différance*', as that which 'blocks every relationship to theology' (that is, to 'transcendental signifieds' such as truth, Being, God). *Différance* is both the operation of *difference* between signifiers that produces meaning, and the structure of indefinite *deferral* which prevents any signifier from finally connecting with a signified.

4 Kemmis (1992: 31), for instance, wonders whether, 'the cure of some postmodernisms is not more deadly than the twin diseases of modernism and postmodernity'. See also MacLure (1994, 1995) for a review of engagements between educational research and postmodernism.

5 See, for example, Luke and Gore (1992: 5): 'Through the naming of our feminism as primary . . . we adamantly resist the hidden agenda of erasure that drives much of current postmodernist theory and analysis.'

6 Thus providing an exception to De Man's (1982: 15) observation that 'criticism by hearsay is only rarely held up as exemplary'. This is perhaps fitting, since de Man is one of the writers who would probably figure on a list of banned books, because of anti-semitic sentiments in his early writing – see Johnson (1994) for a discussion (and deconstruction) of the controversy surrounding De Man's writing. The participants in the seminar reported above, however, were more concerned, as researchers working within feminist perspectives, with Baudrillard, as an instance of the 'undoubted sexist and offensive nature of some post-modern writing' (Paechter and Weiner, 1996: 270).

1

Fashioning postmodernism, finishing modernism: tales from the fitting room

The avant-garde movement, deconstruction, which has for some seasons been quietly subverting established notions of style, reached its logical conclusion in Paris this week. No longer the cutting edge of fashion but the very cut itself, deconstruction is now influencing even mainstream designers. The tailored suit, the mainstay of fashion for a decade, is as dead as a dodo. In its place stands a long, sinuous silhouette of unfinished lines and interleaved layers of featherweight fabric.
(Sally Brampton, *The Guardian*, 14 October 1993)

A central purpose of this chapter is to examine the extent to which the above fashion note could lay mischievous claim to be an allegory for the accommodation of research discourses with postmodernism. Are there those among us who have begun to burn their suits for 'random folds' of 'sheer nylon mesh' (surely a palimpsest?), wear their seams on the outside and sport the simulated recyclings of deconstruction's 'distressed charm', as Brampton puts it. And if there are, should we greet their efforts with contempt, hilarity or acclaim?

Before we turn to an examination of the nature of any such bargains struck between education and postmodernism, it is necessary to locate research and theory in relation to more general debates between modernism and post-modernism. In the increasingly overlapping fields of philosophy, literary theory and social analysis, there has been more than a decade of controversy between the likes of Gadamer, Habermas, Rorty, Foucault and Derrida, as well as more derivative appropriations within individual disciplines, such as anthropology and sociology, and the possibly more illuminating (from the point of view of educational theory) hybrid fields of feminism and post-coloniality, as '... Opening ...' indicated. The latter are perhaps more interesting because, as we've seen, such hybrids often try to reconcile elements of standpoint epistemology, enlightenment critique and deconstruction in ways that are reminiscent of current reworkings of educational 'critical theory' (Giroux, 1988; McLaren, 1993a). In this regard, however, we need to echo deNuvo's somewhat lofty criticism of the laggardly and incomplete nature of the uptake of postmodernist themes in anthropology (for example, in *Writing*

Culture, Clifford and Marcus's watershed publication in 1986; Denüvo, 1992), noting all the while that at least anthropology was gripped by these issues from 1984 (Moore, 1994), whereas educational research could not be said to be more than lightly touched by postmodernism before 1990.[1] There are important issues of translation, resistance and rescue involved in these processes of dissemination/contamination.

The first move in this chapter, however, will be to offer a reading of various alleged boundaries between these 'isms', and to trace the sorts of ways in which those 'boundaries' (if that is the metaphor, and we will shortly argue that it is not) are established and challenged.[2] The intention will be to build a strong case against the 'fit' of the boundary metaphor in relation to modernism/postmodernism and then to consider consequences and alternatives.

Can the boundary between modernism and postmodernism be defended?

Before we clarify some of the confusions that invest that boundary, it might be helpful to create some of them by looking at a number of paradoxes and contradictions, to treat boundary as a question of dissension rather than definition.

The first and most common complaint is that the language of postmodernism is deemed esoteric – concepts like postmodernism itself, deconstruction, essentialism, pastiche, intertextuality, simulacrum, self-referentiality, metanarratives, the flux of meaning and performativity are held to be hopelessly remote from the real world. Thus, for example, a petulant leader in the *Times Higher Education Supplement* (THES), appropriately entitled 'Back to basics in sociology': 'Maybe it is time for the theoretical meanderings and self-indulgent conceits of post-modernist readings to be put aside; we are *not* at the end of the Enlightenment project ... Future Sir Keith Josephs [former UK education minister emblematic of the New Right] are unlikely to be impressed by deconstructionist [*sic*] strategies' (THES, 9 November 1993).

Likewise many academic critics: postmodernism 'has shifted from awkward neologism to derelict cliché without ever attaining to the dignity of a concept' (Hassan, in Seed, 1993: 93). Deconstruction is 'theorrhea' (Verges, 1992: 393); 'it is the divine underside, the Luciferian penumbra, the goat with a thousand faces' (Rasché, 1986: 126). Its anti-foundationalist ideas are the province of the 'zombie philosophers' (Maker, 1992), and so on. The impression is clear: postmodernist ideas are remote from everyday contemporary life. They belong to the monstrous realms of that great enemy of British or 'Anglo-Saxon' political and professional life – 'theory' – and stand in contrast to the real world of business-like practice and common sense. As in most responses to the 'intellectual' in Britain, the old and favoured dichotomy of practical/jargon is used to police the boundary.

Yet the contemporary worlds of architecture, literature, fashion, cinema, business management, market research and advertising are shot through with concepts drawn from postmodernism, or at least its near relative poststructuralism. It is easy to demonstrate that postmodernism exists in practice, whether or not it ought to in theory.

There seem to be a number of ways in which postmodernism turns up in the everyday world: as an action theory (e.g. management prescription, architectural recipe), as a theory of action (e.g. social commentary, critique) and as a kind of theory-as-action, linked to a culture of quotation in which 'it works specifically to promote the audience's theorizing through a visual discourse' (Linstead and Grafton-Small, 1990: 417). In this last instance, postmodernism is a kind of thinking necessary for decoding messages in advertising and literature; for example, in relation to their intertextual reference or their irony.

By way of brief illustration, elements of postmodernist thinking turn up in improbably practical and applied fields, such as management literature. Tom Peters envisages a world of flux, of near anarchy and collapsed metanarratives, wherein the new task of management is to manage disorder and instability (Peters, 1993). Commenting on how management theory has 'gone postmodern', the THES reported that 'today's best selling advocate comes across like a Prozacked Nietzschean who has been locked up in a New Age bookstore all weekend' (Aspden, 1994). Even if the content of that message is nonsense, look at the postmodernist style of writing – a pastiche of character talk from Tom Wolfe's *Bonfire of the Vanities*. And of course postmodernism also builds buildings (Lloyds Building in London; Jamieson, 1988; Jencks, 1991), structures films and books (*Blue Velvet*, Denzin, 1991; Calvino; Borges), and assists advertising and market research (Davidson, 1992). We might conclude that its language may be esoteric but it is certainly in business:

- *Simulacrum.* The Lynn Franks agency recently launched a Sega product through the medium of a spoof advertisement for a new brand of cat food. 'The simulacrum was perfect: press release, publicity shots and television campaign; then they disrupted their own TV adverts with supposed broadcasts from a pirate TV station, pulling off a brilliant media intervention' (Bracewell, in *The Guardian*, 11 November 1994).
- *Performativity.* In a sad little piece of modernist nostalgia by *The Guardian*'s Melanie Phillips, she berated the Research Director of Synergy Brand Values for abandoning the canons of validity in social science. The director was unmoved, echoing – knowingly or not – the views of Lyotard: 'We don't want to prove whether our research is right or wrong. If the stuff doesn't work for our clients, that's the bottom line for us' (*Observer*, 12 September 1994).
- *Self-referentiality.* Mark Edwards's Adwatch column explained the 'ad-literacy' of UK audiences, and their ability to pick up the ways in which advertisements refer ironically to themselves and to each other (*The Guardian*, 25 October 1994). Linstead and Grafton-Small (1990) deconstruct such intertextual references in advertising, showing the widespread nature of symbolic borrowing and commenting.
- *Essentialism.* Barthes, Baudrillard and Eco are cited in the *International Journal of Marketing Research* variously to stress the indexicality of objects, and the notion that what is consumed is the 'idea of relation' between consumer's self as constructed by the product as symbol (Noth, 1988). No room

here for essentialist (i.e. modernist) views of the self: 'Divorced from biography, personal identity becomes located in a perpetual future of consumption self-images' (Goldman, 1987: 712).

Such advertising foregrounds lifestyle rather than product, and appeals to a consumerist sense of self-reference (cf. Baudrillard's *America* (1989: 34) and the 'narcissist refraction'). Of course, it is true that each of these features of contemporary communication cannot unequivocally be said to be 'postmodern', but as a constellation of associated semiotic beliefs and practices they do offer a plausible hypothesis for a 'postmodern culture'.

Even such a brief review of everday manifestations of postmodernism should illuminate the dilemma. On the one hand 'postmodernism' is seen as outrageous, exotic, fanciful; on the other hand, it is everyday, experienced, intimate. In Geertzian terms, postmodernism, seen through the prism of the notion of boundary, is an 'experience-far' object (Geertz, 1983: 59). It is the Other of modernism, but Other in the sense used by Rosaldo – the barbarian, the outcast, the unruly other (Rosaldo, in Apter, 1964): 'Like ethnocentric and racist perspectives on "the other", the colonists' formula – as symbolically potent as it was distorted – was to take a characteristic regarded as morally ideal in their own society and verbally endow the Ilongots with its opposite' (*ibid.*: 254).

Bhabha considers that such conceptualizations of the 'Other' and of difference tend towards a 'strategy of containment where the Other text is forever the exegetical horizon of difference, never the active agent of articulation' (Bhabha, 1994: 31). We later employ that distinction in our deconstruction of the modernism/postmodernism relation, but meanwhile restrict ourselves to noting that it is not surprising that postmodernism as the Other of modernism (in the sense articulated by Rosaldo rather than Bhabha) should provoke a general academic hostility in terms of references to 'zombies', 'goats', 'castration' and 'monsters'. Objects in the distance are always a matter of cultural suspicion – and as Haraway reminds us, 'monsters have always defined the limits of community in Western imagination' (Haraway, 1990: 222). But what ought to surprise us more is how 'experience-near' these objects seem through current communication technologies such as advertising, marketing and human resource development (as opposed to that more pedagogically antiquated communication industry, education). How can they be both esoteric and the 'inner logic' of late capitalism (Jamieson, 1983), or the common sense of the 'new global economic order' (Fox-Genovese, 1993: 253)? And where does that leave the notion of boundary? On the far horizon, or in the heart of late capitalism?

Even greater confusion descends if we retain the popular cartographic metaphors of boundary, border, frontier etc. and attach to it a sense of membership. Who are the postmodernists? More contradictions appear. A central interpretive strategy of postmodernism is deconstruction – as genus is to species, argues Verges (1992: 391). Yet the progenitor of deconstruction, Derrida, declines the label: he is for a 'new International' and will have nothing to do with the death of Enlightenment's Project: 'Nothing seems to me less out-dated than the classic emancipatory ideal' (Derrida, 1992: 28; see also Derrida, 1994a: 37). Nor is the case of Foucault more straightforward. Labelled first as a structuralist, and then as a poststructuralist after *Discipline and Punish*, in the past few years he has experienced a strange post-mortem redefinition – resurrected as a postmodern (almost as if it were a misprint). Even a hermeneuticist like Gadamer makes the occasional, presumably bemused, excursion into the postmodern fold (Risser, 1989).

Nor are the various ideological and philosophical groupings of post-modernists and others easy to understand. Rée, for example, takes Foucault, Derrida, Deleuze and Lacan to be 'neostructuralists' rather than post-modernists, whom he sees as Hegelian corrupters of the latter group's insights (Reé, 1990). Verges (1992) instead lumps postmodernists, poststructuralists and deconstructionists into the same category, while Calhoun (1993: 80) arranges the first two of these chronologically, claiming that poststructural-ism is 'a tributary into the postmodernist current'. Philipse, on the other hand, argues that the core of postmodern philosophy comprises Rorty, Heidegger, Quine and Wittgenstein, and seeks to bind them together in various forms of shared epistemological scepticisms. Yet he goes on to argue a position that other postmodernists would find deeply oxymoronic – advo-cating the development of a 'postmodern metaphysics' (Philipse, 1994: 42). Haraway goes a step beyond postmodernism, arguing that there is a femin-ist 'dialectical shift' from empiricism and postmodernism to 'situated know-ledge' (cited in Sassower, 1993: 437). Meanwhile, Huyssen prefers to think in terms of a postmodernism that is the 'revenant' of modernism in the guise of theory (Huyssen, 1990: 160): 'a postmodernism that works itself out not as a rejection of modernism, but rather as a retrospective reading which, in some cases, is fully aware of modernism's limitations and failed political ambitions' (*ibid*.:162).

We may safely conclude that there is no shortage of boundaries, or of boundary disputes, between modernism and postmodernism. If we were to succumb to the 'mapping' metaphor implicit in the task of this chapter, we would certainly need to locate postmodernism in some disputed enclave of a metaphorical Balkans, while refusing to locate ourselves behind and in front of an epistemological camera mysteriously separate from that cauldron of al-legiances.

The political readings given to these labels are equally eclectic. In Haber-mas's view, Derrida and Foucault are 'young conservatives' (cited by Huyssen, 1990: 253), and critical theorists in general tend to opt for this neoconserva-tive reading of postmodernism – 'a counter-tyranny of invidious leniency' (Connolly, 1987, cited in McCarthy, 1991: 79). Meanwhile, Rorty tends to be pigeon-holed as a liberal puralist, or a 'cavalier elitist' (Haber, 1994: 45). Even where critics have some sympathies with postmodernism they tend to stress the need to go 'beyond' postmodernism towards some notion of a recovered 'oppositional politics' (Haber, 1994: 1). Yet such 'liberal recovery' pigeon-holing is not inevitable. Others have placed the postmodern critique to the left of Marxism, with Shurmann taking an anarchic position in relation to postmodernism, seeing the shift as being 'from a principial economy to an anarchic economy of presence' (Shurmann, 1990: 45).

Doing boundarywork

In general – and this has to be a rather sweeping generalization – there seem to be four broad ways in which the boundary is envisaged. The first takes it to be a polarity, as we have seen, a paradigm-like distinction.[3] For example, Benhabib (1992: 208): 'the paradigm of language has replaced the paradigm of consciousness.' From this dichotomizing position, postmodernism may either be applauded or reviled, as a Rosaldo-like Other. A second group (e.g. Liszka, 1983; Flax, 1990; Shurmann, 1990) prefers a tripartite division, emphasizing the liminality of the transition, but holding on to some version of a stage theory of that transition, a line that can be traced in anthropological thinking from van Gennep through to Victor Turner. A third group also stresses liminality, but from a more deconstructive position, asserting the permanent 'in-between-ness' of liminality (e.g. Spivak, 1988; Bhabha, 1994), a view that this book will favour. The fourth group looks to resolve the contradictions between modernism and postmodernism (e.g. Fraser and Nicholson, 1990; Calhoun, 1993; Parton, 1994), usually through a series of more or less ingenious attempts to rescue modernism from foundationalism and essentialism and to offer 'reconstruction' as deconstruction's cure. Parton (1994: 28) offers one of the less ingenious accounts: 'The postmodern condition is the condition of modernity emancipated from false consciousness, unrealistic aspiration and unrealizable objectives.'

As indicated in '. . . Opening . . .', educational discourse offers its own vanguard of 'rescuers', such as McLaren (1986), Giroux (1988) and Kellner (1988). In general they reflect a tendency for critical theorists to move from the first group (the opposition tendency) to a more accommodationist stance as uneasy members of the fourth group (see also Carr, 1995). These uncertain moves are well captured in McLaren's 'radical pedagogy': 'one foot solidly planted in the Marxist tradition and the other poised somewhat hesitatingly over the antimetaphysical radicalism of post-analytic philosophy' (McLaren, 1986: 393). A kind of intellectual version of the hokey-cokey.

Thus it is not difficult to see why postmodernism's boundaries, membership and affiliations are so hard to pin down. Given the 'ravenous eclecticism' (Huyssen, 1990: 262) of postmodernism, its anti-foundationalism, its concern for movement rather than 'position' and its tendency to name itself in shifting if not shifty metaphors such as 'nomad' (Deleuze and Guattari, 1988; Grossberg, 1988; Shurmann, 1990; Braidotti, 1993), 'subaltern' (Spivak, 1988), 'pagan' (Lyotard, 1984), 'traveller' (Baudrillard, 1975), 'migrant' (Bhabha, 1994) and 'pharmakon' (Liszka, 1983), while appealing to hybrid status and laying claim to new categories such as 'cyborg' (Haraway, 1990) or 'mestiza' (Lugones, 1992), it is hardly surprising that it should be difficult to place, either politically or philosophically. Huyssen adds to the difficulty with the convincing claim that postmodernism simply isn't 'a relational phenomenon' and that, post-Derrida, *either/or* thinking simply confuses the issue, preventing 'the phenomenon from ever coming into focus' (Huyssen, 1990: 236) – which leaves 'boundary' postmodernism barking up the wrong rhizome, as Deleuze and Guattari (1988) might say.

Nevertheless, the argument against postmodernism's slipperiness as a position and a philosophy can be taken further. It is easy to suggest that post-modernism – conceptualized as a bounded entity, a movement, a system of related belief – has set itself an impossible and self-contradictory task. We propose now to offer a critique of that 'bounded' notion of postmodernism and to examine and suggest some alternative conceptions of the relationship. That task is especially important for educational theory and educational research because most accounts of postmodernity and postmodernism within that arena are – misleadingly – couched in terms of such metaphors, and are as a result subject to a number of logical objections (as exemplified in the recent work of Hargreaves (1994) and in Giroux's (1991) 'border pedagogy').

To enumerate some important objections:

1 The logic of 'boundary' (or any other such synonym) requires criteria that can legitimate inclusions and exclusions. Such criteria imply a metanarrative of postmodernism's relation to modernism. But postmodernism asserts the impossibility of such metanarratives. Therefore postmodernism is self-contradictory.
2 Postmodernism attacks dichotomous thinking. Yet without such either/or thinking it cannot create itself against modernism.
3 Postmodernism stands against essentialism and the stability of meaning, and is therefore unable to define itself, yet forced to do so in order to exist as a system of ideas, as an '-ism'.
4 Deconstructive approaches to meaning characterize postmodernist think-ing. Such approaches deny and displace the sorts of originary and causal accounts that are needed in order to explain the historical relationship between modernism and postmodernism.
5 Postmodernism objects to universality in an argument that cannot avoid making the universalist assumption that such a statement against univer-sality (at least) is universally true – and so gets caught in *tu quoque* objec-tions that it cannot avoid.
6 Modernism defines itself as including counter-modernism. Its history is agonistic, a series of revolts against ways of seeing, portraying, building, thinking and writing. Postmodernism is simply another of these rebellions since it does not, and indeed cannot (see first objection), offer criteria to dis-tinguish the radical qualities of its particular rebellion from those in mod-ernity's past.
7 Postmodernism makes a great deal of fuss about the paradoxes of a presence that always implies absences, deferrals and silences. While such displace-ments are worth attending to, the exaggeration of their importance privi-leges the margins at the expense of the centre, creating another arbitrary and equally violent reading: the logic of postmodernism is to define pres-ence through absence, which is a bit like defining Emmenthal cheese by the holes in it and concluding in general that holes define cheese, or that cheese doesn't exist.

In conclusion, such critique successfully poses postmodernism as an imposs-ible object – both asserting the need for, and failing to provide, coherent ratio-nales for definition, boundary, specific meaning and generalization. It cannot be denied that it is a historical phenomenon of some sort, but it marks a kind of *fin de siècle* loss of confidence in the Enlightenment project – a nervous breakdown rather than a breakthrough. (McLeod (1994) sees postmodernism as just that sort of post-imperialist loss of confidence in the West.)

Further 'boundary' problems for postmodernism can be constructed at the level of narrative rather than theory. The first is exemplified above – postmodernism as a singular noun encapsulates just the sort of homogenous reduction that postmodernisms must avoid. 'Postmodernism claims that . . .' (Taylor-Gooby, 1994: 285); 'Postmodernism is guilty of . . .' (Maker, 1992: 319). So texts which in theory recognize the heterogeneity of postmodernism narrate its disputes in ways which contradict that recognition. To give a more specific example, Nicholson at first names postmodernism as plural: 'linked under the label of postmodernist' (Nicholson, 1990: 3). Then the label disappears and 'the postmodernists' are embodied and given an agenda and entered into a dialogue: 'Postmodernists describe modern ideals of science, justice.' Soon these postmodernists are giving 'strictures' (p. 6), and 'urg[ing] us to recognise' their perspectives (p. 4). As Augé points out in relation to Maussian discourse, such personifying usage can be theoretically pregnant with significance, since the notion carries within it assumptions of totality and typicality – as in *the* Melanesian [whose] individuality is a synthesis, the expression of a culture which itself is regarded as a whole' (Augé, 1995: 21). Yet, as Augé would also argue, any poststructuralist notion of individuality must include the notion of 'a figure who is literally unthinkable' (*ibid.*: 23); that is, inherently 'other'. This seduction of theory by narrative has important consequences, also effecting unconsidered changes from the synchronic to the diachronic, making the discontinuous linear by means of emplotment and rendering an inevitable and particular kind of closure (Knight, 1994). Such narrative brings about a kind of hermeneutic recovery, and often results in a simplistic synthesis of the old and the new which owes more to a happily-ever-after narrative reconciliation than a logical outcome: 'the ultimate stake of an encounter between feminism and postmodernism is the prospect of a perspective which integrates their respective strengths while eliminating their respective weaknesses' (Fraser and Nicholson, 1990: 20). Similar dénouements are offered by Nicholson's reviewer (Nye, 1991) and by education theorists such as McLaren (1986), Giroux (1988) and Hargreaves (1994).

An additional and familiar personifying strategy is employed by Haber (1994): she treats Rorty and Lyotard as emblematic postmodernists and conducts her critique of postmodernism against their work, but without real acknowledgement of the range of theorizing that might be said to be covered by the uncertain boundaries of postmodernism and poststructuralism. Maker (1992) is guilty of the same kind of single-minded pursuit of Rorty and universal-minded conclusions about 'postmodernism'. Nor is it only postmodernism that gets such singular and personified reading. The 'Enlightenment Project' is another such reduction, as is 'Modernity' itself (cf. Calhoun, 1993): indeed, the student of Modernism's arrival as an intellectual *concern* might conclude that in many academic arenas Modernism didn't really get going as an idea until after its demise at the hands of Postmodernism (a notion of life-but-only-after-death that Derrida would probably applaud).

Thus far, we have examined constructions of postmodernism that centre

on some notion of 'boundary'. We have done so because it is the dominant
conceptualization of modernism/postmodernism – as frontier, boundary,
border, margin, paradigm, foreign-ness, opposition or historical period. We
have tried to show how difficult it is to maintain that metaphor as a distin-
guishing device. What is 'experience-far' is also 'experience-near', so that it
is hard to tell horizon from heartland; problems of membership and political affiliation seem hopelessly unclear and undecidable; logical problems
abound in trying to justify separations; and discourses on postmodernism are
inclined to offer narratives of definition and engagement that undermine
their own theoretical positions. A final consequence of the notion of the
'boundary' is the narrative tendency to portray activities across such frontiers
in terms of confrontation: 'opposition' (Bauman, 1988), 'cannibalism'
(McCarthy, in Verges, 1992), 'capture' (Shurmann, 1990), 'exorcism' (Maker,
1992), 'kamikaze' (Verges, 1992), 'defense' (Harding, 1990), 'death' (Habermas, 1987) and so on. The narrativization of such separations and conflicts
usually leads to a series of heroic recoveries in which the forces of good and
evil are engaged either in the warlike business of the Enlightenment's rescue
from the postmodern barbarian, or the reduction of modernity's authoritarian battlements of certainty and progress. We might label this the masculinist discourse of modernism/postmodernism. The effect is to reintroduce
just those notions of dialectic and totality that deconstruction sought to
erase. The question therefore remains: how can we think about postmodernism in ways that evade such self-contradicting dénouement? And can
we avoid a logocentric and patriarchal reading of the conundrum 'modern-
ism/postmodernism'?

Re(searching) metaphors of difference

> Breaks are always, and fatally, reinscribed in an old cloth that must con-
> tinually, interminably be undone.
> (Derrida, in McCarthy, 1991: 99)

How else can we conceptualize 'boundaries'?

We intend in this section to give 'boundary' a different reading, and also indicate other notions of definition and distinction that may offer fruitful and less
deterministic ways of thinking about difference. Coetzee offers the starting
point of a postcolonial perspective which redefines the relation of Self and
Other.

In Coetzee's novel *Waiting for the Barbarians* the colonial border beween Self
and Other is allegorically constructed via the Magistrate's relationship with a
Barbarian woman. At first captive and victim, she becomes his servant and
mistress, and witness to the Empire's repression. He is both master and peni-
tent. Their relationship is complex and paradoxical, although always unequal,
and its 'in-between-ness' bears some comparison with the Victorian relationship of Hannah Culwick and Thomas Munby (see Chapter 3). At any rate, the

barbarian woman has been part-blinded through torture and has to squint to see; he sees in her eyes the 'trace' of her injury. He reflects:

> Is it then the case that it is the whole woman that I want, that my pleas-ure in her is spoiled until these marks on her are erased and she is restored to herself; or is it the case (I am not stupid, let me say these things) that it is the marks on her which drew me to her but which, to my dis-appointment, I find, do not go deep enough? . . . No thought that I think, however antonymic, of the origin of my desire seems to upset me. 'I must be tired,' I think. 'Or perhaps whatever can be articulated is falsely put.' My lips move, silently composing and recomposing the words. 'Or perhaps it is the case that only that which has not been articulated has to be lived through.'
>
> (Coetzee, 1982: 64)

It is the magistrate's dilemma that their gaze can never 'meet', that the origins of his desire remain forever deferred: 'So I continue to swoop a circle around the irreducible figure of the girl, casting one net of meaning after another over her' (p. 81). Yet it is through the trace of her disfigurement that he comes to understand that the Barbarian is the internal necessity of the Empire, rather than its external challenge. Personal knowledge is denied, but it is displaced into a political understanding.

Bhabha argues that postcolonial literature is perhaps prefigurative of post-structuralist issues. His deconstructions of Fanon, and his attention to authors like Gordimer and Toni Morrison, pursue the issues of identity and difference, analyse the occlusions and exclusions of the colonial/postcolonial gaze. Bhabha concludes that the truest eye may be the migrant's double gaze. Lugones makes a similar claim in relation to the 'self in germination in the borderlands' (Lugones, 1992: 32). 'But the plurality of the new *mestiza* is anchored in the borders, in that space where critique, rupture, and hybridiza-tion take place' (*ibid.*: 35).

For Bhabha and other postcolonialists, then, the focus is on 'the borderline work of culture' (Bhabha, 1994: 7). But that notion of 'border' – as in Coetzee's novel – is not a looking out at the exotically Other, but the kind of 'unhomely' looking in at the Other (*ibid.*: 8) that Derrida recommends. Reading from the border inwards ('a footnote in search of a text': Barzilai, 1990: 12), Derrida seeks to invert the violent hierarchy of the text's opposition (in this case its sense of boundary, of division). This suggests a paradoxical approach to the distinction between modernism and postmodernism – as a question of articu-lation rather than division: 'an anatomy of articulation . . . rather than an anatomy of punctuation (decision, dissection, closure)' (Johnson, 1993: 154).

A deconstructive reading of such an articulation need have no fixed prop-erties, allowing us to read its shifting properties: it 'de-limits what it (de)limits' (Barzilai, 1990: 11). Thoughts of maps and boundaries and frontiers may deceive us into rigidity, insisting on either/or concessions that we wish to avoid or at least defer, or into definitions that cannot be fixed (Harvey, 1986). The question of definition, as Derrida argues in another context, may need to take into account the unfounded nature of the distinction. It may be as nonsensical to ask 'where is the boundary between modernism and postmodernism?' as it would be to ask 'what is a justice?' [*sic*] since both questions are incalculable, in the same way as justice is incalculable – 'moments in which the decision between just and unjust is never insured by a rule' (Derrida, 1992: 16). By the same token it may be impossible to ask what the 'rule' is for separating modernism and postmodernism, and, if so, some of the philosphical problems raised earlier will not so much be answered as dismissed as irrelevant. If we don't draw the line, we won't need to defend it.

A consequential problem faced by Giroux, McLaren, Kellner and Hargreaves in the field of educational commentary is that they all draw lines between modernity and postmodernity, and between modernism and postmodernism, but make various attempts to rescue a position for their modernistic commentary – an inexplicable vantage point, a core of values, 'buttressed' (McLaren, 1986: 394) by modernity. Whence, of course, to treat with postmodernism's attractive trickery about difference and diversity, and to concede even trickier demotions of 'totality' from ontological to heuristic status (Giroux, 1988: 16). In such modernistic rescues a 'critical and dialectical view' (*ibid.*) reappears like a rabbit out of an (old) hat.

If not a line, then what? We wish here to indicate three possibilities, drawn from Derrida and Augé. What they have in common is that they are notions of difference that are not exercises in exclusion so much as attempts to regard 'inside' and 'outside' and the oscillation between the two in deconstructive terms. For example, it may be that 'inside' and 'outside' are not reliable distinctions: 'A frame may be framed by what it appears to frame' (Derrida, 1992: 12). Derrida further suggests the 'parergon' (a kind of incomplete frame) as a more suitably ambivalent notion of framing, and elsewhere the notion of 'tympan' (the 'sounding board', as it were, of the eardrum) in order to 'complicate the distinction between inside and outside and [to] problematize the question of the limit, the boundary, the margin' (Johnson, 1993: 154). From this perspective deconstruction is the enemy of boundary, and, Derrida (1992: 19) argues, may: 'lead to a reinterpretation of the whole apparatus of boundaries within which a history and a culture have been unable to confine their criteriology.'

Augé offers a different sort of erasing of the line, envisaging some version of the modernist/postmodernist division in terms of juxtaposed and interacting 'spaces' which have the radically different properties of 'place' and 'nonplace': 'If a place can be defined as relational, historical and concerned with identity, then a space which cannot be defined as relational, or historical, or concerned with identity will be a non-place' (Augé, 1995: 78). He emphasizes the impurity of these locations, as related categories of difference, named in and through their contemporaneity in 'supermodern' society, as he calls it (e.g. the different forms of experience that invest such contrasts as the village square/motorway; cathedral/airport lounge). He argues that it is 'possible to grasp the idea of supermodernity without ignoring its complexities and contradictions, but also without treating it as the uncrossable horizon of a lost modernity with which nothing remains to be done except to map its traces, list its isolates and index its files' (Augé, 1995: 40–1).

There is nothing inevitable, then, about representing the distinction between modernism and postmodernism in terms of 'border' or 'boundary', or indeed the related notions of 'paradigm' or 'period'. If the notion of 'border' is to be maintained, then it needs to incorporate Bhabha's notion of hybridity, as Giroux sometimes does (1991), and more often does not. Otherwise, notions of boundary and period take on self-contradictory meanings in relation to postmodernist readings. Hargreaves provides a clear example of this sort of problem in the educational arena (Hargreaves, 1994). He posits a world moving from modernity to postmodernity. He then creates his analytical boundaries by labelling schools 'modern', and society 'postmodern', recommending that the former catch up by adopting the good bits of postmodernity (some forms of flexibility, flatter hierarchies etc.). All this is explicated from a position of alleged modernism ('unapologetically', p. 42) that lapses into postmodernist prescription in a contradictory way, while failing to offer a coherent account of how he can be both inside and outside the postmodernity he claims to analyse: 'While I am interested in such things as the collapse of scientific certainty as a social phenomenon, I do not myself embrace that absence of certainty in the way I analyse it!' (Hargreaves, 1994: 40).

With such underminings of the notions of 'boundary' in mind, particularly in relation to hybridity, oscillation and the contemporaneity of different worlds, we turn now to an examination of the less dominant tropes that critics have deployed in the task of reading modernism/postmodernism. If we are to think deconstructively, then we will have to consider how to read that mysterious 'slash' between the words differently.

What about modernism/postmodernism as a life and death affair?

The first cluster centres on some notion of death. As we've seen, Habermas employs that metaphor. So too do McCarthy (1991) and Benhabib (1992), although the former extends the metaphor, envisaging a postmodernism 'gnawing at the bones of its own carcass' (McCarthy, in Verges, 1992: 391). In a similar conceit Maker criticizes the 'zombie philosophers', by whom he chiefly means Rorty: 'Each has proclaimed himself alive in and through his rejection of dead forebears, a rejection which consists in showing how and why these forebears are still philosophers and thus dead' (Maker, 1992: 317).

Verges prefers the notion of 'philosophical kamikaze' (Verges, 1992: 391), while in a more optimistic vein Denüvo refers to a resurrective 'second coming' (Denüvo, 1992: 44). Lurking in all this talk of death, of course, is the Foucauldian notion of the 'death of the subject' as well as of the Enlightenment project.

A second cluster overlaps the first with the notion of 'eating'. Postmodernism is depicted as 'ravenous' (Huyssen, 1990: 262). Supporters talk of wanting to 'have our cake and eat it' (Distefano, 1990: 77), and critics accuse others of the necrophagic consumption of modernity (Maker, 1992). This metaphor is distended rather than extended by Phillipson in his playful characterization of the body of modernism consumed by cancerous growths and condemned to a 'living death' (Phillipson, 1989: 159; Maker, 1992: 317 for a similar image).

Those who employ the rhetoric of death/cannibalism generally do so to ridicule postmodernist intentions, as they define them. In a sense, what Maker wants us to do in his incisive and witty attack on postmodernist philosophy (as oxymoronic) is to take seriously his philosophical objections and be entertained by the 'zombie' rhetoric. But it is worth contemplating the coincidence of death-like metaphors in these various and unconnected readings of modernism/postmodernism, and in particular the interesting recurrence of cannibalistic charges of one sort or another. Our strategy here will be to take seriously the metaphors of the zombie/living dead etc., and to hope to dismiss, or more accurately displace, some of the philosophical objections. This may seem an arbitrary and indefensible inversion until we note that the theme of death receives an interesting inversion, appearing as theory rather than narrative in other accounts of modernism/postmodernism. For example, Hix reads modernism's reactions to postmodernism against stages of grieving (Hix, 1993; see also Stronach and Torrance, 1995). Derrida also recommends the notion of 'mourning work' and draws on Freudian analogies in discussing the contemporary life/death of Marxism (Derrida, 1994b: 98). He goes further, insisting that Marxism must now be read in terms of its 'spectrality': that Marxism's particular modernist project is more alive (and more necessary to keep alive) as a spectre than it was as a living and somewhat disgracefully embodied dogma. Derrida therefore argues that 'one must assume the inheritance of Marxism', that is, its most 'living' part, read it in a spirit of 'mourning', and attend to 'the spectral, of life-death beyond the opposition between life and death' (Derrida, 1994b: 40).

He asserts the possibility of the superior power of such spectres, refusing to regard them as mere reminders, or fading images, as, for example, in the spectre of the Communist Manifesto: 'What manifests itself in the first place is a specter, this first paternal character, as powerful as it is unreal, a hallucination or simulacrum that is virtually more actual than what is so blithely called a living presence' (Derrida, 1994b: 32).

We have, therefore, an intellectually lively world of the dead, of ghosts invested in theorizing rather than narrating modernism/postmodernism. Such ghosts naturally claim that the necrophagic or spectral metaphor is indeed an interesting way to conceive of a relationship that is not wholly one thing or the other, and assert the necessity of modernism for the project of postmodernism, thereby opening up different ways of envisaging the articulation of the two concepts (or of the many concepts that tend to be reduced to the two concepts).[4] In particular, the fruitfulness of the life/death/ghost metaphors for Derridean readings can be seen: they address the ambiguities and deferrals of presence and absence; refuse to privilege the power of the 'real' over the merely spectral; fail to address one notion as original and any other as copy; and undermine the oppositional notion of life/death in setting up an uncanny oscillation.

Alongside these ultimately disparaging references to 'zombies', 'kamikazes' and the 'living dead' lie the undeconstructed metaphors of ethnocentricity – the unruly and primitive Other dragged metaphorically into the story.[5] Yet the celebratory ritual of a cannibalistic death allows us to invert and displace the implications of death as a loss, as a necessarily negative (or even final) event, without, however, inventing some sort of belated teleological rescue such as a resurrection or second coming.[6] After all, Ruth Benedict has written about the 'excellent ethical use to which cannibalism has been put among the peoples of the world' (Benedict, in Mead, 1959: 45). Cannibalism was a tribute to a worthy enemy, and a highly economical form of killing. Writing shortly after the modernistic triumphs of the First World War it is not surprising that she should take such an ironic view, advocating cannibalism as a more civilized option in human conflict. Following Benedict's argument, we might choose to argue that cannibalism, contrary to Maker's analysis, is a better theory than a rhetoric, and that it is the means through which postmodernism pays its necessary compliments to modernism:

> Certain valiant tribes of the Great Lakes and the prairies long ago made use of it [cannibalism] to this purpose. It was to them their supreme gesture of homage to human excellence. It is told by old travellers that of three enemies whose death made the occasion for such a celebration of their valor, two were eaten with honor, while the one remaining was passed over and untouched. For at the death, this one had marked himself a coward, and cried out under torture. Of such flesh no one would eat.
>
> (Benedict, 1959: 45)

Let Maker and his like beware, lest none consume their flesh.

What is displaced by such a reformulation? We think it can be argued that a number of the seemingly unassailable objections against postmodernism previously rehearsed in this chapter can now be dismissed as irrelevant. If postmodernism posits no singularity or boundary, then the objection that it is the metanarrative of which it denies the possibility falls. Similarly, objections about its either/or status are avoided, along with charges of essentialism. Equally, there is no need to invent an origin and cause for postmodernism because it is not being posited in these terms. Nor is it being argued as just an inversion of modernism, and hence an equally arbitrary privileging of the marginal, since what notions of spectrality offer is an oscillation and deferral of meaning rather than a set of alternatives (for example, between such rejected hierarchies and polarities as body/ghost; real/unreal; present/absent). Now it is true, of course, that such a tactic brings with it different problems that also need to be addressed – including the notion that what does not oscillate, and is not 'spectral', is the only too solid and unyielding privileging of the notions of difference and deconstruction.[7] They become the new arbitrary, the undeconstructible, the foundationalism that denies itself yet lays itself open to charges of neostructuralism. Second, when we consider 'modernism/postmodernism' there is still the need to characterize in more specificity the meaning of that obscure slash or scar that (we now argue) both separates and joins them.

What new metaphors of relationship might be explored?

We need to be careful, or perhaps careless, in our search for metaphor. This cannot be a search for the holy grail of appropriate metaphor, the one true likeness that will enable us at last to recognize the face of postmodernism in the crush of the contemporary. We have rejected the singularity of metaphors of 'boundary' and 'period'. Then we explored some of the heuristic possibilities of regarding modernism/postmodernism within the metaphorical provenance of death/ghosts. Such a conceptualization helped to point up something of the possible connections rather than contrasts between modernism/post-modernism, but there is still something rather final and periodizing about any metaphor of death, however qualified and cancelled. So perhaps we need to explore the conceptualization of that relationship further, to accept that it is not at all a life and death matter, and that we have to put all those zombies and cadavers back into the toy box of imagination, acknowledging their fruit-ful suggestion that we should think in terms of articulation as well as division in order to think the distinction between modernist and postmodernist ways of seeing, thinking and being. Our strategy here is what Sassower has called 'experiment': 'to try out different moves from different perspectives and with different rules, not being concerned with consistency and coherence univer-sally but only locally' (Sassower, 1993: 440).

How, then, can we give modernism/postmodernism that kind of different reading? That is the final task of this introductory chapter, and it sets up a deconstructive agenda that is variously pursued throughout the book.

We began with the notion of deconstruction-as-fashion, and close with an exploration of how metaphors associated with fashion, clothes and the relation of body to clothes may be a fruitful way of considering the relation of modernism to postmodernism. Here we address a cluster of metaphors associated with the notion of 'folding' (Barzilai, 1990), with 'fabric' (Spivak, 1988), 'veil' (Fuss, 1994), 'patches' (Fraser and Nicholson, 1990), 'weave' (Lyotard, 1984). Spivak likewise addresses the public/private distinction in those metaphorical terms, claiming that the private '*is* the weave, or texture, of public activity' (Spivak, 1988: 103; original emphasis).

The usages range from vague gestures towards a relational meaning through more elaborate description and even to specific injuction: 'weave yourself a text' (Barzilai, 1990: 13). In contrast with what we called the masculinist 'boundary' and 'border' talk, this might be regarded as a more feminist telling of the relationship. As might be expected, the notion of 'folding' is also usually associated with some sort of turning or returning (Huyssen, 1990: 'revenant'), a kind of turning back on the past in ways that do not merely recall. Johnson calls that process 'deconstruction': 'at the same time the continuous sifting and transformation of this descendance, a turning back on itself in order to proceed, a continual, elliptical passage through the origin' (Johnson, 1993: 186).

It would be inappropriate, clearly, to sanction any single metaphor. A decon-structive approach would suggest, instead, a more plural strategy, identifying a *field of metaphors* wherein multiple and dynamic possibilities for meaning may be generated. This postmodernist approach would address what we have elsewhere called the 'mobilization of meaning' (Chapter 5). In order to explore what that might mean in this case we turn to an examination of the appro-priateness of 'folding' metaphors within the notion of clothes/body associ-ations. Our purpose is to illustrate the range of articulations and differences that such a couplet can engender, although we also need to acknowledge that such illustration is heuristic rather than exhaustive.

Exclude–include. If we regard the 'fold' as one of a possible field of metaphors relating to clothes and to bodies, it enables us to offer ways of foregrounding and backgrounding relational possibilities in non-exclusive ways. We can say, for a start, that the fold represents a kind of liminality, Bhabha's 'in-between-ness': 'the textile superfluity of folds and wrinkles that typifies the inevitable act of "translation"' (Bhabha, 1994: 227).

But it is made to carry no implication of destruction, death, stage theory or simple repetition (ellipsis and not circle, in Johnson's reading). Nor is it necessarily an exclusive term. We do not need, for example, to censor the notion of 'border' (see 'hem' or better still 'skirt': OED – 'to form the skirt or edge of; to lie alongside of; border of a garment; to bound or border'). In this context, we could argue that the notion of 'border' is more ambivalent and complex than in territorial versions of the metaphor. There are multiple possibilities relating to the fabric itself, such as 'patch' or 'veil', or the border that plays with both concealing and revealing the body (as in hem/collar) while simultaneously legitimating and censoring the gaze. The metaphor, as it were, can be engendered, and made to play between notions of sexuality and gender in a language of concealment that is also a form of revealing.

Surface–depth. Then there is the notion of clothes as a membrane between body and world, a second skin[8] conducting and reflecting the physical properties of both. Such a metaphor can readily be embodied, as well as engendered. In addition, there is the way that fashion/style may express the body's depth (its inner meanings and affiliations) on the surface of the body, thereby inverting the significances of surface and depth. In that reading, clothes are 'deeper' than the body, the heart worn on the sleeve, and the metaphor can be used to explore postmodernist themes concerning the nature of identity. Butler, for example, considers the play of meaning and the relation of body to clothes in the notion of 'drag': 'As imitations which effectively displace the meaning of the original, they imitate the myth of originality itself' (Butler, 1990).

Real–unreal. Equally suggestive is the status of those 'live' characters in Disneyworld. They realize the fictional in their costumes. Yet their realization is doubly fictional and they are less real as presences than their mythic and filmic absences. Berleant interprets such a Disneyworld as a parody of postmodernism, although that may miss the point that postmodernism is already pastiche (Berleant, 1994).

Utility–excess. Nor is the play of body/clothes limited to a 'closed' problematization of notions of depth/shallowness, presence/absence or identity/difference, since it is also possible to regard fashion as an art that demands the consideration of clothes as 'excess', irreducible to mere theory: 'Art is that practice which in its utter uselessness, constantly escapes, exceeds, all attempts to press it into the service of theory and knowledge' (Phillipson, 1989: 166).

Nature–culture. In these sorts of ways, metaphors of body/clothes proliferate. Nor does the body/clothes relation need to be regarded as a hierarchy based on 'nature' over 'culture'. We can think of the body not as 'nature' but fundamentally as 'culture', in terms of 'flexible bodies' – as Martin has recently portrayed the postmodern body (Martin, 1994). In postmodern times the body has to be flexible, reshaped and imaged, immunized and celebrated.

'Appearance skills' become a possibility of 'being', or at least a condition of employability, and it becomes conceivable for journals of advice for aspiring entrepreneurs to write about the need to train people how to 'emotionally clothe' themselves (Crawford, 1992: 18) in ways which are essentially 'performative' in nature. Such a relation between nature and artefact, body and clothes, is not too dissimilar from Haraway's notion of the 'cyborg', that human/machine combination that she takes to characterize postmodernity, and with which she promotes the argument for 'pleasure in the confusion of boundaries' (Haraway, 1990: 191).

History–myth. Finally, we might note that the body/clothes relation is deeply mythologized in ways that ought to be of interest to deconstructionists. After Derrida, we might wish to challenge the sorts of mythic and originary innocence associated with nakedness (Adam and Eve before the Fall), noting that the category of nakedness, far from being prior, could only follow that of clothes. We might say that clothing invented nakedness, as writing preceded speech.[9]

In these sorts of ways, then, this metaphorical space engendered by 'body/clothes' allows us to pose questions about inside and outside, origin and cause, and the relation of the individual to the cultural – but without being dragged towards a singular reading or an essential meaning or a static once-and-for-all interpretation. Such a bricolage of possibilities might not be an incongruent resource with which to begin to narrate postmodernism's 'limits'. It acts not as a definition or frame, but more as a series of semiotic chains, from, through and against which emerge different readings of the complex and shifting articulations and differences that attend the problematic relationship of modernism/postmodernism (see Chapter 5).

Conclusions

In this chapter we have tried to read the 'boundary' between modernism and postmodernism. We have been biased, of course, and offered what Derrida has called a 'performative interpretation' (Derrida, 1994a: 51), reading back from a deliberately shaky investment in postmodernism. Our reading has tried to be a deconstructive one, which means that we have not tried to understand modernism/postmodernism in terms of defining either of these two terms. Instead, we have asked for the meaning of the mysterious 'slash' that both joins and separates them like a scar. Since our approach was deconstructive we approached the 'slash' or scar through the ways in which others had envisaged it, dealing with three clusters of meaning centring on notions of 'boundary', 'death' and 'folding'. Our intention was to inspect the work done by these metaphors. We concluded that metaphors of boundary tend to set up either theoretical or narrative meanings of the 'slash' that contradict poststructuralist or postmodernist assumptions about some pretty central things like essentialism and foundationalism. The choice of boundary-related metaphor carried the representation of a solution, prematurely answering what it had hoped to question. Regarding the boundary as a 'slash' seemed a useful kind of temporary withdrawal from linguistic representation, an unsayable 'slash' that could only be said in writing, as the question rather than the claim of a relationship which it posed in terms that it had not already answered. As a mark between two words, it carried polysemous possibilities. Was it a 'slash' (and thus a severing)? Was it a 'scar' (and hence a healing that acknowledged the inaugurating wound)?

The next move was to inspect the ways in which anti-postmodernists tended to narrate their attacks via the metaphors of death/cannibalism and so on, arguing that these were actually interesting ways of interpreting rather than dismissing the relationship, and ones which allowed the privileging of what was real and what was unreal to be challenged and inverted. We then extended our inspection of the (erstwhile) boundary between modernism and postmodernism by looking at a third cluster of metaphors. Our suggestion here was that we should think in terms of fruitful and at least non-contradictory fields of metaphor (in relation to deconstruction's assumptions about the world), whence to envisage that 'slash' in terms of plural articulations and differences. We do not claim that such metaphors say all there is to be said about modernism/postmodernism, but argue that these open up rather than close down the possibility of multiple readings. They provide a field for exploration in subsequent chapters, and at least we should say that in theories of 'difference' we need to learn to count beyond two.

A question remains: what is the relevance of such deconstructive approaches to understanding? It might be argued on practical grounds that reading the 'boundary' between modernism/postmodernism and claiming that the 'slash' between them was the conundrum to be deciphered is a fairly esoteric preoccupation, and just the sort of thing that future Sir Keith Josephs are going to get riled about. We finish with a brief indication of some possible connections. (The theme of a practical agenda for postmodernist research is developed in Chapter 9.)

There are elements of the contemporary world (whether we call it late capitalist, or postmodern) that suggest that deconstruction is a useful way to understand the sorts of hybridity that characterize the postcolonial condition. The problem of identity, of the de-centred subject, is a central one for social theory and practice. Deconstructive approaches to the notion of identity, therefore, have much to say to feminism about its increasingly precarious notions of woman as an essentialized subject (Butler, 1990; di Stefano, 1990; Haraway, 1991), and also to the gay movement (Eadie, 1994). For example, Eadie discusses identity deconstructively in relation to 'queer' identity:

> The irony of purity is that it generates a kind of eternal crusade against the traces of that outside within its centre, a process of scrutiny and self-scrutiny which induces panic so complete that in the end the centre disappears, its every content marked as a potential – or actual – dangerous transgression.
>
> (Eadie, 1994: 247)

The same is no doubt becoming true of heterosexual men in so far as they begin to lose their status as 'universal subjects' and acquire a less hegemonic gendered self. In addition, issues of national identity, especially in times of plural allegiance, are a fruitful area for debate (McCrone, 1992; Stronach,

1992; Shore, 1993). Deconstruction may therefore be politically useful in helping to read new personal and political situations in terms of hybridity and shifting meaning, rather than in universalistic and totalizing expressions of essential identity and certain truth.

Our concern in this chapter was to deconstruct just such a membership category (the 'modernists' versus the 'postmodernists'), reading how these distinctions were constructed and expressed, and trying to *model* that process of interrogation in ways that might just as well be applied to other questions of identity or definition. (We hoped, therefore, that both the method and the substance of this chapter would have a pedagogic function.) In particular, we sought to begin to elaborate a field of metaphors within which and from which the problem of their articulation and difference could be read differently. Such a task is important if educational appropriations from postmodernism are to avoid crude sorts of boundary-drawing, and contradictory attempts at stuffing modernism and postmodernism (or modernity and postmodernity) into either/or categories, or periodizations that eventually make little chronological or logical sense. We take that task of deconstruction to define a postmodernist approach (although the label can be more of a liability than anything else) to be a subversive one, epistemologically anarchic, yet neither politically conservative nor relativistically acquiescent. And deconstruction, it might be argued, ought to be a central concern of educational research and theory. After all, Derrida defines it as 'a critical culture, a kind of education' (Derrida, cited in Sohm, 1994: 28).

Notes

1 The British Education Index offers no postmodern entries between 1986 and 1991. Thereafter there is one entry for 1992, two for 1993 and fifteen for 1994. The Education Index has no postmodern entries from 1980 to 1985, and thereafter a trickle of citations.
2 A full consideration of this issue would need to address 'modernity', 'postmodernity', 'modernism' and 'postmodernism'. Discussion is restricted here to the perspectival contrasts and similarities between modernism and postmodernism – partly for reasons of space, but also out of a more general scepticism about the usefulness of periodizing contemporary history and current changes into the either/or boxes of modernity or postmodernity. Harvey (1986) and Jamieson (1983) provide useful general accounts of such periodization.
3 Despite the fact that all definitions of the 'paradigm'– disagreement about values and meanings, 'incommensurable' theories, 'continual competition' etc. – are features of a preparadigmatic status in Kuhn's view. That is, what if anything is paradigmatic is the preparadigmatic status of the so-called paradigm (Kuhn, 1962: 4, 178).
4 Anti- or post-modernists also recognize the prevalence of these perceptions of death and decline, e.g. Lyotard's ironic question: 'is postmodernity the pastime of an old man who scrounges in the garbage-heap of finality looking for leftovers?' (Lyotard, in Sassower, 1993: 439). Guattari also rejects the 'easy way out' of dismissing postmodernism as 'the death throes of modernism', cited in Sassower (1993: 438).
5 Perhaps the parallel is with the kind of liberalism that Gordimer noted in South Africa. The white heroine confesses to her black lover: 'because that's what I was told, when

I was being taught not to be prejudiced: underneath, they are all just like us. Nobody said we are just like *you*' (Gordimer, 1988: 207).

6 Or we might draw on Augé's account of interrogating a cadaver in West Africa. 'One of my first ethnological experiences, [was] the interrogation of a cadaver in Alladian country. [The ritual] involved making the cadaver say whether the person responsible for his death was to be found outside the Alladian villages or in one of them; in the village where the ceremony took place or outside it (and in this case, whether to east or west); inside or outside his own lineage, his own house, and so on' (Augé, 1995: 45).

7 We will not seek to answer that objection here, but note its force. Spivak (1988: 107), for example, refers to the 'very law of displacement'. Knorr Cetina makes just that sort of move that *tu quoque* objections pick out. Of deconstruction she writes: 'the very impossibility of unambiguous meanings may become the only "meaning" literally recoverable' (Knorr Cetina, 1994: 4). Nor does Derrida's position seem clear. He argues that deconstruction is undeconstructible – as the notion of justice is, and identifies the two concepts with each other: 'Justice itself, if such a thing exists, outside or beyond law, is not deconstructible. No more than deconstruction itself, if such a thing exists. Deconstruction is justice' (Derrida, 1992: 14–15).

8 Haraway writes perceptively about 'skin' as a false marker for self and other, and about the notion of auto-immune disease as – metaphorically and literally – a postmodern nightmare wherein the body fails to distinguish between self and other at a biological level (Haraway, 1991).

9 Iragaray ironically links the body to clothes in a different sort of association. Woman's sole invention was held to be weaving: 'This would explain the only contribution women have made to "the discoveries and inventions in the history of civilisation" – weaving. Which is, however, more or less, an "imitation" of the "model" *Nature* gives in the pubic hair' (Iragaray, 1985: 115).

2

Jack in two boxes: a postmodern perspective on the transformation of persons into portraits

Introduction

If the first chapter of this book was about signposts for deconstruction, postmodernism and places west, then the second was more of a map, laying out a terrain within which the mythic struggles of modernism and postmodernism were alleged to take place, a paradoxical map apparently best read when folded. But we 'opened' with a promise to be practical in terms of research methodology and praxis, and for that reason we now address a specific 'site' of deconstruction, 'identity'. This chapter begins by questioning the links between accounts and 'reality', and making visible some of the textual devices that writers use to achieve the semblance of coherence and authenticity in their research portraits. (Chapters 5, 8 and 9 also develop different aspects of this theme.)

In this chapter, then, we attempt a practical exploration of methodology in action. We take as our starting point two narrative portraits that we wrote in the course of a 'Teachers' Jobs and Lives' project.[1] These are of particular interest in that they 'portray' the same person: Jack, a primary school headteacher approaching the end of his career. While each of us worked with the same basic 'facts' of Jack's life, as represented in three lengthy biographical interviews that he gave to Maggie MacLure, we assembled these facts into quite distinct portraits.

This raises the question of what might be an appropriate metaphor for the relationship of person to portrait. How should that process of questioning and prompting, editing and selecting, theorizing and storying be characterized? Within naturalistic portrayal, the interactional metaphors tend to be 'dialogue' and 'negotiation'. The more cognitive aspects of the process would be labelled 'inductive' – a grounded, collaborative and ethically justifiable construction of portrait from person. 'Portrait', then, means something like a self-encapsulation, a theorizing in which the researcher facilitates the self-expression of the other, leaving control in the hands of the subject in so far as it is possible. The researcher's task is to 'represent' the subject in a double sense: first, in the artistic meaning of the word, to make a realistic likeness; but, second, to act as a kind of agent for the subject, to 'represent' her interests and ensure that her 'voice' is heard. Linked with this second sense of representation, accounts tend to be celebratory of the individual as person or professional – making a life, rather than taking a life. Indeed, it is tacitly agreed to be bad form to do otherwise: 'Dogs and horses are thus deemed inedible, for, as the Red Queen said, "it isn't etiquette to cut anybody you've been introduced to"' (Sahlins, 1976: 174).[2]

The two stories of Jack were produced according to the usual negotiating procedures: the interview transcripts and the draft stories were negotiated with Jack; and the later discussions offered the opportunity to revise the portrait and to include new stories, as we shall see later. So the task of representation was a collaborative one, and the metaphors of 'dialogue' and 'induction' are appropriate.

Or are they? We will argue that a better metaphor for the relation between subject and researcher might be that of 'struggle', first of all in the sense of a one-sided attempt by the researcher to 'subdue' the raw material of the interview data and bring it under the regime of a tidy, coherent, textual structure, even if this seems to contradict the picture of self offered by the subject; second, in the sense of a rescue attempt by the subject in the subsequent negotiation interview. (This notion of 'struggle', later dignified as 'agonistics', recurs variously in the book – see especially Chapters 3, 8 and 'Mourning' – as an issue between researcher and researched, self and identity, writer and written.) We will question, too, the self-effacing aspirations of the researcher/writer within qualitative research – the idea that the writer can and should get out of the way, textually speaking, and let the subject 'speak for himself'. As the readings of the Jack stories show, the writer is often most visible and intrusive when he or she is trying to be reticent. And authorial 'absence' should, in any case, be treated with scepticism. We suggest below that it is those accounts which seem most 'natural', 'transparent', 'real' or 'rounded' that are most carefully wrought with a view to producing just those effects in the reader – that the writer is never more present in the text than when she seems to be absent, and the subject seldom less audible than when he seems to be speaking for himself. This is not to suggest that there are other, more genuinely innocent or transparent ways of writing, but simply to state that the appearance of artlessness is a rather artful business.

The two stories of Jack are presented below, followed by the commentaries, which use the discrepancies between the two versions to interrogate the notion of a 'life' as a textual product, and to foreground the issue of the links between person and portrait. We also refer in the commentaries to the fieldnotes which preceded the writing of the stories, and to the comments of colleagues (six in all) who gave us their own 'readings' of the texts, and whose remarks provided insights into the ways in which texts convince, or fail to convince, readers of the 'authenticity' of their descriptions. Finally, we refer to Jack's own 'reading' of the stories, and to his attempts, as we see it, to reinstate or rescue his own, preferred version of his life.

Story 1 (Ian Stronach)

Jack's story, or, biographers are ventriloquists whose lips are sealed

1 Jack Nisbett has been a first school headteacher for the past 20 years. Married, mid-50s, grown up family, he's very much his own man. So let him tell his own story:

I can remember talking to the old RSM – he was an ex-RSM who was in charge of weapon-training . . . 'What shall I do when I go in the army, sarge?' you know, and he said, 'Well, why don't you join the education corps? You like teaching – you've got to do a National Service. Make use of it.' And that's what I did.

2 This conversation took place in the late 1940s, at a minor public school. Jack jokes about his academic career at the school ('I was the strongest boy in the school . . . held the rest up'), but enjoyed sports and the cadet force. School was a cloistered existence, and National Service an eye-opener: he met 'men from all walks of life'.

. . . most of my mates, colleagues, whatever you like to call them . . . were North Londoners, Essex people . . . and, you know, they were lorry drivers' mates and things like that . . . and their idea of going out was to go to the pubs, go to the pictures and all that. Totally new to me. But they – 'Come on, better come with us, we'll show you what to do.'

3 He joined in July; by December he was 'a sergeant at 18'. He did an extra three years as a regular. The army gave him the confidence to teach, and also to socialize:

. . . most of the senior NCOs were war veterans in those days. I mean they were people who'd served in World War II, in 1954. And their daughters were about the right age for me! And when we used to have the social, the social function, I mean I was in great demand to dance with.

Interviewer: . . . an eligible bachelor, eh?

That's right. I had a fine service career. (laughs)

4 Jack had stayed in the army in order to be able to pay his way through teacher training college, despite his autocratic father's wishes. His father was a bank manager and wanted him to go into forestry or banking. He did his teacher training at Goldsmith's. Teaching was in the family – his father later told him that his grandfather had become 'one of the first truly qualified teachers in Norfolk'. An aunt was a head of department in a training college; his mother was also a teacher.

5 He spent the rest of his twenties teaching in London, and then in the Black Country, where he became a deputy head in a large primary school. He felt that he was being groomed for headship:

. . . he sort of gently gave me the reins and said, you know, you run it. I'm the Head, but you run it. I mean he could sit on his backside, and when I was sort of pulling the wrong way he'd sort of lean over my shoulder and put it straight, you know.

6 Shortly afterwards, in 1969, Jack was appointed headteacher of a county primary school in East Anglia: it was the right job, in the right place.

I wanted to come into the rural area and I must admit, I'd used my experience in urban areas, in large schools, as stepping stones to come here . . . I didn't think I'd get the job. When I came down and stayed with my parents – attended for the interview – was, I must admit, I won't say blasé about it, I mean I, you get uptight at interviews, and I would have liked the job . . . I was surprised. I mean at 32 I didn't expect it and it was the first time I had been shortlisted, and I didn't expect to get it and there was quite . . . there were a lot of applicants . . . sort of 50 or 60 applied for the job, might have been more . . . It was a long short-list and they were interviewing all day and there were three of us called from away, and quite a lot of local heads and I didn't really when . . . you know when you chat in the interview room, and they all seemed far more experienced than I was – didn't expect to get it. But there we are . . .

7 Jack's career received its first check seven years later, when the county introduced middle and first schools to replace the 5–11 county primary set-up. As a junior secondary trained teacher, he preferred working with older pupils, and he failed to get the headship of the middle school:

I thought they would bring in a newcomer from outside with Middle School experience – which is exactly what they did. I suppose I was mildly disappointed but not very because I wasn't surprised and – you know – I was prepared for it. And I . . . I thought, well, I've still . . . I've still got juniors in the school insomuch as the top class are juniors.

8 In a sense, that's the end of Jack's first story. He has stayed at the first school, tied by a mixture of preference, family and friendship. Is it a story with a happy ending? Sometimes it sounds as if it is; sometimes not. On the one hand, Jack says 'I'm perfectly happy being in a first school.'

I like being with kids . . . I like being with people who like being with kids . . .

. . . I suppose when I was younger I was very ambitious. I'm happy with what I've got now, and I couldn't . . . in my terms, in my opinion I couldn't've . . . I wouldn't've wanted to go anywhere else, because my children then reached the age when I wanted them to have a stable school.

9 But there seems to be another version. He misses the older children, the involvement with sports, the company of male teachers (the first school has been predominantly female):

I do enjoy teaching 8-year-olds but I would probably enjoy teaching 11-year-olds more.

Interviewer: Do you think you'd definitely enjoy teaching 5-year-olds less?

I couldn't do it . . . I'm just not the sort of animal who'd want to do that . . . I wouldn't want to be with children of that age on a day to day basis. No younger than I am with now really. I'm not doing it by choice. I'm doing it because that's the way the situation happened.

Interviewer: Yes, so you definitely . . .

Many of my colleagues, many of my colleagues who've been in the situation that I'm in now have either . . . look, serious . . . have either had nervous breakdowns (laughs).

Interviewer: What? Because of having to trans–

Yes, I think so. I mean, what other implication is there? I mean they . . . they ran good County Primary schools for a good many years and were happy colleagues of mine for a good many years and they were landed in this situation and they had nervous breakdowns. What . . . what's the implication? What's the inference? That it's a situation with which they can't cope . . . Erm, I'm lucky, insomuch that this school is big enough to give me a group of fourth year children of a first school age range which are first school, first year children of the junior age range. I can cope with that . . . The comment I'm making is that I certainly feel that it was – erm – contributory to mental illness among colleagues. Oh, I'm not prepared to name names, I don't think we should go into that, but I mean I don't mean one, I mean more than one. And when I say mental breakdowns I mean – two have actually died . . .

So the first story, of Jack's career, has at least two endings.

10 There is a second story, however, one that centres on his evolving ideas and feelings about his role and his life. Now, in his mid-50s, he looks back on himself as a young teacher who was too hard-working, and who neglected his first wife for the demands of the job. He was 'selfish', 'left her holding the bloody fort', 'while I played schools'.

Alright, they're not young kids for very long, but when you look at it, it's over perhaps – it's 12 years, say 12 years, 15 if you like. But it is a bloody long time . . . It's bad, but there you are.

11 He feels that he now knows how to balance the demands of job and life. His recipe for survival is a mixture of establishing clear priorities and firm boundaries:

There are some of my staff here who I wouldn't recommend for Headship, because if they got it, it would kill them. I feel – I think you could say they're too conscientious, and in modern – in schools today – I'm not saying details aren't important – but if you . . . to take one example: when you come in in the morning, and you've got a pile of mail to do, if you were to sit down and read that, every single one of those letters fully, and make notes on everything that perhaps you ought to make notes on . . . you wouldn't get in the classroom.

12 So he puts his teaching role in front of the administrative one, and relies on the team spirit of the school staff to share the burden of management. He calls himself a coordinator rather than a leader.

. . . the priorities in this school are those kids in that classroom for me – they're my priority. The second priority is the rest of the children in the school.

As far as stress goes, he thinks that he's 'lucky':

I . . . I basically don't give a damn that . . . no, that's too strong . . . I do give a damn, but I don't give a damn what people think (chuckles), which is different. Now I can go home at the end of the day and think, 'Ah well you know, I've earned my pennies today' and my conscience is clear – and everything I've done I've believed in – I don't worry.

13 So concerns like the National Curriculum, assessment, the governors, the area office and their 'forms' all tend to be spoken about in the same kind of way. Above all, Jack paints a picture of himself as a pragmatic man, full of common sense and give-and-take, opposed to jargon and theory, his wisdom home-spun, a believer in simple solutions to practical problems, and sensible limits to a man's involvement with his job. For example, these anecdotes seem typical of Jack:

I said [to one of his staff] you know, you've been here three years, you're 35, time to look at your life. She said, 'I don't want to do it.' I said, 'Why not? You can do it. You can do that.' She said, 'I see a bloody good organiser, much better than me.' Said, 'I'm a lousy organiser – I leave all the bits, all the tying of ends, to you' . . . And she says, 'Yeah, but you know I'll tie them up.' She says, 'What I can't do is this – parents come in the room with me and – just off the top of your head you'll deal with the problems, you'll deal with the accidents. You never seem to flap' . . .

. . . I was saying, 'Oh Christ, I dunno I – I – it's no good asking me where anything is, or' . . . And she said, 'You always seem to know what to do.' And I was sailing by the seat of my pants, and I do. I do tend to go through life by the seat of my pants.

And I said to her, 'I know what I'd do, love. Family first. Put your resignation in' . . . I said, 'You know, there's stacks of people lying in graveyards who thought they were indispensable.'

Everybody who comes in, they're here to do a job and I make it as comfortable for them as I can. And you get back what you give. Always. That's my – that is one of my principles in life.

14 Perhaps there is also the beginning of a third story about Jack. He seems to feel that maybe he's getting a little too old for the job, his attitudes a little old-fashioned – or at least unfashionable in terms of 'modern criteria of thinking'.

I – don't you think, though, seriously Maggie, by the time you're 55 plus, you're too old to be with kids?

15 And some of his stories suggest that he is beginning to think of himself as a survivor. He tells how both the middle school head and the secondary head have had breakdowns. He knows of other headteachers who have found the strain too great. And on two occasions he tells stories of people whose careers have closely paralleled his own, and who have suffered what might be called a kind of professional suicide:

Ronald Rae, who used to be head of [county primary], and they closed his school. And he didn't want to be in the First School. Felt he couldn't. He went to the – he went for a routine op on the gall bladder and died under the anaesthetic. Well, he didn't die under the anaesthetic, he never came out of it, and . . . and it was almost as if he didn't want to live (laughs). They broke his heart . . .

16 He also tells of a recent illness:

He said, 'Keep out of the bloody school.' And he said – funnily enough, when I was in hospital, the sister came to me. I hooted with laughter. And she said, 'Now I've got to come and have a serious discussion with you this morning . . . Are you worried about your job?' And I said, 'Well,' I said, 'it is . . . I said it's a job where you have to be on your toes all day. If you're not feeling well it gets you. There's no doubt about that.' But I said, 'But I'm not ill as a rule. This is an exception.'

17 So that's something about Jack Nisbett. Perhaps a happy man. Perhaps quietly desperate. But there's a lot missing from this sketch; he's been married three times, was a lifeboatman for 12 years and spent several years bringing up four children on his own.

Story 2 (Maggie MacLure)

Jack: A good run

1 When I arrive at the school Jack welcomes me warmly, as always. Usually I bring a sandwich and join him and his colleagues in the staffroom for lunch. There are seven staff altogether in this village first school of which Jack is head, and has been for the past twenty years.

2 There's always a lot of jokey chat over lunch, interspersed with business. Jack tends to dominate, with updates on the progress of his garden, anecdotes about the adventures of the kids or groans about the slow progress of the repairs to the ancient fabric of the school buildings.

3 Jack is a 'teaching head', which means that he gets a mere half-day out of his full timetable for admin and management. He does have an office though, which he shares with his part-time secretary and the photocopier. We hold our meetings there. It's cluttered with books and papers, but cosy. There's always a stream of interruptions: colleagues rummaging for files and forms; the 'nit nurse' reporting on the day's trawl for headlice; a parent and fishing partner of Jack's dropping off a sack of charcoal for the school barbecue; another parent, the local butcher, with a poster to be run off on the copier.

4 Jack moans about the interruptions, but actually he encourages them – especially the dads. Many of them are local businessmen and professionals that Jack knows in connection with his many activities and hobbies. These dads provide various goods and services for the school, and in return, Jack ensures that the school is able to do them a few little favours. For Jack, that's what community involvement is all about:

. . . if I want things I tend to pick phones up and ask for them, you know, I ask people in the community. I always try and – try and use the community to help this school, and if we can use this school to help the community, it's well, you know – it's great.

MM: . . . mm – like the butcher bringing in the, er (copying)?

Jack: oh yeah, I mean, I'll do that for Ronnie, yeah, sure, I'll do that for Ronnie, that's no–, that's no problem. And I won't charge him . . . no way am I going to charge him for that, because he's the local butcher and when it comes to the Christmas party he'll give us – er, all the sausages, for the hot dogs. He'll give us beefburgers for barbecues in the summer, which cost far more than those few sheets of paper.

Likewise, the charcoal comes from a fellow-member of the local branch of the 'Round Table' who, Jack says, owes him a favour.

5 Jack's out-of-school hobbies and activities, and the people he meets through these, are very important to him. He would probably describe himself as a bit of an 'action man', and he prefers the company of like-minded people. He doesn't socialize much with other teachers:

. . . er – and outside school I also – I don't mix much with teachers outside school much . . . I mean, I mix with farmers, because I like farming, and sportsmen – you know, cricketers and hockey players, because I've played a lot of cricket and hockey, and – er, and I've been for the last eight years very much involved in Parish Council work at A and now I've just got on to B and I enjoy that – you know – helping other people. I'm vice chairman of C which is a British Legion Sheltered Home, er, was in the Round Table. I'm – I was a founder member and first secretary of the D Volunteer Rescue which is a lifeboat. Er, I was officer of the coastguard at E for eight years. And that's the sort of activity – working with men, and doing things like that. I love the sea – I love sailing . . . And those sorts of activities I find that I do outside school, um, make it more easy for me to be able to pick up a lot of knowledge which you can use too, in the school.

So Jack sees his activities, not just as leisure, but also as a kind of INSET [in-service education for teachers] – it refreshes his mind, and gives him 'knowledge' which informs his practice.

6 This combined interest in physical pursuits and the company of his own sex goes back a long way in Jack's biography – to his days in the Combined Cadet Force at his public school. And unusually perhaps, it was his enjoyment of these military activities that sparked off his interest in becoming a teacher, in the face of his father's opposition:

. . . he wanted me – either to, as I say, go into forestry, or go into banking, and I said 'no, I want to teach'. And I really think, the love of it, the idea of it came from when I was at school, they had what was called a CCF . . . and er I – I – I did enjoy that. I mean a lot of people hated it. I – I – enjoyed it. I liked handling weapons. My father was always a keen shot so we – I was used to handling guns in the family and it didn't worry me handling guns . . . And – I rather liked the activity – I liked the physical side of it. I enjoyed the field days when you played soldiers and all that and . . . I found that when I'd sort of been in the – the corps some time and had passed the various silly little exams you had to pass, you eventually became an instructor and – er – I really enjoyed the instructing of the other lads who were a bit younger than me. And I felt I did it quite successfully and they told me I did it successfully and I

finished up as a sergeant in the – in the CCF. So I'd got a platoon of my own and all this business. And I really enjoyed the teaching side of it as well. And, er, that's probably what made me decide to go (into teaching).

7 Jack did his National Service, and spent three years after that as a regular officer in the Education Corps, as money was short and he had younger brothers still at school. Then he trained as a school teacher. He was ambitious, and set himself the target of getting a headship within ten years. He made it – returning to his home county, and to the school of which he is still head – though the school itself has gone through changes, as we will see later.

8 Jack's 'action man' identity shows in his educational pronouncements too. He disclaims dedication and enthusiasm, and indeed at times he professes a cynical, 'only here for the beer' attitude to the job, couched in the blunt speech of the ex-soldier:

I mean I'm – I don't even think I'm enthusiastic, you know – I do it because I've got to have – I've got to – feed my family and – put clothes on my back and, you know, get money for a pint of beer. Um, this is the nicest way I can think of doing it. But if I didn't have to do it I'd – I'd retire and I'd go fishing every day and – catch butterflies and do the things I like doing.

9 He takes a similar stance about the effort he puts into organizing governors' meetings. It's not a question of dedication or industriousness, rather:

. . . if you've circulated (the papers) before the meeting, it's merely then a matter of, you know, you can get to the pub quickly, can't you?

10 In fact, at times Jack comes close to claiming that he doesn't 'give a damn' about the job, as here, where he gives this as his reason for not feeling the stress that other teachers appear to be suffering:

. . . erm, I just think I'm lucky. I – I, basically I don't give a damn. Er – no, that's too strong . . . I do give a damn, but I don't give a damn what people think (laughs) which is different. Now, if I can go home at the end of the day and think 'ah well,' you know 'I've earned my pennies today, and my conscience is clear, er – and everything I've done I've believed in' – I don't worry.

11 But in fact Jack does have strongly held educational principles, and again, these are quite congruent with his action man persona. As one might expect, he has little time for intellectuals or specialists, favouring 'breadth' in education:

I think the – the problem with a lot of teachers is that – academic excellence, which I don't – frown upon, and which I – do try and encourage – that academic excellence is(n't) the be-all-and-end-all . . . I think that one of the great things of British Education is its breadth. Er, it could also have elements of disadvantages in that because you spread so far, er, you don't concentrate enough on one, but I, I – it's funny because – you see – it's the breadth in the primary curriculum, and you get to secondary and because of exams it suddenly constricts again. And there's a great change in the ethos and the way of looking at education from primary to secondary and – I wonder whether perhaps we actually specialise too soon, you know? (mm) It's difficult –

you've got to have experts – the word today is experts, isn't it? We have to have experts, er, but, you know, they seem to know more and more about less and less. And a lot of these experts are such narrow-minded people who are – specialists in their own field, and are totally ignorant about every other – every other field.

12 Equally, he has the man-of-action's exasperation with bureaucracies and administrations, whom he sees as impediments to the central task of teaching – that is, being in the classroom with the kids:

And as I've already said to you, the priorities in this school are those kids in that classroom for me. They're my major priority. The second priority is the rest of the children in the school, and everything that I do is towards – them. Um, as far as forms are concerned, when people ring up from County Hall and say, uh, 'form so-and-so, and so-and-so,' er, and then – spew out over a – list of letters and that – and numbers – which I don't recognise, even after seventeen years I don't recognise them, I say 'oh yes, well, I'm sure it's got lost or something.' I mean, then – and I'm sure they're very important to somebody but they are not important to me, because they don't teach kids anything. They don't do anything for kids.

13 'Being there for the kids' is at the centre of Jack's philosophy of teaching:

because the kids come first. And the – the whole of my ethos, if you like, for running the school is that, er, I don't give a monkey's what goes on in here (i.e. the office) really . . . as I say, the classroom is the priority, always.

14 Jack interprets 'the classroom' quite widely though – in fact, he likes to get the kids outside its four walls as often as he can. For him, open-air activities or 'outings' of the sort he himself likes doing help to provide that 'broad' education which he favours:

I am strongly of the belief that outings like that, and I do as many of them as I can in a year . . . I would suggest to you that they, if you could teach all the time like that . . . you could get far better, rounded and more developed kids.

15 These activities can provide the basis for almost every curriculum area: maths, 'nature study', creative writing, etc. Jack shows me some of the worksheets and materials that he has used before and after trips:

. . . and there's all sorts of things in there about lighthouses and uh, how to catch shrimps and – I tend to do – I tend to work that way. I work with, er, that sort of thing with kids, and this is – this is the one I've got on maths. I mean, the other day we went down, uh, Warblers Walk, and we were particularly looking at (inaudible) and things, and that was the mathematics that came out of that.

16 Jack tends to tell his life (hi)story on an up-beat, but it emerges that his career reached a watershed some ten years ago, when the local authority reorganized its primary provision, breaking up the old 5–11 primaries into a system of first and middle schools. This meant that Jack – head for over ten years of the old primary – now found himself forced to apply for the headship of the new middle school in the village. He didn't get the job, and wound up as head of the first school, occupying the same building as the old primary, but now providing for 5–8-year-olds.

17 This was a blow in many ways for Jack. For a start, he'd always preferred teaching the older junior classes, and now the oldest children in the school were no more than 8. More than that, the change struck at the heart of his action man identity, for it removed him simultaneously from the company of male colleagues, and from the school sporting activities which he'd always enjoyed:

. . . the thing that I miss in the first school more than anything really, is contact with men . . . erm when I was younger . . . I was very much involved in sport and man's type, you know, really chauvinist – I was a total chauvinist. And I missed that. I missed the fact that with 11-year-olds I could play cricket and football. Now, I very much miss the – social interplay which used to go on between the – the – the junior schools, and you had your football matches with orange and biscuits afterwards.

18 These social events were also an important preparation for adult life (at least for the boys):

All those sorts of activities which people just – brush aside. They – they're not important. They were, they were very important and they were very good for the kids. And it was, if you like, an introduction to, er, club and society activity after leaving school. It was a facet of that. And it was a shame they ever went.

19 So now, Jack sees his career as static, if not in decline. He feels out of step with the aims of contemporary education, especially as interpreted by his local authority:

When I finish at this school, I shall be damn glad to go and I shall be the first out the door. I really will.

. . .

MM: Would you take early retirement if it was on offer? I mean gladly?

Jack: Well I quite honestly think that some of us, of my age group, we're invited to take early retirement because we don't suit the pattern that's needed.

MM: What d'you reckon the county would be looking for?

Jack: (pause) They won't be looking for me . . . They'll want somebody in the modern idiom, doing the things that – are being advocated in education now.

20 So Jack sees his career as winding down. He reckons that he won't be around for long after the national assessment programme is fully 'on line': and in the meantime, he views the immediate future with resignation:

By the time we get there (i.e. testing at age 7) I haven't many years to do, have I! (MM: Yeah, well I'm sure quite a few people are thinking that way.) I will do what I've always done, Maggie. I will give each, to this school and to these children, a fair percentage of each day. And when I get to the end of the day and I've had enough and I'm tired, I'll go home, and I'll have the other side of my life.

21 But the 'other side' of Jack's life is winding down a bit too. He hasn't

played hockey for some years, and he had to give up cricket because his eyesight deteriorated, suddenly and inexplicably, a couple of years previously. It's been a long time since he and his mates took the boat out for one of their deep-sea sailing jaunts. And other activities have stopped too:

. . . and I've given up coastguarding . . . and 12 and a half years as a member of a lifeboat crew. That's gone, past. I don't play cricket now, I don't play hockey now. I don't play anything now.

22 But he does still have many interests. He's taken up fly-fishing, and he still greatly enjoys everything to do with the countryside. More and more of his time these days is spent in leisurely activities that he can share with his wife:

Well now, Gillian and I married, what, three years ago come March. We're very, very happy. Erm – we never get on each other's nerves. We love gardening and do a lot of gardening, and we're quite good at gardening. And, you know, I've set myself up a little workshop. I like bodging about with wood and mucking about. (mm) She's got her knitting machine, and we get involved in the local community. I'm on the village hall management committee and playing field and parish council.

23 It's perhaps poignant that, as Jack comes to terms with the remainder of his career, and with the effects of the passing of time, he has taken up one other hobby – collecting and mending clocks. Jack himself chooses a different metaphor. Characteristically, it is a sporting one:

Well, your mid-fifties, you've had a good run.

A note of caution

What the commentaries offer are two further 'readings' of the Jack stories. They are, of course, 'privileged' readings – first, in the sense that they are produced and controlled by the authors of the chapter into which they have been inserted, and are therefore inevitably accorded a higher textual 'authority' than those other readings of the stories that are dimly visible throughout. They are also 'privileged' in the sense that the 'readers' in this case were also the writers. Not only did we have access to the interview data from which the portraits were drawn, but we also had access to our own differential intuitions and intentions (as we think/claim we recall them) at the time of writing (MacLure had done the interviewing, Stronach had never met Jack). This may, however, be a double-edged privilege: as authors who cannot always remember that we are dead, even though it is some time since Barthes and others proclaimed 'the death of the author', we have no doubt been guilty of mixing (respectable) text analysis with (disreputable) special pleadings as to our original authorial intentions, or our peculiar personal biases. At any event, the argument that we develop in the readings/commentaries that follow is one which would have to question the authority of those readings themselves – a paradox that we return to in the concluding section.

Commentary on story 1

The reading developed here concentrates on the sorts of analytical and narrative strategies involved in the construction of 'Jack' in story 1. That account is constructed according to the methodological and ethical canons of qualitative research: that is to say, it purports to offer 'grounded' theory based on a series of open and unstructured interviews with Jack. The transcripts (136 pages) were subject to content analysis, and reduced to 18 pages of closely written notes about categories (self, career, social life, classroom persona, teaching philosophy, head's role etc.) and themes (sense of status, attitudes to authority, boundaries between job and life, cases of 'professional suicide' etc.). Illustrative quotation was noted, and the first draft was produced in the form in which it is presented in this chapter (though we cannot fully reproduce the aura of 'provisionality' of the originals, with their typing errors and lack of attention to layout).

The writer – Ian Stronach – constructed the account knowing that it was naturalistic in approach, and that he had criticisms to make of that approach. Nevertheless, it was a form of research writing with which he had been familiar in the past, and which typified the approach of the research centre in which he worked at that time (CARE). In so far as it is possible or justifiable to have access to one's own intentions and motivations, the account was researched and written with 'integrity', although the original title, scored out in the first draft, clearly shows the writer's scepticism. It read: *'Jack's story: or, biographers are ventriloquists whose lips are sealed'*.

Let us look first at the narrative strategies that are embedded in the account. Story 1 begins with a pattern of three triumphs for Jack. Each triumph is a resolution of opposites. In the first opposition (paragraph 2) – 'cloistered'/'eye-opener' – the young Jack passes from the socially closed existence of public school to a very different army world ('totally new to me'; 'all walks of life'). The opposites register in his uncertain translation of the status of these new people ('mates, colleagues, whatever you like to call them'). But he is accepted ('we'll show you what to do') and becomes a sergeant at the age of 18. The second triumph contains the opposition of the assertive son against the autocratic father. Again, Jack triumphs and becomes a teacher against his father's wishes (paragraph 4). The third opposition is between the experienced and local headteacher applicants and the young aspirant who is also an outsider (paragraph 6). And it is Jack who wins the headship of the county primary.

In the storying of these triumphs, however, the writer sets out to exact a cost. In a fieldnote written just after completing the account Ian Stronach noted 'I don't quote J. so that you can believe him – often it's to allow a sceptical "deeper" reading in the clues about status, career, emotions etc.' Thus the apparently authentic mode – Jack 'speaking for himself' – and the inauthentic – the author speaking about Jack – change places. When Jack speaks, he is being invited, unwittingly, to confess. The writer notes: 'feel that I comment more when I'm quoting Jack than when I'm linking the quotes. The links feel more like summaries than judgements, whereas the quotes are a series of summary judgements.'

What is the researcher trying to say about Jack? The notes that make up the pre-text of Jack's story give some indication. He is struck by Jack's habit of ordering people in terms of a social hierarchy: 'five men in a boat, hierarchically listed (two doctors, one headteacher, probationer officer, and "a chap who runs a nursery")'. Or, in relation to a later interview in which Jack refers to the same circle of friends, the notes record: 'two local doctors, a probation officer, a nursery owner, myself and an ex-nature conservancy warden'. Jack was certain of the doctor's status, uncertain of his own placing, interested in 'rank'. So he was made to speak 'for himself' in narratives about class and career (and never mind Jack the lifeboatman, father, husband, widow, cricketer, hockey-player, councillor, Norfolk man born and bred . . .). He is allowed his triumphs, but they are deemed a form of pride. And pride comes before a fall.

Thus, this story of Jack is given its fulcrum in the events that surround Jack's failure to become headteacher of the middle school, and his ambivalence towards that circumstance. Again, Jack is 'summarized' in paragraphs 8 and 9 through the data that suggest his contentment with his lot. But he is made to 'speak for himself' about his doubts, in the extended quotation in paragraph 9 – about how he misses the older children, the company of male teachers, not doing it by choice, the nervous breakdowns of colleagues 'in the situation that I'm in now'. These data are left to 'speak for themselves', but Stronach's original fieldnotes in the pre-text indicate a more certain emplotment: Jack, he hypothesized, was offering a 'serial confession', and he went on to list the elements of that confession:

'I enjoy teaching 8-year-olds'
'I'm not doing it by choice'
'nervous breakdowns for others'
'I can cope with that'
'two have actually died'

Later in the portrait, these 'broken heart' stories are accompanied by the notion of 'professional suicide' (paragraph 15). In the pre-text, the researcher settled on the 'quietly desperate' (paragraph 17) version of the story, claiming that 'Jack talks about himself through these surrogate heads'.

It is clear that this is an 'author-saturated' text in Geertz's term (unlike story 2, in all but its introduction). Jack is manipulated. The author declares the presence of stories, and claims to identify endings. The author offers to lead the reader to meaning: 'so . . .' this, and 'thus . . .' that. A tremendous amount of ordering goes on; surface data are implicitly rejected as a cover-up on Jack's part, and a depth theory is introduced (i.e. beneath the surface of contentment lies an unhappy man). Further, it might be argued that this is 'male-author-saturated' because the considerable amount of data on Jack's sports, hobbies and family life is glossed over. It is a male status story – preoccupied with career in a way that Jack wasn't, or not in terms of the bulk of the data.

So far, we have analysed this story in two different ways. We have examined it as a narrative, considering its construction – how Jack was emplotted and explained. We have also looked at the notes out of which that story was created – the pre-text – in order to throw some light on the sorts of strategies that seem to have been employed by the writer in creating this first draft. A further way of trying to understand what was going on in the construction of this portrait would be to establish the relation between plot and theory. The interview data about Jack's life could in principle be treated as ambivalent rather than oppositional. Yet the author seeks a satisfactory emplotment that will lead, ultimately, to narrative closure, by choosing to regard Jack's early life as a series of three triumphs, centring on the career dimension. This narrative structure demands a dénouement: the opposition implies a struggle that must be resolved. Jack must be accepted or rejected by his mates in the army; he has to get his own way with his father or succumb to his will; he has to win or lose his job. And, most significantly, he has either to be content with his lot in the end, or to be unhappy. Having led him through three trials whose oppositions revolve around Jack's purported desire for social status and recognition, the author cannot then 'unstory' that plot by characterizing his failure to become headteacher of the middle school as anything other than significant to his life. This would be to go against the narrative logic established in the three previous incidents. That logic makes a 'critical incident' or 'epiphany' (Denzin, 1989) out of the unsuccessful job interview, and predisposes the author to sort positive views and comments by Jack ('contented', 'happy') into a box marked surface data, and to sort negative ones, along with some ambivalent associations, into a 'depth' reading that provides a watershed for Jack's life, allowing the rest of his life to be portrayed in terms of decline, disappointment or even despair. The narrative logic encodes, therefore, a *theory* which explains the 'meaning' of that critical incident, and its implications for the rest of Jack's (professional) life to date. As we show below, the second story also locates its turning point or watershed in Jack's failure to get the middle school headship, but its theory of the meaning of that failure, and of the resulting course of Jack's life, is a rather different one. The story–theory nexus is at work in both stories: telling Jack and explaining Jack become the same thing.

Yet another way of looking at the story would be to ask: how did others read it? Some complained of the intrusive and pre-emptive author: 'let Jack tell his own story'. In rejecting the author-saturated version of the account, however, they sought to read Jack's words directly – over the shoulder of the researcher, as it were. Both found an authentic reading in Jack's words: the first taking Jack at face value, a man who is as he seems; the second offering more of a depth theory, a man slightly at odds with himself, revealed by his 'odd tones' etc. But the reach for authenticity, based on the question 'how do I understand a man who sounds like that?', ignores the editing and the subverting that went into the researcher's presentation of Jack in the account. 'Naturalistic generalization', in this instance, means no more than to succumb to a double bias: the idiosyncracy of one's own reading in terms of prior experiences, background, prejudices etc., and also the bias of the selection presented for interpretation by the author to the reader. What turns out to be interesting about the process of naturalistic generalization is only the ways in which it provokes a naive reading in otherwise sceptical minds.

So why is 'struggle' a metaphor for the relationship of the writer to the text and to the subject?

1 There is a covert critique in the researcher's reading of Jack's life, a bias which operates even if methodological canons are respected.
2 That hostility is manifested in a desire to sort the data into oppositions.
3 These oppositions take on (already have) a dialectic narrative quality (Jack is/Jack is not . . .).
4 The juxtaposing of opposites provokes depth theories of what Jack really is like (reading the data as a 'presentation of self' through which shafts of revelation can be seen).
5 An opposition posited must become an opposition resolved: the story must have an ending, and given (1) and (2), an 'unhappily ever after'. At any rate, endings are singular things.

But the struggle may be over the wrong thing. The problem is not what will count as an authentic portrait, but the assumptions that we make about personhood. We think of the problem as one of representation (the person as given, the portrait as problematic) and we struggle with forms of ethics, social interaction, data analysis and reporting that will 'express' the person, squeeze his essence from the body of data. But perhaps the problem is one of conceptualization, of making problematic what we mean by a 'person'. Are 'persons' an ontological rather than a methodological problem? We return to that issue at the end of this chapter.

Commentary on story 2

Like the first portrayal of Jack, this one is amply 'substantiated' by excerpts from the interview transcripts. In fact the excerpts account, again, for more than 50 per cent of the overall text – a strong indicator in itself, one might think, of the 'likeness' of the portrait. It suggests, surely, that Jack has been given a decent chance of 'speaking for himself'. Well, not really of course. But of the two stories, this one certainly seemed more convincing, more 'authentic', to several of those who read them for us. People said things like 'You get a strong feeling of what he was like.' One person, comparing the two versions, found this one more 'rounded'; the first, she wrote, 'feels it's on the outside, looking in at Jack [while this one] feels more in there, with Jack, looking out.' Most affirmative of all perhaps: someone who happened to know Jack identified him instantly ('It's just him!'). Responses such as these are generally gratifying to the naturalistic researcher, as testimony to the authenticity and validity of a portrayal. They are just what a researcher is looking for when she or he is collecting warrants for the methodological soundness and the ethical probity of an account, for they suggest a good fit between the portrait and the 'real person' – that the author has done everything possible to reduce that troubling gap between language and reality, and in so doing, to efface the writer from the account.

We want to suggest, however, that the gratifications offered by responses such as these are misplaced, or at least overvalued: that recognition, authenticity and validity are not methodological or ethical phenomena at all, as far as the reader is concerned, but rather *textual* ones – the effects of particular generic conventions for representing reality.

Let us take a closer look, then, at the discourse strategies that have been used in 'A good run' to make sense, quite literally, of Jack and his life. There are many things that could be said about this text, but the reading offered here will pay particular attention to the textual devices that are used to establish a 'core identity' for Jack, and the ways in which this identity is then used as an *explanatory mechanism* – a means of accounting for Jack's actions and choices as rational, consistent and intelligible.

We can start by noting that this account is recognizably a *story*: it has plot, characterization, causality and coherence. It has a 'beginning' which sets the scene and introduces the protagonist, a 'middle' which elaborates Jack's character and delineates the main episodes in his life, and an 'end' which brings his life to a close – textually at any rate. The storied nature of this account is not, we suggest, a trivial fact; and the story features that we identify below are not mere stylistic flourishes superimposed on a bald sequence of events to make them warm, friendly, empathetic and accessible (though they may accomplish these things). Stories, as Ricoeur (1981) showed, are powerful explanatory structures: while episodes seem to 'follow' one another in a sequence that leads ineluctably to the story's conclusion, the overarching structure of the story, and its end-point, gives meaning to the individual episodes. So stories always work backwards as well as forwards: as the text accumulates, it spins itself into the form of a story; but it is also its overall structure *as* a story that allows us to make sense, retrospectively, of the individual elements. A simple example of this can be seen in the title to this particular story, which faces 'forwards' to the story to come, issuing a kind of instruction as to how to read it, and setting up a small mystery as to what the title's full meaning will turn out to be. But that meaning is, in turn, fully interpretable only in the last line, which therefore turns the text back full circle to its beginning. The implications of this sort of thing for life (hi)stories is clear: they may look like simple chronologies (first this happened, then that) but only the 'bed-to-bed' stories of young children are like that. As we have already seen above, life stories are inevitably theoretical – assembling the 'facts' of the life into an explanatory structure that ranges backwards and forwards over the text.

The first three paragraphs of the story, as noted, set the scene: they introduce Jack, sketch in a few details about his job and the context in which he works. They do more than this though. Note the scattering of words and phrases that suggest repetition and recurrence: 'Usually, I bring a sandwich; Jack tends to dominate'; the three instances of 'always'. Recurrence is indicated throughout these opening paragraphs, in fact, in the choice of the present tense rather than one of the past tenses: 'we hold our meetings there' in Jack's office, rather than 'we held them there'. These features act as warrants for the representativeness of the account: they suggest that what Maggie MacLure saw on the days she visited, and the characteristics that she discerned in Jack, were typical, routine, familiar. They are part, therefore, of the naturalistic researcher's armoury of stylistic devices that say, implicitly, 'trust me, and trust my account'.

There are other features of this opening section that fulfil a similar function: the vividness of the descriptive detail, for example – the busy colleagues rummaging, the nit-nurse, the sack of charcoal. This is journalistic 'local colour' of course, but it also serves a key function within the research text: in the words of Geertz, it gives the sense of 'being there', ethnographically speaking. As Geertz (1988: 16) says, one of the main problems facing ethnographers is 'to convince us . . . not merely that they themselves have truly "been there", but . . . that had we been there we should have seen what they saw, felt what they felt, concluded what they concluded'.

As well as setting the scene and presenting the writer's credentials for having been there, this introductory section begins, towards the end, to announce the themes that will give coherence and intelligibility to the narrative as a whole. The last sentence of paragraph 3 introduces the parents from the local community, who are also personal friends of Jack. This is immediately elaborated in the next paragraph (4), where a further theme is casually gestured towards in the throw-away comment 'especially the dads'. Though the reader does not, of course, fully know it at this point, the text has already begun to shape up three themes or dimensions of Jack's 'life' that are going to figure prominently as organizing devices: (a) his community involvement; (b) his sporting and leisure interests; (c) his preference for the company of men. These three themes are elaborated in the remainder of the lengthy quotation in paragraph 4, and still further in paragraph 5.

More importantly, paragraph 5 marks the first instance of the core identity which is fashioned for Jack in this text – that of 'action man'. This term is used to 'collect' together different dimensions of Jack, and give them coherence and unity as facets of a single identity. At this point of its first appearance, it collects together the three themes we have noted so far: community, (active) leisure interests and male company. The ensuing quote gives details of those community and leisure activities and 'allows' Jack to spell out the point about his preference for 'working with men'. The meaning of the action man label continues to develop, however, over the course of the story: as the text accumulates, the label 'collects together' further dimensions of Jack and, as we show below, progressively extends its explanatory scope as a device for understanding Jack's life and the choices he has made.

For the moment, though, we can note another textual strategy accompanying that first appearance of 'action man' in paragraph 5. The phrase 'He would probably describe himself as a bit of an "action man" not only introduces the term, it virtually puts it into Jack's mouth. This authorial sleight of hand works, if it does, because of the introductory credentialing work described above: readers will be prepared to accept this act of ventriloquism (see story 1 above) to the extent that they are convinced of the writer's authority to make such claims about Jack's predispositions and internal states.

Paragraph 6 contains an interesting new development in the structuring of the story. Once established, the action man identity is now available to cast a *retrospective* interpretive slant over Jack's early life: 'This combined interest in physical pursuits and the company of his own sex goes back a long way in Jack's biography.' By the forging of a link between Jack's contemporary 'identity' and his adolescent experiences, the present is used to construct the past, while making it look as if the process had worked in reverse. At the same time, this paragraph grafts on to the action man identity a further element – that of military enthusiasm. In Britain at least, one meaning of the term 'action man' has militaristic connotations (and also a slightly comical flavour: it is the name given to the soldier doll for boys that is known as GI Joe in the USA). This military theme, as the ensuing quote makes clear, provides the biographical 'bridge' into teaching as Jack's career choice.

The military theme also comes in useful a little later on in the text: at paragraph 8 it is used to weave a further strand into the fabric of Jack's story. Here the text spells out a connection between Jack's action man identity and his educational pronouncements – namely, his disclaiming of enthusiasm and his 'only-here-for-the-beer' attitude. The textual strategy seems particularly visible here (to us at least; it did not seem to attract much attention from the other readers). Would readers ordinarily assume a link between such attitudes and the term 'action man', had not the text spelled this out in a rather heavy-handed authorial intervention: 'couched in the blunt speech of the ex-soldier'? And a similar authorial 'nudge' occurs at paragraph 11, where, after the statement that Jack does in fact hold strong educational principles, it is claimed that these 'too' are 'quite congruent with his action man persona'. Indeed, the authorial nudge is slightly more forceful here: the comment 'As one might expect, he has little time for intellectuals . . .' recruits the reader to the writer's vantage point, and invites her or him right inside the discursive frame. The implication is that the reader now 'knows' Jack well enough to make predictions about his preferences and predispositions, or at least that reader and writer are like-minded persons whose interpretations would 'naturally' coincide.

Passing over paragraphs 12 to 15 (except to note that, in 12, 'exasperation with bureaucracies' is added to the list of action man characteristics), we come to paragraph 16, which introduces the event which is presented as a turning point or epiphany in both versions of Jack's story – namely, his failure in the mid-1970s to get the headship of the new middle school. The epiphany – described here as a 'watershed' – amounts to nothing less than an identity crisis for Jack: a change which 'struck at the heart of his action man identity' (paragraph 17), by removing him from male company and sporting events. The identity that has been carefully fashioned for Jack in this portrayal is now, finally, used therefore to 'explain' the force of a key event in his life, and thus to prepare the grounds for a 'reading' of the remainder of his life to date as a gentle decline or 'winding down'.

Returning to our text, what remains is for the story itself to 'wind down'. Some of the narrative means for doing this are quite clear: note how the term 'winding down' is twice 'seeded' metaphorically in the text, at paragraphs 20 and 21, foreshadowing the mention in the final paragraph of Jack's latest hobby of collecting and mending clocks. This careful seeding allows the writer to characterize that choice of hobby as 'perhaps poignant', before ending with a sentence which marks the last, if veiled, appearance of the action man identity. So firmly established is this textual identity that it is possible to use the word 'characteristically' of Jack's 'final' comment – though that finality is itself entirely a narrative artefact. It was not, of course, the last thing that Jack said to the interviewer, and its placement as the 'last word' of the narrative gives it a nostalgic retrospection that it would be difficult to read into the original interview data. Placed here as the closure of the tale, it seems to sum up the 'point' of the whole life story.

Covering over the cracks: the tyranny of the text?

Jack 2 is a simple story, by any literary or ethnographic criteria. It is an example of 'classic realism' which, as Belsey (1980: 73) notes, 'tends to offer as the "obvious" basis of its intelligibility the assumption that character, unified and coherent, is the source of action'. Such an assumption runs through the second story of Jack: it is put together in a way that establishes (a) that Jack is the 'same person' now that he was 40-odd years ago; and (b) that this stable identity is the well-spring of the choices he made and the things he did (or failed to do). He fits the description of individuals as constructed in classic realism, 'whose traits of character, understood as essential and predominantly given, constrain the choices they make' (Belsey, 1980: 74).

If most of the readers of Jack 2 found the portrait plausible, then, this is more easily attributable to the tyranny of the text and its control over the reader's options than to methodological astuteness or empathy between the writer and the subject. Realist writing aims to resolve contradictions, smooth over inconsistencies and achieve a sense of closure. In order to be revelatory, therefore, realist texts have to conceal: they have to iron out inconsistencies, establish coherence and insinuate a shared point of view between reader and writer that convinces the former that both see the world in much the same way.

As we have noted, most of the readers of this story did seem to be seduced by its narrative pretensions into taking the portrayal of Jack at face value. Unlike the previous version, the presence of the author here attracted almost no attention; on the contrary, readers generally felt they were getting a clear and untrammelled view of Jack. Yet, as deconstructionists insist (see, for example, Lather, 1991), it is always worth asking what the text is *concealing* – what it has had to suppress, or make a detour round, in order to achieve its sense of completeness. This is not to suggest that there is some true or ideal story waiting to be written, whose fate is usually to be 'distorted' by base interest or poor literary skills; simply that to engage in the act of writing one story, in one way, is always to opt (consciously or not) *not* to write something else. And that choice will carry ethical or ideological implications. Macherey (1978) argues that the absences, elisions and silences in texts are generally ideologically motivated, and that to read against the grain – to interrogate texts for what they fail to say, but cannot fully cover up – is to reassert the existence of a plurality of voices, values and perspectives, in the face of the universalizing tendencies of the dominant culture.

As a privileged reader of this particular tale, the writer knows some of what she has chosen to exclude.[3] One of the most notable exclusions, hinted at above in the first story, is the episode (or what might have become, in the story, an episode) in Jack's life during which he was a single parent, combining his job with the care of his two young children following the death of his first wife. One might have expected such an experience to figure in a life history, however brief – especially since male single parenthood is still less than common in our culture. Other omissions are equally curious: there is almost no mention in the story of any of the women in Jack's life, with the exception, at the end, of his second wife. Yet in the interviews Jack spoke at some length about his mother, his aunts, his daughter.

We can speculate on some of the textual reasons for these omissions: it is fairly obvious (or so we would claim on the basis of the particular reading of Jack 2 above) that such data would not have fitted well with the action man thesis elaborated in the story. To include them would have contradicted, or at least muddied the clarity of, the themes of sporting interests, preference for male company etc. that were foregrounded in the telling. Speculation as to why the writer should have wanted to portray Jack in this way takes us into the realms of intentionality rather than textual analysis. But it is not inconceivable that some kind of covert feminist critique was intended – that in a manner similar to that suggested in the first story, the writer wanted to allude to Jack's sexism, as she perceived it, without directly telling it. There is one faint hint of this in the story, at paragraph 18: 'These social events were also an important preparation for adult life (at least for the boys).'

Jack: rescuing the life from the text

So far we have written two stories about Jack, commented on them and referred to the comments of other readers. But we have not so far heard from Jack. How did he respond to these attempts on his life?

In the four hours of tape-recorded follow-up discussion, he did a lot of 'work' on them – tidying up the facts and the interpretations, challenging, confirming, admitting, excusing, confiding. He felt at the mercy of our interpretations – a 'guinea pig', he said. On the other hand, he still felt in control: 'Well I don't think it really matters whether it's a biography or an autobiography. Because all you get is what you're given.' It was his choice, he said, when and if to release stories; and he could also control through mocking or rubbishing ('this load of crap' he called one of the stories at one point, without rancour). Or he could deny the surface of the text: 'It's me hiding behind words, isn't it?'

The issue of control and who 'has' it – researcher or subject – is a complex one. There were interesting political switches in the relationship between researcher and subject at different points in the research process. The original three interviews took place under the rubrics of a democratic regime: collegial atmosphere, collaborative intent, negotiated draft. But the stories, as we know, were authoritarian: imposed, devious, unilateral. The subsequent interaction reverted to the democratic appearances of the first. Maggie MacLure asked questions like 'Where did we get it wrong?' and retracted or modified strong interpretive claims. She even expressed bewilderment that the text had turned out the way it did: 'What on earth possessed me to write that?' And now, of course, Jack is once more at our mercy. These are neglected disjunctions in the politics of the research process, and one way of interpreting them is as a covert struggle: the authors conciliatory in face-to-face encounters, but implacable in the construction of their texts.

Jack had claimed to have been 'hiding behind words'. What had he been hiding behind his words? He gave examples of his dedication, his enthusiasm – for his job, but also for his hobbies. He was concerned to undermine the 'only here for the beer' impressions, and offered many examples – worksheets, school trips, testimonials – and ended: 'so we've shot that one down'. We had got it wrong, he felt, because for him the surface stories were really about his powerful sense of boundary – between work and home ('I'm a changing man as I travel'), between work and play. They marked a way of switching off from work, putting it into its place. He had used them to mark the sensible limits a man must place on his job – if he was to avoid a nervous breakdown.

And that was another thing. He agreed with the idea of 'professional suicides'. It was 'virtually true', and had happened again to a colleague who would have been the 'last person' you would have expected. But it had nothing to do with him. There was no watershed, no sense of disappointment: 'I'd achieved what I wanted to achieve within the time scale'; 'I'm doing what I want to do.' (But 'time scale': what note was that?)

In tidying up his stories Jack had in mind a rather different plot structure from the ones that we had offered: he read his life as a 'main trunk': 'there's a central thread with many branches.' He seemed to define his enthusiasm and positive nature as the central account – fighting against the narrower 'action man' and 'professional suicide' cores. Towards the end of this final interview Jack was more inclined than he had been previously to take an overall, summary view of his life. He seemed to be moving towards a more rounded realization of his life as a text. But perhaps the negotiation procedures in life history research leave subjects with little choice in the matter: they may disagree with the 'facts' of the history/story; or they may disagree with the interpretation; but they are more or less obliged to treat their 'life' as some sort of narrative. The negotiation process itself tended, therefore, towards a realist dénouement for Jack's story.

... And with one bound, Jack was free?

In this last section we want to sketch out some of the possibilities for different approaches to biography in educational research.

One way to tell Jack's story would be through his notion of his life as a 'trunk' or a 'central thread', building on the implicit continuities of that concept. But another way to approach the problem of representation might be to see his story in discontinuous terms, and again on grounds that Jack himself had supplied. We had asked Jack to look back. But he was not a 'back-looker'. He was a 'mover-onner': 'I tend to look to tomorrow in all aspects of my life.' So perhaps we had asked him to do something that did not come naturally, when we asked him to look back. That might imply a more episodic writing of his life, raising the possibility that we might explore (with reason rather than arbitrarily) different narrative forms within which to represent his life – forms that took as their justification different aspects of his own subjective experience, and his own partial theories of himself. Working in this way, contradictory versions of Jack might be developed – the continuity thesis of the 'trunk' story undermined by the discontinuities implicit in the 'mover-onner' story, and so on.

Or alternatively, we might conclude that the accumulation of evidence from Jack suggests plots that were finally irresolvable. There was ambivalence in his accounts: 'I enjoy what I do now' would be confronted, in a short space of time, with 'I shall be damn glad to go when I go and I will be the first one out of the door' (a sentiment that appears in more than one interview). The resolvability of such contradictions was in doubt. Both of our stories had privileged a negative version, and Jack had sought redress. But his rescue attempts kept re-telling the negative as well as the positive themes. And new themes and concerns were still proliferating throughout the follow-up interview: 'winning' seemed to be elaborated as an important issue for Jack; or the need to 'control' his life. It seemed arbitrary to offer core identities for Jack, and increasingly necessary to find ways of representing the plurality and contradiction of his – and no doubt everyone's – ideas and selves.

Another possible strategy for biographical research would be to explore the problems of reflexivity more thoroughly. What kinds of involvement do authors have in the construction of the text? How secure is their methodological position? Ashmore (1989) formulates the problem in the following way: we know that all accounts are contextual, defeasible, inconcludable and reflexive in the realities they invoke and address. But we also accept the paradox that they are routinely accepted and analysed as unproblematic. This kind of fundamental problem is – somehow – 'signally unsuccessful in making life as impossible as its existence would lead us to suspect' (Ashmore, 1989: 176). A central task for research, therefore, is to understand how that paradox comes to be accepted: to try to uncover the methods and sense-making procedures that members of a culture apply in order to find/create regularity and stability in the phenomenal world. So far, so good: we might feel that we have tried to do some of that in this chapter, showing the self-effacement of authors, reductive analyses, prejudiced emplotments and their various textual disguises. But the carrying out of that research task itself proceeds, as we have already hinted, through the creation and use of documents that are themselves contextual, defeasible etc., and contains the same necessary paradox whose acceptance is the legitimate focus for research. It follows that this account, too, must necessarily be read and critiqued for its treatment of evidence as fixed and reliable, its glossing over of ambivalence and uncertainty. We cannot claim that the paradox does not apply to our own work.

A qualifying point needs to be registered. We have argued that authenticity, validity and recognition are textual accomplishments: that they are not 'really' methodological, stressing the 'tyranny of the text'. This raises the question of whether methodological questions are reducible to textual ones. There are two answers. For the *reader,* texts can only be authenticated in themselves: the reader has no other resource than the persuasiveness of the text. But for the *researcher,* the problem of the interrelationship of methodology and text remains important (see Geertz, 1988; Measor and Sikes, 1992). We do not seek to dismiss methodology, but rather to bring its textual properties to light; to ask what sorts of stories are implicated in a particular methodology, and what sorts of stories are suppressed or made un-tellable.

There are good reasons, therefore, for attending to the *forms* in which teachers are portrayed in research accounts, whether by themselves or by other people. Narratives that promote coherence, singularity and closure, and which aim to set up a cosy camaraderie with the reader, are ultimately conservative and uncritical of prevailing ideological and representational arrangements. If we refuse to 'interrogate' these forms, we run the risk of promoting an uncritical research practice which, in seeming to describe teachers as they 'really are', simply perpetuates whatever iconographies of teacher-hood happen to be circulating in the various professional cultures (research, practitioner, academic) at any given time.

One goal must be to produce accounts which deny the reader that comfort of a shared ground with the author, foreground ambivalence and undermine the authority of their own assertions. Yet, as Geertz wryly observes, proposals to abandon the 'easy realism' of ethnography have prompted a 'pervasive nervousness', 'moral hypochondria' and 'authorial self-doubt' among anthropologists, as they have done among those of us who profess other disciplines, including education. There is, however, no going back. As Geertz acknowledges, citing what he calls a 'small shower of dropping names, which could easily be whipped into a tropical downpour . . . "telling it like it is" is hardly adequate as a slogan for ethnography than [it has been] for philosophy since Wittgenstein (or Gadamer), history since Collingwood (or Ricoeur), literature since Auerbach (or Barthes), painting since Gombrich (or Goodman), politics since Foucault (or Skinner), or physics since Kuhn (or Hesse)' (Geertz, 1988: 137).

Notes

1 Supported by the Economic and Social Research Council, award nos C00232405 and R000231257. An account of the project can be found in MacLure *et al.* (1990). A version of the present chapter was originally presented to the Annual Meeting of the American Educational Research Association, San Francisco, April 1992.

2 In fact, there is a hidden tension between the celebratory impulse, which requires the researcher to take the subject's account more or less at face value, and the methodological commitment to validity, which recommends triangulation and other verification procedures to make sure that people are not pulling the wool over the researcher's eyes (e.g. Goodson, 1983: 141; Sikes *et al.*, 1985: 15). Accounts are often, then, celebratory in terms of their substance, but faintly punitive at the methodological level.

3 As Steele (1986: 268) notes, in a deconstruction of the narratives of Freud and Jung, 'Omissions are difficult for the strict deconstructionists to analyze because if the leaving out is done well it leaves no traces of its disappearance.'

3

Eccentric subject, impossible object: a postmodern reading of Hannah Cullwick

Preamble

> But, the figure is complex and ambiguous from the start, enmeshed in translation, staging, miming, disguises and evasions.
>
> (Haraway, 1992: 90)

Donna Haraway, in writing these words, is writing about Jesus – the 'suffering servant' of the Christian salvation narrative. She goes on to speak of another exemplary suffering servant – Sojourner Truth, the peripatetic nineteenth-century feminist, abolitionist and former slave whose famous 'Ain't I a Woman?' speech now circulates in the form of posters on the walls of women's studies offices across the US (Haraway, 1992: 90, 92). Haraway's point, in offering a poststructuralist reading of these incalculably powerful reclamation narratives, is that Jesus and Sojourner Truth are transgressive figures, 'eccentric subjects' who repeatedly exceed the limits of their identities as suffering servants, and their exemplary status as 'bearers of the promise of humanity'. Both figures are palimpsests – texts endlessly translated and overwritten in a way that makes questions of their 'true' origins and their 'real' identities unaskable. Both are, in Haraway's words, trickster figures and shape changers, 'who might trouble our notions – all of them: classical, biblical, scientific, modernist, postmodernist, and feminist – of "the human"' (p. 98). It is this perspective on identity as a shifting and erratic performance that we intend to develop in this chapter, taking as our starting point the problems we encountered in trying to 'write' Jack, and giving them a more positive reading as hybrid and oscillating features of identity. To an extent, Chapter 2 inverted the hierarchies of a powerful 'realist' tradition in writing and researching, while this chapter seeks to displace that inversion with a more positive reading of the instabilities it produced.

Like Sojourner Truth, Hannah Cullwick was a suffering servant – a Victorian 'maid of all work' who did the hardest and most menial of the jobs available to women 'in service' all her working life. And like Sojourner Truth (although Hannah's story is much less widely known), her identity as suffering servant has become *exemplary* of women's condition and women's humanity in several of the texts about Hannah and her life. The reading that we propose here has much in common with Haraway's in its intent to interrupt that singular version of Hannah's identity. We suggest that Hannah too can be read as a shape-changer and trickster figure: a mistress of disguise, simulation and dissimulation; a boundary dweller who lived, painfully but irresolvably, *in-between* the binary oppositions that structure Enlightenment thought – private/public, wife/servant, master/slave, clean/dirty, man/woman, personal/social, high/low, self/other, appearance/reality. And because of this unresolvable in-between-ness, we suggest, Hannah too is a transgressive figure, an eccentric subject, liable to trouble and destabilize the foundational categories that shore up our theories of class, culture, subjectivity, sexuality and identity.

In focusing on *in-between-ness* as the space (or the absent, negative space) that Hannah inhabits, our reading draws also on the writing of theorists of postcolonialism such as Gayatri Spivak and, especially, Homi Bhabha, who identify the condition (psychic and social) of postcolonial subjects as just such a (non)state of in-between-ness or hybridity. Bhabha (1994) argues that formerly colonized, 'subaltern' peoples experience a profound splitting of identity, an irreparable dislocation and displacement of the self, as the traumatic legacy of colonialism. But, he also argues, this dislocation acts 'back' upon the colonialist too. By failing 'properly' to return the objectivizing gaze of the colonizer, to provide the fully delineated, and perversely desired, Other that would secure the Self of the colonizer, the fractured identity of the subaltern profoundly destabilizes, in turn, the Western idea (ideal) of the universal human subject. The postcolonial discourse, then, is a discourse of *otherness* – a liminal space 'where the shadow of the other falls upon the self' (*ibid.*: 60). 'It is not the colonialist Self or the colonized Other, but the *disturbing distance in-between* that constitutes the figure of colonial otherness – the white man's artifice inscribed on the black man's body. It is in relation to this impossible object that the liminal problem of colonial identity and its vicissitudes emerges' (*ibid.*: 45; our emphasis). This seems to us a powerful way to read Hannah's relationship with Arthur Munby, the rich barrister and poet who was her secret companion and, subsequently and equally secretly, her husband. For although the borderlines on which Hannah and Munby lived did not span racial difference and were not located (not directly anyway) in a colonial context, aspects of Hannah's engagement with Munby can be read in ways similar to that of the displaced, subaltern woman confronting the otherness of the colonizer, and vice versa. We suggest below that, as the object of Munby's possessive gaze (and the pleasure/power of looking, as we shall see, was a significant element in their relationship), Hannah was nevertheless an 'impossible object', in Bhabha's words – a dislocated, and therefore dislocating, identity. Impossible object. Eccentric subject.

'Coming across clearly'? Photographs and the staging of the real

> In these diaries Hannah comes across very clearly as a woman of great character and of much power and pride.
>
> (Stanley, 1984: 9)[1]

> Her name was Hannah Cullwick and she wrote diaries which bring home
> to us with a quite unique freshness and immediacy what it meant to live
> and work as a lower-class woman 'in service' in early and middle Victorian
> England.
>
> (Stanley, 1984: 1)

Hannah wrote detailed diaries of her daily life and work from 1854, when she
was 21 and had recently met Arthur Munby, until just after her marriage to
him in 1873. For Liz Stanley, the editor of the diaries, one of the enchant-
ments is how fully visible Hannah is in these pages: she 'comes across very
clearly' as a certain sort of person, as the first quote above states. For Stanley,
as for many other people, a diary is a kind of window, offering an unimpeded
view, not just of the deeds of the person who writes it, but of the person
herself. The text and the person are unified in the first person journal
('Hannah's text speaks for itself,' she writes later: p. 28). Moreover, as the
second quote suggests, in seeing Hannah with a 'quite unique freshness and
immediacy' we are not just seeing one unique individual, but also a repre-
sentative of a class of women of her time. Such exemplarity involves negotiating around some tricky details documented in Hannah's diaries, such as
licking Munby's boots, wearing a padlocked chain around her neck and
coating herself in black lead to enact more fully her role as slave to Munby's
'Massa' – as she named him throughout the diaries. This, however, Stanley
attempts, by counting such details exceptional, and arguing that many of the
other aspects of Hannah's routine practices were typical of the condition of
subordinated women. Moreover, in an audacious move, Stanley claims that
Hannah's 'service' to Munby is in many respects 'no more and no less than
what millions of women still do for their husbands/lovers and children'
(p. 13). In this way Hannah becomes a figure of women's transhistorical condition as suffering servant, as the dedication to the diaries has already
instructed us: 'This book is dedicated to the memory of Hannah Cullwick and
all the many thousands of women who lived, and live, lives not so very different from hers' (p. vi).

We have not done justice to the complexity of Stanley's account, and will
return to this below. But for the moment we want to focus on the claim she
makes about the visibility of Hannah in the diaries – the claim on which her
argument about Hannah's exemplary status rests, for Hannah must paradoxically be shown to be self-evidently 'real', a palpable presence, in order to stand
metaphorically as a substitute for universal woman. Whom do we see when
we see Hannah? As a first approach to that question we look not at the written
text of her diaries, but at another remarkable source of documentary 'evidence' of Hannah – the numerous photographs that were taken of her during
her relationship with Munby, and at Munby's request. A few of them are presented in this chapter.

We see Hannah as maidservant – 'in her dirt' and cleaning the boots of the
(disappeared) Munby. And we also see her in various disguises – 'Gainsborough' lady, man, semi-naked chimney sweep. Hannah as shape changer.
The photographs, like much else in Hannah's and Munby's relationship,
stage a play across the boundaries of reality and appearance – Hannah

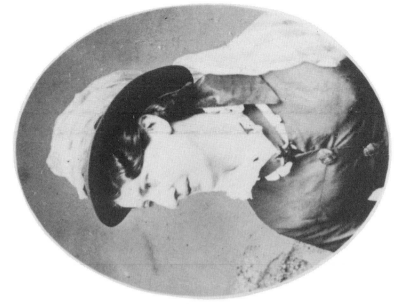

Figure 3

Figure 2

Figure 1

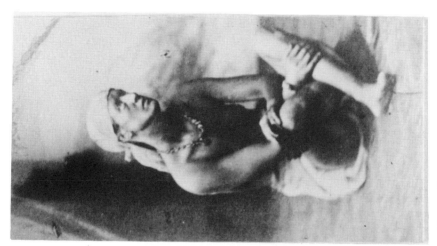

Figure 4

Figure 5

appearing/made to appear as something *other* than herself. This has the curious effect of lending even those photographs in which Hannah represents her 'real' self, as maidservant, the status of simulacra. Hannah as maidservant impersonating a maidservant. Or forging her own signature, as Clifford Geertz once wrote in a different context. For these are not 'naturalistic' photographs of Hannah at her work: they are studio portraits. Like all the others, they are carefully staged. In both Hannah's and Munby's diaries there are numerous references to discussions about poses and props; how 'black' Hannah should look 'in her dirt' etc.

Other aspects of the photographs are worthy of mention. The first is the absence from them of Munby himself. Indeed in two of them (numbers 2 and 5) he has actually *erased* himself, although in both the trace of his presence (or, rather, his absence) remains, in the form of the toe of his boot intruding into the frame. It is difficult not to read these photographs as implicated in the voyeuristic desire of the Self to fix the 'Other' – i.e. Hannah – in an object position from which she can be safely and wholly known in her 'difference'. As Bhabha notes of the colonial relation (and the argument is equally familiar in feminist analyses of the disciplinary ambition of the male gaze; e.g. Kaplan, 1990), 'the problematic of seeing/being seen' runs through the entire story of encounters between the powerful and the powerless, and as Foucault asserted, is the source of 'the crucial bind of pleasure and power' through which surveillance operates:

> in order to conceive of the colonial subject as the effect of power that is productive – disciplinary and 'pleasurable' – one has to see the *surveillance* of colonial power as functioning in relation to the regime of the *scopic drive* . . . the drive that represents the pleasure in 'seeing' [and] which has the look as its object of desire . . . Like voyeurism, *surveillance* must depend for its effectivity on the *active consent* which is its real or mythical correlate (but always real as myth).
>
> (Bhabha, 1994: 76, original emphasis)

The pleasure of looking recurs in entries in Munby's diaries, which we turn to below; and it was a pleasure in which Hannah happily participated on innumerable occasions, although not, crucially, without ambivalence. Before we turn to the diary extracts however, there is one further suggestive characteristic of the photographs: namely, that Munby carried two contrasting ones bound together in a travelling frame (numbers 4 and 5). As Hiley (1979) points out in the photographic essay in which these photographs appear, one of the main interests for Munby seems to have been in the play of *difference* which the photographs provoked: Hannah as, simultaneously, working girl and fine young lady; as both 'Gainsborough' beauty and chimney sweep. That 'difference' also insinuates itself into some of the single photographs which are not reproduced here. For instance, the leather strap which Hannah wore as a sign of her bondage to Munby – visible in photographs 2 and 5 – is also apparent in some of the 'fine lady' photographs (see Hiley, 1979: 27).

The play of difference

Hiley, in his provocative essay, assembles numerous instances from Munby's diaries of his abiding preoccupation with 'suggestive contrasts' – with the pleasurable difference released in the contemplation and juxtaposition of women of the highest and lowest status. Moreover, this difference was enacted in the visual plane: Munby was an avid spectator of difference, deliberately seeking out and observing kitchen wenches and maidservants in situations which dramatized their utter difference from the high-born women whom they serviced. Here is a diary description (not discussed in Hiley) of Munby's encounter with a chambermaid:

> Going up to my room after breakfast, I passed the open door of another bedroom, in which a housemaid was doing her work. I went in, and spoke to her about some washing, without observing what she was doing. She was a stout, lusty country lass, with a rosy honest face, and with large coarse arms and hands: bare thick red arms, rough in texture, and all one tint of pure healthy vermilion, from the shoulder to the finger tips. A most wholesome and blooming rustic maid, and just in the bloom of eighteen – the very hour of virgin bashfulness. What was she doing? Cleaning out a chamberpot! And when I entered, she did not drop it, or hide it, or look confused, or blush. On the contrary; she stood still, looking at me with frank blue eyes, answering my questions, telling me (in good broad Cumbrian) how things could be washed; and all the time she continued holding the vessel in one hand. And, as she ceased speaking, she calmly emptied it, and replaced it under the bed.
>
> Consider the difference which this implies, between her mental condition and that of a young lady, even of the humblest order.[2]
>
> (Hudson, 1974: 399)

This passage is characteristic of many others in Munby's diaries. It turns on the observation of a working girl and the contemplation of her 'difference' to the highborn. It includes detailed description of her physical appearance (bare arms and rough hands are always particularly noted features). It inverts (or seems to: see below) the moral code of nineteenth-century womanhood by claiming virtue and grace for the sturdy, degraded wench. And, in its focus on her work, it dwells on *dirt and uncleanliness*. The opposition between wench and lady is almost always, for Munby, also the opposition between dirt and cleanliness, black and white.

Hiley notes other instances of Munby's 'love of suggestive contrasts' (Munby's own words). The diary extracts mirror the structure of opposition and difference of the photographs, in which Hannah is bound in her difference as lady and wench, clean and dirty, clothed and naked, strong and submissive. And despite taking up a position that attempts to invert the moral, aesthetic, spiritual and emotional codes that excluded Victorian working women from the name of womanhood, it seems that it was, or was also, the ambiguous space *in-between* that fascinated Munby. The following extract reads like a manifesto of difference (or at least reads so under the light that our interpretation casts over Munby). On a summer afternoon at the botanical gardens, Munby appreciatively observes the 'pretty girlish faces and tasteful dress' of the young women 'swelling' round. But, he continues:

> to be often amongst such scenes which are wellknown and always alike: which have nothing to show but a *deadlevel of serene gentility*, with no picturesque ruggedness of aspect, no salient trait of character, to catch the mind's eye: that would indeed make one wish for some pricks to kick against. Good heavens! To have married Laura Matilda[3] and all her relations, and found life one vast platitude of tarlatan and small talk and pap!
>
> (Hiley, 1979: 25, our emphasis)

Munby chose the delights of difference, then, over the *'deadlevel'* of serene gentility and the familiar. This, we would argue, is the ambivalent ground on which his relationship with Hannah was played: the tension of irreconcilable opposites. For example, throughout their 21 year courtship, and well into their marriage, Hannah would, as already noted, 'black up', or otherwise get as dirty as she could, while Munby watched her at her work. For example:

> Massa told me to black my face like it was that night I clean'd after the coalmen. So I did, & got the dinner & cleaned the boots & washed up things & Massa's feet with it black, & M. seem'd pleased with it so but said my hands wasn't looking so thick & red as they did the Sunday when he read them verses to me.
>
> (Stanley, 1984: 138)

The extract points again to the centrality of 'the desire of the look' in the fantasy of slavery that Munby called upon Hannah to engage in – with Munby, again, as the spectator of Hannah 'in her dirt'. It also shows his magisterial interventions in the orchestration of that look. However, Hannah's servitude, and her willingness to enact the 'active consent' which Bhabha (1994) described as essential to the effectivity of surveillance, did not require the actual presence of Munby. Nor indeed of Hannah. For the diary itself was a means of representing (re-presenting) Hannah to Munby's gaze. As Stanley notes, Hannah wrote her diaries at the express request of Munby. There are passing references to Munby's demands for his regular instalments; for example, 'Massa sent me a note to say he should go away if he didn't get my diary a Saturday night, & I had only written a letter to him' (Stanley, 1984: 116). The diary, then, functioned as a substitute scene for the enactment of the gaze, and the contemplation of the transgressive differences released in the serious game of the drudge/slave. In this extract from a longer essay that Hannah wrote about her life as a servant, she describes a scene in which she cleaned the grate with her bare hands in front of her invalid mistress, Miss Knight (who was thus also a spectator across the boundary of class difference):

> I had taken care to get my arms black & I rubb'd them across my face, & having my striped apron on & frock pinned up, *you may guess how I looked* as I crawl'd on my knees to & from the bedside & holding my hand up for the water. [Her] been so delicate, as white as a lily & her face too, from been in bed so many years, & I suppose never soil'd her fingers ever,

except perhaps with a dirty book or paper, & the white coverlet & all standing out against my dirty black hands, & my *big* [Hannah's emphasis] red & black arms, & my face red too & sweating till the drops tumbled off, or stood on little drops o' crystal again the greasy black.

I wish'd much that M. could see me for I knew he would o' liked to see me so, & have loved me the more for it. But still I was satisfied that I was doing it for him & I could *give him a nice account of it in writing.*

(Stanley, 1984: 66, our emphasis)

Here the diary account takes on a quality of mirrors within mirrors. Munby becomes the (imagined) spectator of the spectator observing Hannah,[4] as she (re)creates another drama of opposites: lilywhite lady and black servant; white coverlet 'standing out against' dirty black hands; sickness and health, unsoiled fingers and big red arms. Hannah even writes her sweat into this text of difference and displacement – 'little drops o' crystal against the greasy black'.

Like the preceding fragment, this next one also disrupts the scene of looking. Here, the displacement is effected in Hannah's simultaneous (re)creation of the scene, her representation to 'herself', and thereby to Munby as reader/spectator of the diary, of the contrasts of black and white that it invokes, her (depiction of her) picturing of Munby's imaginary enjoyment of the scene, and her report of Munby's written response to her (presumably spoken) account of the event, in which he reportedly was simultaneously picturing *her*. So the extract is a text that both incorporates and refers to a text about looking, at the 'same' scene in each case, from the viewpoints of both the spectator and the observed, and their mutual imaginings of each other's viewpoints. The status of reality and appearance is diffused in a way that has nothing to do with the facticity of the depicted scene. (Why should we doubt that it happened?) What is challenged is the transparency of the text as a window through which, as Stanley asserted, Hannah 'comes across clearly'. The boundaries between 'self' and 'other', subject and object, are blurred in the overlapping layers of representation in the text. Hannah is the subject both of the depicted action and of the 'enunciation', as the author of the text; but as author she writes herself also as the object of Munby's gaze. Yet he too is the imaginary object of *her* gaze as she pictures him watching her (as in Coetzee's representation of the Barbarian woman in Chapter 1). And the text itself (it is true of the diaries in their entirety) is ambiguously addressed both to her 'self' (as personal journals always putatively are) and to Munby as the reader/spectator over her shoulder.

'The secret arts of invisibleness'

The theme of concealment in the above fragment invokes a final, and in some ways obvious, dimension of difference which runs through Hannah's and Munby's relationship: that of invisibleness (and its opposite, visibility). Theirs was a secret courtship and marriage (their 'stolen love' as Hannah called it), transacted across the boundaries of private and public, legitimate and illegitimate. We look in more detail below at the pleasures, and ultimately the intolerable stresses, that Hannah and Munby seem to have experienced through the play of appearance and 'reality'.

A recurring game of invisibleness, in the early years of their marriage, involved Hannah scrubbing the yard outside their house, getting as dirty as possible in the process, while Munby watched her from inside, through the window. Hudson (1974: 357) notes that 'This was a feat Munby particularly enjoyed' and one which he later described in one of his highly (but again secretly) autobiographical poems. It was also, as we discuss below, one such scene which occasioned a fierce argument between Hannah and Munby, when she became angry at his treating her as a 'real' servant. Again, the yard is a liminal space between inside and outside, between the secret, domestic realm of the private, and the external world of public appearances – a world in which, as both Munby and Hannah reiterate many times, women such as Hannah are literally invisible to the passers by on the 'outside'.

One of the primary scenes for enacting the game of invisibleness, in the early years of their marriage, was Hannah's double role of wife and servant. Several entries from Munby's diary describe incidents revolving round visits by Munby's friends, during which Hannah would act as servant, to the gratification of both (as reported by Munby, at any rate), as they contemplated the irony of Hannah's hidden identity. In the following reported incident from Munby's diary, which is worth quoting at length, Munby's friend Peacock has arrived, and Hannah is preparing breakfast for them:

Meanwhile the unconscious Peacock talked archaeology to me, till I rang the bell: then came footsteps on the stairs, and a respectful tap at the door, and enter the mistress of the house . . . carrying a tray of dishes. She was clean and neat now, in her Sunday servant's dress . . . She set down the tray, arranged the dishes, gave hot plates to her husband and his guest, and moved quietly about, as a neathanded Phyllis, behind their chairs . . . One would have thought that, even as a servant, her unusual stature and her quiet and graceful ways would have attracted attention; and from ladies, they certainly would; but such is the stupidity of men, that Peacock continued to talk to his distracted host, and never noticed nor looked at the tall neat servantmaid who respectfully changed his plate, or stood in the background, waiting. He talked of this new novel 'John Markenfield', while all the time, a romance such as few could dream of was being enacted before his eyes. 'You like rustic scenes – I have a scene of a servant girl and her master,' said he. 'It is hard to describe servants aright,' I said: 'the life of a kitchen is so different to that of our class!' 'Yes,' he answered, 'and unhappily they have not culture enough to describe it.' This was when the tall maidservant had just left the room, after clearing away our breakfast things in silence; and she had stooped in front of Peacock, as he sat in the easy chair, to remove the kettle and sweep the hearth; and then she had withdrawn, on tiptoe and walking backwards . . . with her hands full of dishes, and her countenance demure and respectful. But he noted not her countenance nor her movements: nor knew that she, without any culture at all, has described her own life effectively for nearly twenty years, 'When do you have your dinner?' I thought it best to say, as she retired. 'About one 'clock, Sir,' my wife answered. 'Then perhaps you had better do the bedroom'. 'Very well, Sir,' said she, quite gravely: and soon she reappeared with all her housemaid's gear, and slid as quiet as a mouse behind our backs into the bedroom, and drew the curtain behind her but did not shut the door: for I knew that she was secretly enjoying the conversation, though I could hear her vigorously emptying slops and lustily making the bed. Peacock, however, took no more notice of her presence than if she had been a dog: he continued talking, in his clever, rambling way; pouring out miscellaneous learning antiquarian and philosophical, talking Spinoza and Berkeley, reading Kingsley's poems aloud, reciting ballads of his own: and all this while, the lady of the house, to whom he should have been introduced, was doing housemaid's work in a servant's dress behind a curtain, as if unfit to be mentioned before him. At last she came out, with her bare arms and her face flushed with work; tall, silent, carrying her full pail, but out of sight; and stole one look of love at her husband, as she passed out of the room to go downstairs . . .

At last, after 3 p.m., I persuaded my guest to go out with me; and in Piccadilly we parted . . . home, by nine, to tea. Now at last, the wife was free to talk with her husband as an equal . . . 'What a strange gentleman he is – and how he did quote poetry, and make clever talk! I was listening to it all, when you thought I was only thumping the pillow and wiping the basins out. But as for him, he'll go mad, with his talk about not trusting our senses, and the things we see not being real! How do I know it's *you* that kiss me, or *you* I've loved these twenty years? Why, God gave us our senses, & if we can't trust them, what *can* we trust?' Such was the verdict of Hannah's plain common sense: so much notice had that lowly waiting maid of this morning taken of the clever gentleman who ignored her.

(Hudson, 1974: 365)

Munby is visible to Peacock as master, hidden as husband. For Hannah, the invisibility is doubled: she is invisible to Peacock both as servant (because the upper classes never 'see' the servant class) and as wife. The description is riddled with irony. There is the primary irony of Hannah as the wife masquerading as a servant; and here the irony is again doubled, since Hannah is also 'really' a servant. Then there is the irony of the exchange about servants and the difficulty of describing them 'aright', where, again, the joke is that Munby (and Hannah) know something that Peacock does not. There is the irony of engaging in a philosophical discussion which Peacock would have assumed to be beyond Hannah, but which (Munby knows) Hannah is listening to, and later displays her understanding of. Munby ironicizes his own status as simultaneously participant and spectator, moving between the engaged first-person 'I' of the participant-narrator and the distanced third-person stance of the spectator-narrator who remains 'outside' of the action, referring not just to Hannah as 'the wife' and 'the tall maidservant', but to himself as 'her husband'. There is the further irony that the philosophical discussion between Peacock and Munby (overheard by Hannah, who is thus also a concealed spectator) is a disquisition on the nature of the 'real'.

But there are signs in both diaries that the game of invisibleness was a difficult and dangerous one to sustain. Although it was a source of exciting play-
fulness, it also became a source of irresolvable tensions between them. Or that,
at any rate, is the reading that we propose. Munby, for instance, while deriv-
ing what seems to have been a considerable emotional charge from observing
Hannah's invisibility to people of his own class, also found that invisibility an
offence to her 'true' status as a woman fully deserving of acknowledgement.
He tried more and more frequently after their marriage to 'arrest' the play of
difference which had enchanted both of them for so many years, by trying to
install one of Hannah's identities – the fine lady – as the 'real' one. Hannah,
however, was deeply resistant to this Pygmalion-like transformation. As
Stanley notes, she thwarted his attempts to get her to act the part of the fine
lady, refusing, increasingly, to dress up and go out with him (i.e. make herself
visible) in polite society. But even this resolve on Munby's part was fragile:
although he came to regret his lifelong educational project (so-called) of
preaching salvation to Hannah through servitude and degradation (Hudson,
1974: 369), he continued to require her to act out the game of drudge for his
secret gratification.

Hannah, for her part, attempted the 'arrest' in the opposite direction –
increasingly insisting on fully inhabiting the identity of drudge, and cherish-
ing her social invisibility. As Stanley (1984: 16) points out, such invisibility
had, and has, its advantages for marginalized women. As social outcasts, they
are also free from certain social constraints. A month into her marriage,
Hannah writes: 'That's the best o' being dressed rough, & looking "nobody"
– you can go anywhere & not be wonder'd at' (ibid.: 274, Hannah's emphasis). It could also be argued that, around this time, she also began to make
herself invisible to Munby, for she *stopped writing her diary*:

> This is the last day o' the month [30 September 1873], & Massa only
> wishes for me to write to the end. And I am glad of it somehow, for I've
> got so thoroughly tired o' writing what I think to most people must be
> very tiresome & certainly *disinteresting* ... And so I've told M. that by
> making me write for so many years he has quite tired me of it, & yet for
> some things I am most glad that he's not tired of reading it.
>
> (*ibid.*: 279, Hannah's emphasis)

Hannah finally resisted, then, Munby's insatiable 'demand for narrative', as
Bhabha (1994: 99) calls it, referring to the colonizer's strategy of surveillance,
through 'confession', of the native. It was a demand that Hannah had ful-
filled, although not without occasional complaint, for 20 years. But there are
signs elsewhere in her diaries of her willed refusal to make herself intelligible,
through narrative, to the surveillance of her 'superiors'. One such refusal occasioned her dismissal from her job as maidservant to the Hendersons – employers with whom Hannah had in many ways a good relationship, and whom
she visited with Munby after her marriage in her new (semi)public role as his
wife. Mrs Henderson discovered, while Hannah was in her service, that she
was involved in a clandestine relationship; and on the pious grounds that 'my
servants' souls are in my charge', asked to know more of her history (Stanley,
1984: 191).

Hannah refused to explain. That refusal can be understood, in Bhabha's terms, as the refusal to accede to the 'narcissistic, colonialist demand that it should be addressed directly, that the Other should authorize the self, recognize its priority, fulfil its outlines . . . and still its fractured gaze' (Bhabha, 1994: 98). In Bhabha's analysis, the colonialist, driven by the paranoid fantasy of possession, needs to know the natives – to render them 'calculable' – in order to fix them, in their difference, as the 'moralized "others" of truth'. By refusing to return the gaze and satisfy the narrative demand of the colonialist, the native refuses to grant the 'authorization' that the colonialist needs in order to sustain his own identity as both oppressor and father (Bhabha, 1994: 98–9). What Bhabha has to say about the role of fantasy and ambivalence in the unstable power relation of colonialism is equally applicable to the analysis of class and patriarchy. Hannah too, in practising what Bhabha calls 'the secret art of Invisibleness',[5] has the power to subvert the totalizing ambition of the master's (or mistress's) gaze. Bhabha notes that the subversive identity of the 'missing person' – of being *less* than meets the eye – is a strategy available to subaltern women in particular, as a way of subverting the masculinist gaze.

Hannah resisted Munby, then, by 'absenting' herself, both in writing, by stopping the diaries, and in deed, by refusing Munby's attempt to make her fully visible as a lady. But her attempt to arrest the play of difference by coming to rest in the identity of (invisible) servant was equally problematic. It was no more possible, finally, for Hannah to be 'really' a servant than it was for her to become truly a lady. Her servant identity had become a simulacrum too, in the 'now you see it now you don't' game of appearance and reality, in which it became ever more difficult to tell which was which. For instance, Hannah insisted that Munby should continue to pay her a servant's 'wages' of £10 per year, even after they were married. However, these 'wages' were in fact her own money, which, as Munby reports, he dispensed from the interest on her life savings (Hudson, 1974: 364). To claim her identity as servant, Hannah had to earn pretend wages from Munby. But, again, the pretence is doubled, for the money is her own in the first place. This was no trivial matter for Hannah, since one of the ways in which she could assert some independence was as a waged servant. She writes more than once of the loss which she incurred in giving up this independence, as the obverse of her happiness in her utter servility to Munby.

> But tho' I'm never so happy as when I'm with him or working for *him*, yet I want to be still a servant & working so as to be independent & get my own living. To do both *is* a trouble, the same as it's a trouble to M. loving me & still having to be above me.
>
> (Stanley, 1984: 193, Hannah's emphasis)

Although throughout her diaries Hannah repeatedly claimed her identity as servant to be her true 'ground of presence' – her real self – even that identity was fragile and ambivalent, troubled by the double game of reality and pretence within which it was embedded. This is highlighted in a critical event that occurred on the day that she moved into Munby's house, in the year prior to their marriage. Hannah had agreed to play the game of scrubbing the yard, described above, for Munby to witness on his return home ('Massah said he sh'd like to see me scrubbing outside when he come at 1/2 past 4 or so and I planned it'; *ibid.*: 254). But Hannah's pleasure in playing the game of the lowly servant and 'looking a regular drudge' was ruined when Munby treated her as a *real* servant, and reprimanded her for not addressing him as 'sir' in the presence of the boy clerk to the barrister who shared Munby's house. Hannah's account of the incident continues:

> Then M. went upstairs and rang the bell, & I thought, Well that is showing off certainly, & I went upstairs with my temper up to its highest, & M. began to question me about not saying '*sir*' to him, as the lad was on the stairs. I felt so *angry* 'cause I thought if M. knew the boy was on the stairs he oughtn't to o' come down, not only for the humiliation on the first day, but because I didn't even know Mr Rees kept a lad as a clerk. So I was really in a passion & said a great deal I didn't mean, & declar'd that if M. tantalised me in that way again I would leave him whether we was married or not, for I didn't care a straw for that.
>
> (*ibid.*: 254, Hannah's emphasis)

Hannah here seems caught in the double bind of being 'really & truly a servant' and being treated as a 'nothing'. She is trapped in the impossible in-between – simultaneously claiming and rejecting her status of servant, asserting and relinquishing her independence.

Munby did not forget, nor did he forgive for several days, even though he presumably read Hannah's petition in the closing sentences of the diary entry. Indeed, he wrote her a letter the next morning, telling her to go back to her old post; and although that crisis was smoothed over, it delayed the marriage. And a few days later Hannah, still miserable, was further humiliated over trivial misdemeanours such as failing to open the windows, blowing out a candle rather than using an extinguisher and not bringing up Munby's boots on time (*ibid.*: 257). Hannah writes: 'So I was altogether in the wrong, & I was dispirited & I felt almost afraid that after all it was a mistake my trying to do so much for M. & wishing to be only a servant' (*ibid.*).

Hannah's and Munby's relationship had been sustained by the playing off of appearance against reality. But their 'reality' was, or was partly, the ambiguous space in-between appearances. That space in-between Hannah's identity as servant and as lady was dissolved, geographically at least, when impending marriage brought them together under the same roof.[6] But each of those identities was, individually, untenable. Unrealistic. Although both of them seem to have wanted to resolve the tension of difference that had fuelled their attraction, such an impossible resolution also represented a profound loss. If that seems a fanciful reading, consider this account by Hannah of a conversation that she had, not long before her marriage, with a friend of Munby's who knew their secret:

> I got up & went nearer to Mr. B. I said, 'This is the first time I've ever been shown to any o' M.'s friends & I never wish'd, indeed hop'd never *to* be. Massa & I have spent so many hours together in this room *alone*,

& ours is like a *stolen* love you know, & when it's known it seems like a
shame, it seems as if the *charm* was broken.'

(*ibid.*: 250–1, Hannah's emphasis)

The charm was broken. Munby's diary account of this conversation is remark-
ably close to Hannah's (Hudson, 1974: 315); and although he resisted her
interpretation at the time ('No, no, don't say that'), Hannah's sad insistence,
'Ah, but it *is*', echoes through the rest of their story.

Postscript

This chapter is an argument about different ways of reading lives, and the
different claims that can be advanced about identity, about truth, about the
relationship between writing and reality. What, then, can we say about our
particular strategy in reading the texts about Hannah? We could bring it under
the name of postmodernism, as we indeed do in the title, or perhaps poststructuralism or deconstruction. We don't want here to define or arbitrate
among these names, for, as Chapter 1 suggested, each resists definition – every
attempt to pin down meaning releases something indefinable that returns to
haunt that particular fantasy of possession. Postmodernism is itself an
'impossible object'. Nor can we delineate what each of us brings to the act of
reading in the way of 'intellectual baggage', since this would be to suggest that
the meaning we make in the reading is somehow an expression of our pre-
existing selves.

But perhaps we could briefly comment on what we were *likely* to have asked
of the Hannah texts. We were disposed (a good word, for it places us as both
the subjects and the objects of the act of reading/writing) to look for boundaries, margins, ambivalence, difference. We were inclined (ditto) to be more
interested in what Barthes called the effect of the real, and how this functions,
than in the decidability of what is, or is not real. In that sense, we 'found'
what we were disposed to look for in the Hannah texts.

What we found is not, of course, the only possible reading. It is not a 'complete' reading that tries to take account of all the texts, in all their details, and
to assemble a master narrative that the texts have secretly been longing to
reveal. Indeed, it is in resistance to that kind of reading that we have worked
somewhat against Stanley's attempt to rescue Hannah as an exemplar which
will instruct and mobilize, in as didactic a way as the Victorian strictures of
Munby to Hannah Cullwick were intended to do. In contrast, our concern has
been for the margins of identity in the relationship between Hannah and
Arthur. We have looked for the in-between-ness of what Bhabha (1994: 44),
after Lacan, calls the 'space of splitting' – an unstable space where identities
are unable to resolve into whole, fully present, reciprocating 'selves' mirrored
in their 'others'. Such identities, being always necessarily incomplete and
intransigently specific, cannot deliver themselves up, in their 'ordinariness',
as exemplars in the stories of emancipation, reclamation or the triumph of
the human subject. In their different ways, Stanley and Hudson, on behalf of
Hannah and Munby respectively, celebrate the ordinariness of their subjects,

making them exemplars of their gender, class or occupation, although we have said little in this chapter about Hudson's rescue of Munby. Each becomes a kind of Stakhanovite figure, morally or politically or productively a paradoxical giant in their ordinariness. But we chose instead to stress the extraordinariness of the relationship, to read it for its specificity and difference rather than its susceptibility to parable of one kind of another.

How does such a reading contrast with 'modernist' approaches other than the emancipatory ones just discussed? We might have adopted a more Foucauldian interest in Munby, as a truly comprehensive practitioner of surveillance, and a most ingenious constructor of his 'subject', in whom he invests, from a number of different perspectives – as master, as super-master (Massa), as husband, as tutor, as co-conspirator in the great game of Victorian hypocrisy. Not only is Hannah made to play her role and fulfil her determined function in these games, she is required to *write* herself for her master. We could also argue that Munby practises his epistemic violence on his own class as well as on Hannah and her class. His creative display of power/knowledge, it could be argued under such a reading, makes what is invisible to them visible to himself. He mocks their ignorance, posits them as dupes (recall 'the unconscious Peacock' of Munby's diary, above), and celebrates the totality of his gaze across the social and sexual divides that characterize that age. Munby, we might claim in this voice, was his own panopticon. This was indeed a punitive household worthy of Foucault's punitive city. And, still through Foucault's gaze, we might have interpreted Hannah's responses to and her rebellion against such manipulation and surveillance as 'local resistance'. That, too, might be represented as a modernist story – but without the illusion of emancipation. Instead, Hannah would be written in this story as a disciplinary exemplar, an illusory project of enlightenment, rescued in vain first by Munby in the name of the age of improvement, and second by Stanley in the name of the feminist project of emancipation.

Or we might have tried a Marxist-feminist materialist reading, as does Swindells (1989) in her brief reading of Hannah Cullwick, seeing Hannah as a woman who sold (under ideological duress) her labour to Munby thrice over – as servant to his bodily needs, as the satisfier of his fetishistic gaze in the doing of that work and as the producer of the diaries which intensified this male fantasy of 'labour as sexual aesthetic' (Swindells, 1989: 32). Hannah's diaries would become, on such a reading, a further instance of women's alienated labour, and as such 'very material – the woman's work for the man's pleasure' (*ibid*.: 32). To produce such a reading we would need, as Swindells instructs us, to abandon the 'seduction' of paradox (for instance, of freedom through exclusion). For this is a reading utterly (and moralistically) without (and against) irony: one which feels able unequivocally to distinguish between sexuality and textuality (*ibid*.: 25), between the ideological and the material (*ibid*.: 34). Swindells takes issue with Stanley's comment, quoted also by us near the outset of this chapter, about the 'freshness and immediacy' with which the diaries 'bring home to us' the condition of Victorian working women (Stanley, 1984: 1). But the objection in a materialist reading such as this would be that Hannah is utterly obscured by the hegemony exerted in Munby's ventriloquizing control over her labour as writer. Indeed, in reading

Hannah's diaries, we would not be reading 'Hannah' at all, but the manipulated 'subject as the subject of Arthur Munby's narrative' (Swindells, 1989: 35).

Lastly, in this list of possible 'modernist' alternatives, we might have given the texts a more anthropological reading, suppressing the emancipatory 'story for' in favour of the 'story of'. An obvious theme of such an anthropological reading would be the notion of *pollution*. Mary Douglas and other Durkheimian analysts would make much of all the juicy polarities that these texts express: rough/smooth, black/white, dirty/clean etc. Are they not the polarities and exchanges of ritual, expressive of 'key values and cultural orientations (Turner, 1981: 6)? The theme of 'hygiene' is vivid in these accounts (Douglas, 1966: 122). And so is the notion of *risk* – for the status and position of both Hannah and Munby, in relation to each other and to their peers. The players of this game are involved in constructing an indefinable status, an interstitial position, full of social ambiguity and – hence – danger. Munby creates, and Hannah enacts, a series of rituals of abasement that deepen the separation between them, and between Hannah and other women. As Turner would put it, those rituals are creative as well as expressive, and dramatize a series of 'categories through which men [*sic*] perceive reality' (Turner, 1981: 7). So, in this anthropological story, what Munby and Cullwick have created is a kind of private theatre for the celebration of certain kinds of ritualized differences.

What separates these sketches of possible modernist analyses from the deconstructive account that we have tried to give? The first thing that we could point to is their eagerness to be done with ambiguity, to find ways of purging accounts of their discrepancies, or of finding mechanisms for explaining the nature of transitions across boundaries, and fixing them in terms of liminality or in concepts such as ritual and surveillance. The central project is to make Hannah Cullwick into some kind of transhistorical figure of representativeness – whether in the name of emancipation or subjection. Instead, we have tried to take Derrida's advice – to 'dig in' from the margins and footnotes of the texts, to look at differences within similarity, and displacements within positions, on the grounds that it is in their difference (to each other, within each other, between their writing and our reading) that 'plausible misreadings' (Spivak, 1988) can be made. Such differences are repressed in the commentaries we have inspected; yet they are – we have argued – necessary for any reading of the complexity of the relation between Munby and Cullwick. In this way, we express our resistance both to the kind of naturalistic naiveté that claims the ability to allow anyone to 'speak for themselves', and to the kind of analytical strategy that is – to return to Foucault – already deeply implicated in normative assumptions about human nature and identity.

So in reading/writing (about) Hannah, we already come to that act with a deep uncertainty about the notion of the universal human subject, and equally, about the simultaneously singular, complete individual who resides in, or can be seen through, the text. We no longer hope to get 'behind' Stanley's or Hudson's interpretative interventions, and read Hannah's diaries in the 'original'. We have tried to show that there is no way of getting through the mediations of language to the person behind, even when the text is a first-person journal. And we have tried to work with these irresolvable ambiguities, rather than merely bring them out as we did in the earlier excursion into 'identity' in Jack's case (Chapter 2). Yet it could be argued that we too have subjected Hannah to a singular reading – that we have brought her identity under the rubric of the shape-changer, the dislocated self. This has to be a valid point: if our argument about identity is right, it has to be wrong. 'Hannah' must always exceed the boundaries of *our* reading too.

Haraway, in the essay on Sojourner Truth with which we opened this chapter, is also engaged by the dilemma of our need for 'something called humanity' which at the same time must be fractured rather than whole, specific rather than generic. She poses a question, and partly answers it with the ambivalent figure of Sojourner Truth. A similar question animates the reading of Hannah Cullwick that we have made here. The question is this: 'So, how can humanity have a figure outside the narratives of humanism; what language would such a figure speak?' (Haraway, 1992: 88).

Notes

1 Page numbers throughout refer to the Virago edition.

2 This passage of 'elementary yet telling observation' as Hudson characterizes it, prompts the latter to the somewhat surprising (to us) assertion that 'This admirer of working women was a pioneer sociologist no less inspired than the amateur collectors of folk-song' (Hudson, 1974: 399). We do not have the space here to discuss fully Hudson's attempts to rescue Munby's identity from ascriptions of (sexual) oddity and/or misogyny by 'normalizing' it under the rubric of the scholar/amateur sociologist/philanthropist/writer. It is, we think, a similar strategy of rendering the subject 'ordinary' to the one that Stanley attempts, with quite opposing intent, on behalf of Hannah. Another such instance is Hudson's comments about the photographic session in which the chimney sweep photograph was taken. Placing this rather risqué (again, to us) photograph in the context of Munby's habitual recourse to studio photographers, Hudson remarks that 'Munby insisted that the photographs he commissioned should be entirely respectable.' Even Hudson is momentarily brought up short in this opinion when he adds, parenthetically, that these photographs 'did, however, include a number of gruesome records – which did not survive – of the features of disfigured women' (*ibid.*: 134).

3 According to Hiley (1979: 22), 'one of [Munby's] nicknames for the skilled exponents of what he called "fineladyism"'.

4 And of course 'we' the authors and 'you' the readers are now further spectators.

5 Bhabha borrows the phrase 'the secret art of Invisibleness' from a poem by Meilin Jin: 'Strangers in a hostile landscape', in R. Cobham and M. Collins (eds) *Watchers and Seekers* (London: Women's Press, 1987). 'Missing person' is the title of a poem by Adil Jussawalla (Clearing House, 1976). Bhabha's reading of these poems develops the notion of the elusive/evasive postcolonial subject who, in failing to return the gaze of the colonialist, introduces a psychic dislocation of identity into the postcolonial relation.

6 Our reading is close to Stanley's (1984: 23) here: 'Marriage would have ended the very conditions [Munby] strove throughout his life to create, because the separations both created and confused in Hannah's double life (and in his) would have begun to be dissolved.'

4

Is Halloween postmodern?

Thus far, our deconstructive/postmodernist quest has involved some sign-posts, a map and two 'sites' of deconstruction, both of which relate to a post-modernist concern for the problematics of 'identity' and the notion of the 'subject'. Our next excursion concerns a calendrical event, Halloween, and its translation into a curricular event. Such translations are the stuff of which School History is made, and our purpose is to give a postmodernist reading to an event and its curricular manifestation which seems at first sight to be so absolutely resistant to such a reading.

We might say: Halloween is the most pre-modern day in the calendar, a strange day on which to discuss the postmodern.[1] But let's exploit that coinci-dence and claim that we can give even Halloween, that most ancient of cal-endrical rituals, a postmodern reading, and contrast that kind of reading with a 'modernist' reading of the ritual. The intention will not be rudely to update Halloween to the postmodern, to ask what it is now, but rather to unsettle a modernist reading with a deconstruction that shows how that ancient, fixed and singular event in our calendar can also be understood as an event in flux. From that vantage point, a few introductory observations can be made on the nature and relation of modernism to postmodernism, and how that connects to curriculum issues. The theme is later developed in Chapter 5. Our interest, then, is in how Halloween can be represented as an event in history, and of History, and in how it turns up as a learning event in the formal and infor-mal education of children.[2]

First, a modernist reading.[2] At first sight, it seems certain that we can say that Halloween is archaic, immemorial, singular and backward-looking. It stands as the fixed Other of Modernity. Cosman points to its origins in the pagan 'samhain' and offers a medieval picture whose outline we moderns can nevertheless easily recognize; children go 'souling from door to door, singing and begging for soul cakes for wandering spirits' (Cosman, 1981: 81–2), just as they did at the beginning of the twentieth century in Shropshire (Ditch-field, 1901: 167). Such narratives of calendar ritual are full of continuity, 'a very ancient custom, which still lingers amongst us' (ibid.: 28). These conti-nuities run back through time, of course, but also across cultures. As the last day of the Old Year, the festival invokes more universal folk rites of death and birth through the metaphor of fire. The Feast of the Dead is a time to extinguish old fires and make 'new fire' (Hole, 1960: 221). As Hutton comments: 'In this way the opening of the season of darkness and cold was made into an opportunity to confront the greatest fear known to humans, that of death, and the greatest known to Christians, that of damnation' (Hutton, 1994: 45). Plenty of reason, then, for the initial hypothesis that informed Hutton's scrutiny of the calendar of celebrations: the search for Halloween as part of an 'immemorial folk festival culture' (Hutton, 1994: 260). That celebration seems to typify the permanence of ancient ritual, and to endure because it addressed the deepest of preoccupations.

Within the ritual, however, looking backwards was a way of preparing for the future, although a future that would obey the general rules of the past even if it might be unpredictable and risky in terms of individual fates. According to MacLeod Banks's *British Calendar Customs* (1946) these rituals were regarded as a time of danger and also a time of divination. He relates an instance of such divination in Shetland: 'This was performed by dropping a small portion of the white of an egg into a glass of water. The forms assumed prognosticated the future in matters of love, fortune and death' (*ibid.:* 75). That practice also suggests a visual metaphor for Halloween's movement in history, as a slow dissipation of meaning and efficacy, the gradual attrition of old customs, the loss – in this particular instance – of the Old Norse ways in nineteenth-century Shetland. Such a notion of the fading essence of ritual and custom is prominent in all accounts. Celebration becomes a 'rarity' (Shuel, 1985: 183), or something of an enigma (Cawte, 1978), but in itself still a cause for both rejoicing and regret: 'Nowadays, children playing at witches for example, may have little idea of the original meaning of what they are doing' (Ennew, 1994: 139).

So if Halloween is a residual ritual, the trace of past belief on the face of our modernity, then what's left for us? A 'modernist' answer might be that it is a way of remembering who we are by remembering who we no longer are, a recollection of the Other that displays the distance we have come, yet which we feel receding in the power of its performance even in our own lifetimes ('kids these days don't even finish the song', 'it's just begging'). According to Augé (1995: 75), 'The presence of the past in a present that supercedes it but still lays claim to it [is] the essence of modernity.' But it should puzzle us a little to find that our nostalgia is historically recurrent: eighteenth- and nineteenth-century commentators expressed both a historical and a social distance from such rites, and developed a nostalgia for a more convivial and communal past. It seems that Halloween both is for ever, and is forever disappearing – like the receding stars of a galaxy, perhaps.

Certainly it is the case that such a view of Halloween, and of other calendar rituals, is embedded in our education system. School texts and popular accounts (e.g. Harland and Wilkinson, 1882; Trent, 1966; Pearson, 1972; Hunt, 1984; May, 1984; Shuel, 1985) emphasize the immemorial-yet-sadly-disappearing version of the calendar ritual as all the more worth celebrating for its antiquity and associated fragility, for the virtue of 'carrying out a custom that is one thousand years old'. Antiquity is signalled as another world – 'olden days' (May, 1984: 29), 'ancient times' (Hunt, 1984: 26) – while the fading of the ritual is carried in recurring phrases like 'until quite recent times' (Hunt, 1984: 40). In these accounts, the ritual objects provide the 'trace' or 'link' to that original time. The apples in the water link the present to the apples-and-water imagery of the Druid Avalon, or alternatively to the Roman goddess Pomona, just as the masks 'indicate' the guising associated with the Celtic Festival of the Dead. Such recollection is often both didactic and pro-gressive in its evocation of history. For example, Ladybird Books offer Special Days as 'the day each year when we remember' (Pearson, 1972: 28), a recol-lection that concentrates on Christian events and their success in replacing pagan ritual (as in the case of May Day, Mothering Sunday, Halloween and St Valentine's Day). They stress a continuity 'traced back to remote times' (p. 20), accompanied by a sense of attrition: 'all that remains of . . .' (p. 14) 'a custom that continued right up to . . .' (p. 8). Thus the Ladybird ritual: (a) takes as its starting point annual 'treats' for children; (b) explains these as mnemonics for mainly Christian feasts; (c) whose objects and rites (e.g. nuts, apples, fire) can be decoded in terms of their pagan origins; (d) which are subject to attrition; but (e) which are fortunately restored to our heritage by Ladybird Books. What culture forgets, education recalls. In this way Halloween, like History, repeats itself: first as a witching ritual, and finally as a Ladybird.

Other educational accounts are equally firm on continuity, but seek the imaginative involvement of the child in the original 'magic' of the ritual day (Ladybirds are relentlessly informative). This can be attempted seriously, or playfully. A serious example involves All Saints' Day itself, where the account of Father and Mother and their only son Brian going to church on that day involves: (a) a rehearsal of the sacred facts about saints, via the stained glass depictions of saints in the church windows; (b) the vision of saints by the dreaming child ('"I saw them," thought Brian, "These saints are not just pic-tures"'); (c) the confirmation of belief, and example to others – 'I really felt as if all the saints were there with us on their special day' (Smith, 1971: 112). More playfully, such empathic renderings treat pagan myth merely as excit-ing fairy tale, with a cast of devils-on-goats, witches, Fairy Queens, goblins and spells (e.g. Manning-Sanders, 1972; Adams et al., 1977). A striking feature of these ritual depictions is the very firm way in which they separate Christian from pagan, real from unreal, and hence 'history' from 'fairy tale'. Hunt's account of Halloween does even more – not content with the fading of the ritual and an educative reading of the runes, it offers a recipe for developing and celebrating the ritual which includes a history of the ritual, and instruc-tions on how to hold a 'spooky party' (Hunt, 1984: 16).

All in all, educational portrayals of calendar rituals like Halloween and its associated festivals imply a notion of what we called (problematically, but we'll come to that) 'modernist' ritual: frozen events, singular in meaning, determined in their outcome, recurrent in nature and subject only to a kind of creeping amnesia over time. They offer continuity as morality, the implicit virtue of tradition and the pedagogic importance of an enduring cultural identity: 'you will understand a little more how people thought and felt in early times' (Hunt, 1984: 6).

On the other hand, a reading of such events as a manifestation of post-modernity rather than modernity would seem to offer an entirely different picture. Too ephemeral for ritual, or perhaps even for rationality, postmodern events are allegedly things of flux and plurality, always forward-looking, continuously emerging, forever absorbing the past as pastiche (Lyotard, 1984). They stand as black holes do to stars. Thus if we think modernistically about Halloween we contrast it with the postmodern in a dichotomizing move that typifies modern Western thought (or so says Derrida): and the templates of a Durkheim, or a Mary Douglas (Douglas, 1966), then naturally invite us to understand such differences by dividing, clarifying, defining. Indeed, Mary Douglas's invitation is a double temptation, for the act of clarifying is both intellectual and moral, an act of hygiene against the polluting possibility of confusion, overlap and uncertainty, as we noted in Chapter 3.

So what would a *postmodernist* reading of Halloween look like? Well, we might take as our starting point the merest tremble in the fixity of what we called the modernist reading of Halloween, that contradiction we feel about the permanence of the ritual and our equally permanent experience of its loss, a ritual which fades before our eyes – demands for 'treats' without 'tricks', the shameful overlap of Halloween with Guy Fawkes in the amorphous 'Bonfire Spectacular' complete with BBQ and bouncy castle (*South Manchester Express Advertiser*, 2 November 1995), the casual augmentation of the witches with Morticia Addams – a rate of loss that confounds the notion that it is thirteen centuries since Pope Boniface first inaugurated the effacement of that pagan ritual. In the language of postmodernism, we might wonder if that continually reappearing and simultaneously disappearing ritual was not a palimpsest. And, in so doing, we would not be the first. Earlier this century, C. S. Burne claimed, in the *Handbook of Folklore*: 'Our British calendar is a palimpsest' (Burne, 1914: 238).

Such authors point to the overlaying of pagan custom by Christian liturgy, to Boniface's attempt to appropriate the festivals of the dead (Leach, 1949) and to the hotly contested movements of festival days such as Halloween that accompanied the introduction of the Julian calendar, such as the 'Give us back our eleven days' riots of 1752 (O'Neil, 1975). In this perspective, Halloween was always an event of movement and struggle across time and meaning: no passive recurrence of the past, neither fixed nor singular; an element of institutional innovation, cultural invention and political struggle written into its ancient forms, somewhat akin to other 'ancient' institutions, like the British monarchy (Hobsbawm, 1983) or even the attempts by the early Soviet government to invent rituals to replace Tsarist and Orthodox festivals (Lane, 1981). Similarly, we find that in the past Halloween and Guy Fawkes were also read as somewhat 'merged' over time, taking in not only aspects of each other's ritual in what Hole (1960: 223) regards as 'a clear case of transfer', but absorbing elements of other neighbouring festival days such as St Crispin's day, the day of the patron saint of shoemakers, by appropriating games such as hunt-the-slipper (Cosman, 1981). Storch (1982: 11) argues that events in popular culture such as Halloween, and particularly Guy Fawkes, followed an 'often jerky or zig-zag trajectory'. As contests between civic groups and classes, they acted as cockpits in local or national disputes, as reflections of relations between elites and commoners, open to the acquisition of 'new meanings and new uses' (*ibid.*: 9). His version of the nineteenth-century evolution of Guy

Fawkes celebrations ends with middle classes and radical working class conspiring, for rather different reasons, to domesticate as passive 'spectacles' the unruly effigy-burning organized by bonfire gangs: 'to end a popular version of the event and stop everything unsanctioned, unlicensed and unforeseen' (*ibid.*: 95). Rites, then, 'clashed' and were 'suppressed', 'merged' and 'transferred'. They were also open to forms of 'revival': sometimes they grew brighter rather than faded, as in the growing strength of the Guy Fawkes celebrations in the seventeenth century, fuelled by continuing religious divisions. As we'll see, Halloween currently also seems to be expanding, overlapping with Guy Fawkes and absorbing a host of media representations of 'horror'. The forms of these rites were politically as well as culturally pliable – the suppression of street bonfires quickly provoking the response of placing candles in windows to make the same anti-papist message. On the other hand, other aspects of the rituals that surrounded Halloween – such as 'Nutcrack Night', a divination ritual concerning the casting of two nuts into the fire in order to predict future love – could simply disappear:

> If she loves me, pop and fly;
> If she hates me, lie and die.[3]

(Cosman, 1981: 85)

Such disappearances, however, were not necessarily inexplicable. Indeed, a Presbyterian drive against divinations associated with Halloween and All Souls' Day sometimes actively suppressed such rituals – Banks instancing such a trial in sixteenth-century Aberdeen (Banks, 1939). In a similar sort of way, Halloween is currently challenged as a non-PC festival incorporating elements of ethnocentricity (an 'English', 'Scottish' or 'Welsh' identity), religious bias (anti-Christian, anti-Catholic or anti-Muslim) and sexism (witches).

It is not difficult, therefore, to invert the commonly held, and 'educationally' promoted, supposition that celebrations such as Halloween are fixed and immemorial practices, subject only to attrition and gradual loss. Hutton (1994: 225) also concludes that such festivals were a matter of 'symbolic flexibility', and that the 'vestigial' view of popular culture is a deceptive one. He cites Sharpe approvingly:

> the decline of popular culture . . . is probably one of those phenomena which can be found in any period where historians seek it determinedly enough. Popular culture is something which changes, adapts and assimilates, and it would perhaps make more sense to approach its history in those terms rather than by using any simple model of decline.

(*ibid.*: 228)

We can add to those movements in the form, function and boundaries of such rites with even a cursory ethnographic glance at contemporary Halloween, watching its slide in the past century or so from a world of adult ritual to a kind of infantilized and carnivalesque post-Christian game (e.g. Storch, 1982: 75). For example, a content analysis of a Manchester primary school class's Halloween essays (year 7) indicates that the most frequently cited symbol of the ritual for these young children is the 'witch'. Halloween is 'when all the witches get burnt', although Guy Fawkes is sometimes thrown in the bonfire as well, along with the Houses of Parliament. These adjacent celebrations are not entirely distinct. Indeed, it is interesting that Halloween songs and Christmas songs follow the same incantation, merely substituting different themes within the same narrative plot:

Halloween is coming	Christmas is coming
The treacle is getting hot	The goose is getting fat
If you haven't got a penny	Please put a penny . . .
A fiver will do . . .	

The notion of 'transfer', of customs constantly if sometimes imperceptibly rewritten as well as repeated, is evident in such accounts. Most obvious in the data is the accretion of new themes to the contemporary ritual. Halloween's old horrors of 'scary stories', ghosts and witches seem to have attracted the New Horrors – Frankenstein, monsters, horror films on TV, the Addams family, Dracula and the consumption of: 'horible foods like tomato sorce with hot dogs and call it fingers in blood'.

Further innovations include the widespread prevalence of 'trick or treat' for sweets and money, the substitution of the pumpkin for the turnip and the use of vampire masks ('they joke to become evil people'). The ritual also has the power to recruit across religious and ethnic boundaries:

Interviewer: Did you do any of this?
Respondent: No we didn't do this . . . because first of all my religion is different.
Interviewer: And that is?
Respondent: Hindu. And then we didn't know much people then and basically because . . . well, we did do some things . . . played with the sheets . . . ghosts, scaring friends.

Halloween, it seems, is alive and well, and in a state of inventive growth and overlap with a more generalized 'bonfire season'. But this is not to claim an unproblematic continuity, because there is a pervasive sense that even its enthusiastic practitioners are sometimes uncertain or unconvinced about script and roles:

They said, 'we'll have the trick'. I shouted over to my mum and said, 'Mum, what shall we do if they say trick?' She said, 'Just run back and get a pack of cards from the house and show them one of your tricks.' And sometimes they asked me to sing so I sang: Trick or treat/Smell my feet/Give me something good to eat.

A rather different version of soul/sole singing, but there may be a thesis in that translation.

Halloween simultaneously retains an element of carnival and abandons it. The inversions of carnival are present in the children who may stay out late, accost strangers, fool about, dress up, paint their faces with chewing gum ('the red stuff goes on your face and you can eat it and draw on your face'), as well as beg for money ('and I got some sweets off this man that's opposite me, he lives at No. 25'). Even strong taboos are suspended.

But the child who said 'Oh come on, *please*, nobody's given us anything yet' is acting *with* rather than *within* the ritual, appealing as it were over the head of the ritual performance for the collusion of an adult in what they both take to be a distancing from the original 'game'. 'Ritual' as pretext rather than text. Another shift in meaning, then, as the ritual becomes a kind of quotation (like those snatches of carols that preface demands for money later in the year), a licence to beg that merely gives its licence number.

Such an account, however, does not imply that Halloween has become a wholly anodyne child carnival. It has not lost all capacity for fear ('And I hate Halloween so much'), nor even perhaps for malice: 'Some Muslims do not open the door because Muslims do not like it' (ethnic Asian girl). From monocultural relic to multicultural mischief. In our didactic age, of course, various attempts at 'schooling' the ritual are evident. School children may well regard the chore of subsequently having to write about such festivals as part of the ritual, the reassertion of the normal and an adult expropriation of their fun. It is pleasing to record that such adult tactics are sometimes resisted. One child subverted the introductory rubric for the 'Halloween' essay thus:

> One day Mrs Rule came in our classroom and she brought a girl with her and said, 'This is a new girl and her name is Bushra now everybody be kind to her, OK?' Mrs Rule yelled. Bushra said 'What is Halloween?' I said to her . . .

If only it had been Miss Rule, the carnival would have been complete.

There is further evidence of resistance, of elements of confrontation that should reassure us as to the current potency of the rituals of fireworks that surround Halloween/Guy Fawkes. The resistance of the young to attempts to make fireworks merely a passive and public spectacle by continuing to buy and set off their own are an assertion of the active, subversive and carnivalesque role of fireworks as licensed cultural deviance. There is little difficulty in lining up Storch's account of the socially contested nature of the nineteenth-century bonfire 'season' with the contemporary Manchester headteacher standing outside the fireworks shop to prevent his pupils from entering. Like his nineteenth-century forerunners, he anticipates an event 'frighteningly lacking in normative regulation and moral authority' (Storch, 1982: 3), and stands in a tradition of élite disapproval which can only bode well for the continuation of the ritual: 'it was an absurd decision to allow fireworks to be sold opposite a school . . . but as it has been allowed to open, I am standing outside the shop every night and every lunchtime. I am determined that none of our children are going in' (*South Manchester Express Advertiser,* 2 November 1995).

In this sort of way, then, we can read the fixity and the singularity of the ritual against a more fluid, emergent, and contested rendering. Even a ritual as ancient as Halloween can be read as a plural set of meanings spinning itself out in the slow flux of the centuries. But that is not the only story to be told. We can read the old as new, in that way, or the new as old. For what is *postmodernism*, from the imagined perspective of some future retrospective, other than a contemporary act of divination, yet another epistemological eggwhite drifting through the medium of time? To pose such a question is to challenge the boundary that separates rationality from ritual, that privileges any inspection of the event and offers to sort reason from superstitition. It raises the prospect of 'postmodernism' (as ritual) as a kind of narrative that offers a way of condensing meaning, collecting allegiances, scapegoating outsiders and reasserting differences. We might regard such mobilizations of meaning as containing at least the trace of ritual, of a 'sacrificial crisis' (Girard, 1977: 39) enacting the discursive death of modernism and the triumph of a new difference in a narrative that deploys all the old ritual markers of initiation (embedded in discourse rather than practice as befits the domination of the text in our times) – death, cut, scar, break.[4] In this way, then, the relation between modernism and postmodernism parallels the hybridity and ambivalence of Halloween, as a question of shifting inventory rather than definition.

That takes us to a last point. We intend no either/or in this account. Halloween *is* neither modernist nor postmodernist, if we see these as opposites, clashing paradigms or contrasting periods. Indeed, this deconstruction of calendar rituals would have to acknowledge that unfixing concepts like 'ritual', rejecting the 'continuity' of recurrent events in history, doubting the implications of a 'progress' from primitive to modern etc. (an epistemological Mischief Night) can also be depicted as 'modernist' ploys. There is nothing avowedly postmodernist about those such as Turner, or Schechner, who assert the 'liminoid' over the fixed, the discontinuous over the continuous, or choose to define terminology like 'ritual' in terms of what it is not: 'rituals are not safe deposit vaults of accepted ideas but in many cases dynamic performative systems generating new materials and recombining traditional actions in new ways' (Schechner, 1993: 228).

There are a number of implications that follow from such blurring of 'boundaries'. The first is temporal. Like 'Halloween', 'postmodernism' is not best thought of as a label; in both cases the label obscures a disparate flux of the old and the new, and lacks the correspondence that labels demand. Contemporary postmodernism, like 'Halloween', is interesting as a continuous rewriting, as movement rather than stasis.

The second is relational. A postmodern deconstruction is a reading against, but not instead of, a modern reading: it is an articulation on the old, a reading of one against the other, more usefully represented metaphorically as a 'fold' rather than a 'break' or 'boundary', and as a pollution and intermingling that refuses a final resolution of meaning. (See 'Mourning', where 'Reader' argues with 'Author' about such dilemmas, and our own related but less fictional arguments in Chapter 8.) Breaks – whether between Old and New Halloween, or Old and New (or post) modernism – reinstate the polarities they seek to deny. Even in inverting these polarities (fixed/fluid; singular/plural etc.) we retain a nostalgia for the 'original' condition, whether a ritual or a philosophy, and for the dichotomizing of the sacred against the profane. There is no abolition in inversion (a point developed in Chapter 5). Perhaps it is better to say of Halloween, or of the relations of modernism and postmodernism, that we need a middle language, a vocabulary of *both/and* rather than *either/or* – like the language of 'viscosity' (a metaphor of internal dynamics and surface tensions) and of 'proliferation' (a constellation and flux of remembering, forgetting, inventing and suppressing). Such a language might tell us more about ritual and belief, or the nature of tradition and identity, in our contemporary culture.

It might even have educational implications. We teach our children such a rigid, true-or-false, this-then-that, view of history: they learn the fictions of 'facts' and 'truth' along with fantasies of cultural identity and tradition. Yet what kind of ontology is that for the postmodern age? If the young in post-modernity are to have 'flexible bodies' (Martin, 1994), better to give them flex-ible foundations for their self-making than the superstructural fantasies of 'adaptable skills' schooled into the supposedly stable 'base' of their being. If we really want to go back to the basics, then forget school history, kings and queens, and the ravings of contemporary politicians. Teach kids a subversive anthropology of their rulers' fantasies of tradition and identity. Help them to 'deconstruct' ritual and myth. And if they have to obey, let them at least some-times obey the Lords of Misrule.

Notes

1 This chapter is based on a seminar conribution on 31 October 1995, at Crewe and Alsager School of Education, The Manchester Metropolitan University. The paper, and this chapter, is co-authored by Ian Stronach and Liz Jones.
2 It is conventionally the case that postmodernists seek to differentiate themselves from modernists by asserting the 'death of the metanarrative', after Lyotard, by doubting the progressive and evolutionary nature of history – the 'death of the Enlightenment project' – and by seeking new ways of expressing or refusing to express notions of 'difference', 'identity', 'validity', 'truth' and so on. That convention is accepted here in order to introduce the distinction, but modified later in the chapter, and in the 'mapping' chapter of this book (see Chapter 1 and chapters subsequent to this one).
3 See also nineteenth-century Lancashire: 'As blazed the nut, so may thy passion grow/For 'twas *thy* nut that did so brightly glow' (Harland and Wilkinson, 1882: 223). But the nut divination seems not only to have disappeared, but to have re-appeared upside down: 'burns quietly, all is well' (Manning-Sanders, 1972: 130). Accordingly, readers are advised not to try this out at home.
4 Another way of articulating that relationship can perhaps be read from Girard's analy-sis of the 'sacrificial crisis'. His account stresses both the separation and the similarity of the sacrificial object. It must be close enough to be recognized and potent, but distant enough to insulate itself from impure violence and a general breakdown of order. In that sense, the antagonism between modernism and postmodernism can be read as a necessary dispute, just as Halloween itself can be depicted as a 'necessary dispute' between its modernistic and postmodernistic possible readings. Such a reading abandons correspondence as an arbiter of true meaning, folds one set of aspects of the ritual against another set, and seeks to understand the play of differ-ences between them. In the metaphor that Deleuze employs, Halloween is a 'knot' whose meanings can only be self-referential: 'the thought of a knot is given in its alge-braic group' (Deleuze, in Boundas and Olkowski, 1994: 52).

5

Mobilizing meaning, demobilizing critique? Dilemmas in the deconstruction of educational discourse

This book is already a story of irredemption, of sins that cannot not be committed, binarisms attacked yet never destroyed, ideologies in oppositions that are irresolvable in any classic dialectical sense, solutions that are never final. That was, if the opening chapter be recalled, our promise of disappointment. A promise that was not utopian, and a disappointment that was not intended to be negative. In this chapter we begin an exploration of policy, and policy analysis, in relation to that utopianism (as expressed in an instance of 'critique', or 'critical theory') and articulate an instance and an account of that disappointment, seeking to unsettle a polarization of critique and deconstruction while still resisting accommodationist reconciliations of modernism and postmodernism that make the latter into a kind of modernist baroque. Our intention, then, is not to dismiss policy critique but to argue that deconstruction is a necessary part of reading the relations and shifts of meaning that produce critical discourse, and a way of reconceptualizing what may count as critique. In prospect, accordingly, a more positive rendering of the negative. After all, the act of deconstruction, as Spivak insists, is not a negation of critique or an exposure of 'error', as much as an opening-up of critique to more comprehensive and less complicitous formulations. It acknowledges 'the dangerousness of something one cannot *not* use' (Spivak, 1993: 5, our emphasis).

It follows that we do not wish deconstruction and the undermining of 'critical' foundations to be seen as a conservative manoeuvre. Such a mobilization of meaning has its own political intentions, as Denüvo argues: 'Justification . . . requires, as the term suggests, a realignment (political and epistemological) of phrasal or discursive regimes and strategies of communication that can *respond* to the sound-byte hyperspin new-speak, the current (electrified) idiom of advertising and politics' (Denüvo, 1992: 43, author's emphasis).

There is a further condition that we wish to set ourselves in this search for a de-radicalized yet unconservative practice of inquiry. We wish this inquiry to be a practical one, focusing on specific examples and making reference to everyday educational events and processes, rather than succumbing to the byzantine riddling that typifies much deconstructive writing, and which is nicely illustrated by Harvey: 'The point here is simply that deconstruction (a) is not nothing, and (b) is not metaphysical, yet (c) it is not something and (d) is somewhat metaphysical' (Harvey, 1986: 36). Future Sir Keith Josephs are unlikely to be impressed by such excesses.

In the light of these perspectives, and alibis, we pose our central question for this chapter: *what is the nature of the relationship between a policy-related theory and its postmodernist deconstruction?* We intend to approach that question as follows. The first section of the chapter explores the possibilities of postmodernism as a reading practice – a way of making sense of a discursive formation. We take as our deconstructive subject the educational discourse of vocationalism, first offering a conventional, critical analysis of that discourse which characterizes it as a case of 'policy hysteria'. We then subject that analysis to a deconstruction. Following Derrida, Deleuze and to some extent Foucault, we seek to identify the nature of the silences and repressions that underlie critical notions such as 'policy hysteria'. Our aim is to give a more heteronomic reading that 'exceeds' the text (Clark, 1992) and goes beyond hermeneutic exegesis.

In the final part of the chapter we consider the ways in which deconstruction enables us to think differently about the business of reading discourses – through an emphasis on shifts and movements in meaning within and between discourses, and through a concern for those ambiguous trajectories of meaning. In this we follow Foster, who argues that we should deploy postmodernism as follows: 'Think of the difference this way: if the "essence" of modernism is to use the methods of a discipline in order to entrench it more firmly in its area of competence then the "essence" of postmodernism is to do the same but in order, precisely, to subvert the discipline' (Foster, 1984: 75).

Thus we seek to subvert the implicitly modernist elements in the thinking behind 'policy hysteria', and to suggest different ways of interpreting notions of 'disorder' from postmodern perspectives.

First, why pick on vocationalism from the plethora of educational discourses? Is it in some way exemplary?

1 Vocationalism is certainly part of an important discursive formation. That formation connects education to the future of the capitalist economy, and so reflects a central ideological concern of the state in late capitalism/disorganized capitalism/postmodernity. That concern is obvious in countries such as the UK, the USA and Australia. As Wilding points out in his review of social policy in the UK, numerous discrete policy areas (e.g. health, social security) are now also becoming more integrated with economic policy issues (Wilding, 1993) – in terms of both rationales and management procedures.

2 In addition, 'vocationalism' in education is a central discourse of 'crisis' – that is, it may be regarded as a characteristic act of 'problematization' by the state (cf. 'youth', 'single parent', 'foreigner', 'scrounger' etc.): 'the history of government might well be written as a history of problematization, in which politicians, intellectuals, philosophers, medics, military men, feminists and philanthropists have measured the real against the ideal and found it wanting' (Rose and Miller, 1992: 182).

3 Vocationalism can be regarded as a discursive 'space' rather than an object, or indeed a 'subject' in the curricular sense. We mean that notion in the

sense employed by Donzelot: a 'relational technology' linking different institutions (Donzelot, 1980). It also has the apparent characteristics of a fluid rather than a fixed entity, and thus stands as an 'opposite' to 'Halloween'. This enables a focus on these aspects of the discourse which depart from the more static analyses of modernity that Foucault and Donzelot offer, examining, for example, the ways in which vocationalism recruits agendas, interventions and audiences.

4 A further point of interest is that the discourse is subject to a multiple series of 'translations' between ideology, policy, programme and practice. These 'translations' are effected through processes of professional and managerial redefinition that also exist in other spheres of public service, like social work. In this way, 'political rationalities' and 'governmental technologies' intersect (Rose and Miller, 1992: 175), and raise the central problem of what Foucault called 'governmentality' (Foucault, 1977).

5 Thus far, these issues represent questions of reference and space, but the vocational discourse also allows us to address the sorts of problems of temporality raised by Falk (1988), such as: what relations of past, present and future are projected within the discourse? How do these relations construct explanation and prediction? Or questions of our own, such as: how does the temporal structure of the discourse help determine questions of validity or performativity?

So what we are proposing is that we should focus on vocationalist discourse as an interesting postmodern 'space' where (a) meanings are transformed, (b) processes of meaning-transformation are themselves transformed, (c) notions of postmodern time are constructed, (d) elements of sponsorship and contestation provoke both meaning-making and meaning-shifting. Let's call that a preoccupation with postmodernism as a *mobilization of meaning*.

With that in mind, we first offer a 'critique' of aspects of vocationalism, in which we construct the notion of 'policy hysteria', and from which we later develop a deconstruction.

First reading: constructing 'policy hysteria'

During recent evaluation work (Stronach and Morris, 1994; Turner *et al.*, 1994), we developed the notion of 'policy hysteria', and mean the term to refer to a cluster of related features in UK educational policy development, although we suspect the phenomenon is a more general one. It can be identified by a number of related features, which we briefly rehearse.

UK educational change in the 1980s and 1990s was characterized by *recurring waves of reform*. These developed increasingly short-term patterns, based on three to five year cycles of development. The policy cycle grew more frenetic, and gave rise to what respondents in the arena of education/business links called *'sunburst' and 'dieback' effects*. Recent work on the legacy of a billion pound project like TVEI (a broadly vocationalist reform of secondary education) also suggests serious 'dieback' effects (Merson, 1992; Williams and Yeomans, 1993). Cuban (1990) noted similar wave-like patterns in the USA.

Multiple innovation became the norm, with the next set of reforming initiatives overtaking and overlapping the last before their effect was known or knowable. In Scottish schools it was not unusual for state secondary schools in 1993 to be doing 13 different kinds of vocationalist activity, as well as other major curriculum and assessment developments. Things were even more dramatic in England and Wales, where the subject-based National Curriculum threw the skills-based vocational curricula into either contradiction or hasty *post hoc* rationalization, and where inter-school collaboration (e.g. inter-school consortia) clashed with increased inter-school competition for clients brought about by the Education Reform Act.

These waves of *policy changes were often inconsistent and incoherent.* The same government agency led the charge towards basic skills in 1980, and away again in 1984. The government supported 'generic competencies' in 1984 and reverted to basic subjects and standards in 1988. Records of Achievement (a student-centred record of experiences and qualifications) became the hitch-hiker of the educational galaxy, forever being picked up and put down in a different place – as a vocational guide, as personal development, as curriculum vitae, as a counselling instrument, as individual action planning. Traditional attitudes were the problem in 1989, and the solution in 1993.

Reform initiatives became more symbolic in nature, answering a need to dramatize a political 'response', rather than 'solve' an educational problem (Stronach, 1989; Kliebard, 1990). They offered far too simple versions both of the 'problems' they addressed and the 'solutions' they promised. Elements of *scapegoating* became embedded as policy. As such, initiatives were politically important at the beginning of each reform when they needed to be projected within the media as potential 'solutions', and much less important at the end, when they tended to be ignored. As a result the oversimplifications of blaming and curing set up cycles of initiatives designed to respond to crises that were formulated in terms more imaginary than real (in educational if not political terms) and so destined to fail.

In addition, reforms were politically contested within the education system, interpreted differently at different programme levels (Bates, 1989) and developed a language of 'enterprise', 'relevance', 'student-centredness' that came to have as many definitions as it had voices (Williamson, 1992; Turner *et al.*, 1994). This process was characterized by radical *shifts in meaning.* The government tended to introduce educational reforms and ideas whose rhetorics were business-oriented and instrumental. 'Relevance' meant the needs of employers: 'enterprise' meant the need to encourage an 'enterprise culture'; 'competence' meant the accountability of professions to more managerial audiences (Stronach and Morris, 1994). But developers and teachers translated such words into more comfortable and familiar definitions. *Enterprise*: 'Enterprise carries with it no official values; morally it is neutral. Probably the best simple definition is the "ability to make things happen"' (Warwick, 1989: v).

The speed and overlap of reform waves meant that few of these initiatives could succeed. They were never in uncontested place long enough, often poorly conceived and hastily implemented, imposed on the teaching force and subject to marketing strategies that provoked cynicism in professional staff. The result was an *endemic crisis of legitimation* which meant that each 'solution' quickly lost its persuasiveness and had to be replaced by another. In the vocationalist arena, the effect was a kind of *rotation* of various themes of 'blame' and 'cure' – from basic skills to generic skills to subject excellence and 'back to the basics'.

These conditions clearly amount to extreme *turbulence* at the policy level, and in relation to curriculum and assessment. By the early 1990s the contents, processes and structures of education were all in a state of flux. That turbulence was aggravated by a series of management ideologies that swept through (or over) the field of professional action. Performance indicators, total quality management, school effectiveness, school improvement, British Standard 5750, all jostled with curriculum reforms in an attempt to measure and promote the effectiveness of education, although there was barely an independent variable left in the system.

The intention of these policy and management reforms was to *shift educational debate out of professional arenas,* where it was felt to be a closed and oligarchic discussion, and into the realms of a more 'open' populist debate, led by politicians, right-wing ideologues and media pundits. In addition, the education system was simultaneously charged with *tremendous but unsubstantiated successes in its specific reforms,* and an underlying but somehow never contradictory demand from politicians for more change and higher standards in the face of competition from foreigners (few of whom were behaving quite like this). Specific innovations always 'succeeded', and the general situation always grew worse.

A final feature of 'policy hysteria' requires some elaboration. It concerns the ways in which time is represented in the discourse. Within vocationalist discourse, we can identify three different notions of temporality. Generally speaking, proponents within the discourse see time as a *linear* kind of 'progress-thinking' (Falk, 1988). The clock of this kind of 'time' is capitalist development, and especially increasing international competition that puts the wealth and dominance of established capitalist economies at risk: 'Today it is one minute to midnight, when we become a second-rate industrial nation' (Grand Met Chairman, *Observer,* April 1993).

A second kind of time located within the discourse is *cyclical* rather than linear. It envisages a return to lost individualist virtues such as those represented in the work ethic, or personal qualities such as honesty, morality, thrift etc. It posits time as a circular return to past virtues (historical or mythic) and a projection of those timeless virtues into the future.

The contrast between these two versions of vocationalist time is vividly seen in the different responses, for example, of the expanding and modernizing state of Malaysia, and that of the UK. Malaysia celebrates the future in a government-backed drive called 'Vision 20/20', while UK Prime Minister Major's 'Back to Basics' campaign was accompanied by invocations of warm beer, cricket and old ladies cycling to church in the early morning mist (Vision 1920).

The third notion of time is Falk's (1988) 'catastrophic future time', in which present events are overwritten by the apprehension of a 'super event', aided by the accelerating capacity of the media to produce instantaneous stories, and thus to invade the space in which historical investigation might have taken place. Falk's example is the shooting down of the Korean Airline flight 007, in which the super (non) event of nuclear war coloured all accounts of the incident, blurring fact with fiction, film and fantasy. In catastrophic future time the story *is* the meaning of the event (see also Bruck, 1992): the 'truth' of what happened becomes a 'performative' matter, in Lyotard's terms, a matter for the most successful projection of the story at any given moment. History, says Falk, has become a casualty of the present/future: we now live by 'futurostorical' accounts (Falk, 1988: 388).

There are interesting parallels in UK vocationalist discourse, wherein economic decline is a 'super event'. This oppressive sense of future time has rewritten educational futures in the language of competition, productivity and competence, dumping the old Grand Narratives of educational philosophy as a justification for educational activity. The encroachment of the 'future' on the present has been accompanied by a parallel erosion from the 'past'. 'Past time' has contributed to the erasure of present time by the cyclical notions of blame and cure, through the effects of scapegoating and moral panics. Attacked on two fronts (past and future), the present seems to have given up the ghost.

Falk's concern was that history itself was eroded by 'future thinking'. Our analysis of vocationalist time would see that erosion as double-sided, a deception based on nostalgia as well as nightmare, and possibly helping to explain why interest in defining or researching the isthmus of the 'present' is given such low priority, and why current policy debates and public perceptions are so subject to both amnesia and hysteria.

That is the nature and some of the consequences, then, of *'policy hysteria'* in the vocationalist field, and in education more generally. It involves a flux of successive and evanescent reforms, designed to construct short-term political support for current policies that address reflections and deflections of the real problems society faces. The discourses of 'policy hysteria' also displace 'present' time in favour of a mixture of nostalgia and catastrophic future time. On current showing, 'policy hysteria' begins in tragedy and ends in farce. Presumably, it results from a politically necessary displacement of economic problems into the education system, more or less as Habermas suggested (Habermas, 1976).

Second reading: deconstruction

The notion of 'policy hysteria' collects together a range of phenomena defined in terms of movement in time/space (short-term cycles; overlapping innovations; policy switches; meaning shifts; displacement of professional expertise; rotation of themes; oscillation of 'time'). In trying to 'read' vocationalism not as a static 'ism' but as a constantly changing discursive formation, we tried to depict a space in which different kinds of movement take place. Our aim in developing that notion of 'hysteria' was pragmatic as well as textual: the intention was to make a tactical intervention in the discourses of vocationalism that would expose the routine irrationality behind the vaunted rationality of both policy and policy analysis. We also intended to work 'inside' the discourses of vocationalism – to develop an immanent critique that would destabilize these discourses on their 'own' terms.

We want now to propose a different 'reading' of vocationalist time/space – one which deconstructs our own textual practices and challenges our own first reading. We shall argue that, in trying to represent movement, we have 'arrested' it; that, indeed, all the dichotomies that we started out by trying to invert – object/space, stasis/movement, stability/instability, certainty/uncertainty – have reinstated themselves 'behind our backs' as general organizing principles of our own arguments. Our 'reading' of vocationalism in terms of metaphors of movement conceals a pervasive nostalgia, we argue below, for the opposite of movement and its cognates – for stability, order, certainty and the 'present' as reality.

Let us look, then, at some of the individual terms of motion that we have used to construct activity within the vocationalist space.

- *Shortening cycles of recurrent reforms*: contains two, slightly different nostalgic appeals. First, the wave-form ascribed to contemporary change entertains the ideal possibility of arresting policy, so that it avoids repeating itself, at least for considerable lengths of time. Second, the description of the cycle as speeding up ('frenetic') contains within it the notion of a departure from 'proper' or orderly speed. And acceleration implies loss of control, crisis and the potential for future catastrophe, as we saw. In this way, the notion of catastrophic future time is installed, but as an uncontrollable process, rather than a looming event.
- *Multiple innovation*: constructs the vocational space as cluttered and disorderly, with innovations jostling and leapfrogging one another, against an ideal topography where innovations are disposed in a more linear and orderly arrangement. The covert appeal is to the possibility of a singular and coherent progress.
- *Frequent policy switches*: again, contains an implicit pathology of movement, which reads oscillation against stasis, and inconsistency against consistency. Against that pathology, the text offers the definitive account of the process, one of 'policy hysteria'. Policies may come and go, but the interpretation is here to stay.
- *Rotation of themes*: a cynical reading of movement as irrational. Policy becomes merely an opportunistic carousel of solutions which happen to succeed one another, against an implied ideal condition where a solution is properly and permanently connected to its antecedent analysis or rationale. There is an appeal here, not just to the idea of movement as orderly succession, but to cause-and-effect as the basic mechanism of that succession, linking problems with solutions. There is also a covert appeal to those 'experts' who know how to connect the latter to the former, including the authors.
- *Scapegoating*: as one of the phenomena that cause oscillations between false blame and baseless cure, this notion too is invested with the nostalgia for 'rational movement' described above. In implying an improper retreat from the modern to the primitive, from rationality to ritual, the new scapegoats are renamed – as 'policy-makers' rather than 'lone parents' or 'youth'.

- *Shifting meanings within the central vocabulary of the reform*: again, invoking a pathology of movement – in this case, of meanings – within the discursive space. There is a clear nostalgia here for a lost condition of stability of meaning – for a time when words were securely and singly connected with 'their' meanings; or, at least, where the instability of meaning was much less 'radical'.
- *Displacing of professional discretion by managerial and centralized control*: implies a kind of ideological invasion of the discursive space (i.e. by the forces of centralization) that again disrupts a 'proper' disposition of elements, or overruns protected areas of operation within the overall space, such spaces including those more properly occupied by the professional rather than the manager.

The same might be said of other terms used in our critical analysis, such as flux, or turbulence. But the line of argument is clear: at every instant of trying to talk of movement, we have whispered about order, propriety, normality, stability. Our stories of shift, displacement and rotation contain repressed fantasies of devices for keeping things in place and curbing excess. They also establish a commentary box from where researchers can confidently pronounce. We have constructed, in other words, a full-blown 'metaphysics of presence' – the characteristic turn of Western thinking/philosophizing, according to Derrida, in which analysis becomes: 'the enterprise of returning "strategically", in idealization, to an origin or to a "priority" seen as simple, intact, normal, pure, standard, self-identical, in order then to conceive of . . . derivation, complication, deterioration, accident etc.'(Derrida, 1977: 236).

In our critical analysis of vocationalism, we collected together all the movements that we discerned in the vocationalist space under the name of 'policy hysteria'. This term seems, on reflection (or rather, on deconstruction), more apt than we knew at the time, for it contains within it virtually all the dichotomies of presence/absence noted above. 'Hysteria' is the negative 'other' in a whole range of dichotomies: it stands for disorder, instability, abnormality, unpredictability, excess, sickness, unreason. Its etymology and its significance within Freudian psychoanalysis allows it to be read, further, in gendered terms – as the disorderly female principle that challenges male rationality and control.

'Hysteria', then, is underwritten by the metaphysics of presence: it reads the contemporary policy scene, or space, as an aberration from an ideal condition of health, normality and reason. Yet the initial analysis of vocationalism was undertaken to point to the impossibility of such static and essentialist aspirations on the part of a postmodern critique. We were convinced by Derrida's argument that the search for 'presence' – for those principles or entities that will ground theory and end uncertainty – is always, endlessly, deferred. Whatever is proposed as the first, last or fundamental thing always turns out to be itself dependent on something else: 'a product, dependent or derived in ways that deprive it of the authority of simple or pure presence' (Culler, 1983: 94).

How, then, to rescue ourselves from the dichotomizing and paradoxically circular logic that turns out to have organized our argument against dichotomies? How to read motion without, at the same time, freezing it?

Clearly we need to displace the implicit 'hysteria–stability' axis that fixes our notion of policy hysteria, and to develop a different kind of connection that will reflect postmodernist perspectives.

Third reading: remobilizing critique

What sorts of criteria must such an enterprise meet? First, we cannot hope for a definitive account. Second, the account must make no appeal to an explicit or implicit foundational state of recovery. Third, we have to avoid the privileging of one or other aspect of a dichotomizing analysis. Finally, *this* reading should not dismiss the notion of 'policy hysteria' so much as increase our understanding of the provisionality of meanings (including our own), and of the 'positive' nature of this stage of the deconstruction. As Liszka puts it, deconstruction has to hold in play 'an opposition between an overturning deconstruction and a positively displacing, transgressive deconstruction' (Liszka, 1983: 245).

These are formidable obstacles, but we can begin by considering meaning in terms of movement and in terms of relationship. The notion of 'policy hysteria' – as we have discussed it so far – has three elements of stability that we might wish to 'unfreeze'. These concern the notions of policy hysteria as a *state* (a stable, defined meaning), a potential *inversion* (capable of reversal: hysteria/calmness) and a *progression* (from cosmos to chaos or vice versa, a sense of direction). Each of these conjures elements of a modernist world moved by cause and effect, defined by rationality, and capable of definition and transformation. But, according to Shurmann, the postmodern appears as flux rather than freeze, and the task of deconstruction is to: 'liberate the constellations of the political (words, things, deeds) from any present referent whose rule would freeze them into constant presence' (Shurmann, 1990: 93). The three elements of 'policy hysteria' – state/inversion/progression – are just such present referents.

But what would such an 'unfreezing' look like? Deleuze and Guattari suggest we might envisage such meaning movements thus: meanings 'no longer constitute placards that mark a territory, but motifs and counterpoints that express the relation of the territory to interior impulses or exterior circumstances' (Deleuze and Guattari, 1988: 318).

Thus meaning is a matter of adjacency as well as movement. It has territory (or ceaselessly establishes, loses and re-establishes territory), and contested boundaries. Neighbouring concepts, which may be very different yet still adjacent, invest each other in a series of 'semiotic chains of every nature [which] are connected to very diverse modes of coding (biological, political, economic etc.) that bring into play not only different régimes of signs but also states of things of different status' (Deleuze and Guattari, 1988: 7). Nor should we see these relationships in linear cause-and-effect ways. Their metaphor is the rhizome rather than the root (although we should not forget to ask in turn if rhizome may also aspire to be a root metaphor).

We have, then, a plea for flux, uncertainty, inter-relatedness, a concern for how meaning is made between rather than within words, and various invocations of 'pliant being' (Shurmann, 1990), 'nomadic' approaches (Deleuze and Guattari, 1988) and 'svelte discourse' (Lyotard: see Sim, 1988).

> In an economy deprived of an epochal principle ... responsible action will be a response to the ever new modes in which things unite in the world and differ from it. One answers the 'call of the difference' by inscribing one's acts within the play of identity and difference between world and thing.
>
> (Shurmann, 1990: 264)

That injunction points us, as did Chapter 3, in the direction of indeterminacy, but in an indeterminate kind of way typical of such postmodern writing. We need, therefore, to return to vocationalist discourse in order to try to realize some of these general prescriptions by mapping some of the meanings within a specific discursive space, even if only provisionally.

A good place to start thinking about that might be to ask what kind of ordering and disordering principles and tropes apply to such discourse. We certainly want to avoid the kinds of order represented in Foucault's totalizing and 'freezing' metaphors: 'surveillance', 'gaze'. They are metaphors for the modernist condition, and they stand on some unexplicated Foucauldian vantage point. But the notion of 'regulated freedom' has more appeal (Rose and Miller, 1992: 174). It is less determined, paradoxical, if not ironic. It juxtaposes a condition of 'unfreezing' (freedom) with a qualification of 'freezing' (regulation) and also has a more general interest because versions of such a dichotomy underpin much sociological and anthropological thinking – as in agency/structure (Giddens, 1982), or communitas/structure (Turner, 1981).

A first point to note is that the term cannot be separated into its component notions

1 freedom   2 regulation

without creating an external and 'grounding' reference to some principle of 'freedom' (e.g. Habermas), or 'subjection' (Foucault). As an interdependent notion, however, 'regulated freedom' points both constituent concepts inwards in a mutually deconstructive relationship. The two concepts take their meaning in shifting combination with each other and with associated notions. There is no foundational appeal. They occupy a 'site' (Shurmann, 1990: 42), they define a 'space' (Deleuze and Guattari, 1988) but they do not have a 'ground'. In terms of both power and knowledge, we might say that such meanings 'lean' on each other in a kind of deconstructive relationship which, as Tresize puts it, 'seeks to articulate a relation other than that of opposition itself, a relation of differential intrication in which the involvement of terms with each other constitutes their only identity or quidity' (Trezise, 1993). It follows that the 'grounding' metaphors of, say, 'demystification' or 'penetration' give way to new tropes such as 'intrication' and 'imbrication', words which seek to express involvement rather than implicit resolution.[1]

We might also set up the notions of regulation and freedom against other deconstructing possibilities – like 'licence' and 'subjection' – and consider the whole cluster of relations among terms as a suitable resource for deconstruction, taking into account the various combinations that they offer, acknowledging that such a cluster would be one of many possibilities, and connected to other discourses. Such a representation includes the sorts of semiotic chains, diverse modes of coding and absence of 'rootedness' (foundation; origin) that characterize the rhizome: 'A rhizome ceaselessly establishes connections between semiotic chains, organisations of power, and circumstances relevant to the arts, science, and social struggles' (Deleuze and Guattari, 1988: 7).

What we have been trying to explore are the ways in which a deconstruction can start from a conceptual pairing such as 'regulated freedom' and extend – from that 'middle' (Deleuze and Guattari, 1988) – to other possible connections, such as 'licensed freedom' and 'regulated subjection', thus generating a postmodern reading of power/knowledge configuring, and an account of movements and relationships in the making and unmaking of meaning. Such an approach carries the possibility not of defining a new kind of 'prescencing' (as Shurmann would call it) or a new régime (as Foucault might prefer), but of indicating the play of meaning within and between concepts and discourses.

Does such a reconceptualization offer new deconstructive possibilities that we can plausibly connect with educational or social practices? Our last task is to rethink movement within the space of vocationalist discourse. What does a deconstructive praxis now look like?

The paired concepts denote possible forms of movement/stasis, structure/agency that can be employed to characterize objects and relations within (for example) vocationalist discourse, and to express shifts in meaning. They allow us to think about these objects in terms of inherent (rather than aberrant) movement within the discourse (a notion 'unprincipled' by the meta-evaluative notion of order/hysteria), because they carry out a series of translations within and between discourses, grafting different combinations of power and knowledge into temporary structures of application. An example might be the case of Records of Achievement, which has turned up in many different ideological forms and rationales – from licensed freedom (open recording within the insistence to record) to regulated subjection (compulsory, supervisor-assessed, pre-ordained categories and scales, atomized performances). Again, we first reported this circumstance as an aberration (why don't they make their minds up?), but it might be more useful to see those shifts also as a condition of necessary movement, rather than a pathological case. The task of research would then be to track the trajectories of these meanings in the local/national/global configurations of power and knowledge that define and redefine them.

This may connect better with recent vocationalist developments because what has been striking about innovation within the vocationalist discourse over the past decade or so is just that mutability of the meaning of concepts, initiatives and pedagogies. Thus the manifestation of discursive 'movement', hitherto characterized as an aberration in the critical analysis offered earlier – exiled as 'hysteria' – can be domesticated once more. The condition of the vocationalist discourse is 'disordered', but not in a sense that permits the nostalgic recovery of 'order'. That 'disordering' may more fruitfully be linked to notions such as 'disordered' capitalism (Lash, 1987).

Let us now explore the usefulness of these perspectives on 'disorder' in vocationalist discourse in more detail, taking the notion of 'work experience' as the focus for our discussion.

An example: work experience as a 'disordered' curricular subject

Vocationalist discourse has much to say about 'work experience' – the placing of school-age students in workplace settings for educational purposes. It seeks to 'fix' work experience as a definable 'state' (type of educational experience) capable of creating an 'inversion' (recognition of the oppositions of school and work), and of delivering a 'progression' (variously expressed in terms of vocational, personal or economic outcomes for the participants).[2] The rationales for work experience are various, but usually make reference to maturational or preparatory arguments, theories of vocational choice, or claims as to the superior relevance or reality of the experience. Most impute the backwardness of schooling institutions and the need to remedy such deficits in relation to the 'needs of industry'. These appeal to some version of the modernist project – whether a pragmatic capitalist one, or notions of empowerment, or even more critical notions of emancipation (Simon *et al.*, 1991).

If we initiate a parallel concern for the postmodern agenda of move-ment/boundary/relationship with state/inversion/progression, we can address different questions. A movement question: how might the story of the for-mation of work experience be retold? A boundary question: what does the shifting liminality of school/work experience deliver? A relationship question: how do school and work invest each other, and what changes in meaning occur?

We can only sketch an answer to such questions here. But we would suggest that one possible narrative of the shaping of work experience is a story which begins in the 'middle' and which challenges the various narratives of rational progress from a fixed origin which circulate among its advocates. The 'work experience' (WE) event was initially situated in the fourth year of UK second-ary schooling for legal reasons, connected to the regulation of child labour and also to safety regulations in the workplace. It was legally rather than edu-cationally situated. It then developed as a bridging rationale (school-to-work), and became the 'fulcrum' of the subsequent development of the vocational-ist curriculum. It remains in that position of 'fulcrum' even now that the bridging rationale has withered away as school-leaving at age 16 decreases, as the youth labour market disappears and as 'training' offers to duplicate many of the vocational aspects of school-based learning. Further, the 'fulcrum' results in the development of both a pre-WE and a post-WE curriculum. The curriculum prepares *for* work experience through occupational and personal matching exercises, visits, personal and social education and so on, and then subsequently follows up the work experience with more individual sampling of 'work' through 'work shadowing' or more active simulacra of 'work' in terms of entrepreneurial activity. Thus the WE rationale begins in the middle and spreads in one direction down to the vocational créche (see the pre-five

Noddy magazine, BBC publication, December 1992, for the earliest sighting), and in the other direction into upper secondary and further and higher education. As a result, the vocationalist field, in trying to deny its origins in the 'middle' and to assert a rationality of 'ends' (needs of industry) or 'needs' (nature of learners) struggles to sort a collection of initiatives into a theory of 'progression' and 'coherence', and offers a wide range of *post hoc* rationalizations of why events take place in a particular order, or at all. Thus vocationalism – in this account – begins in the middle and develops outwards. The discourse is polyvalent and unstable, and overdetermined in the sense that work experience can be given a very wide range of ideological and educational justifications, both by its organizers and by the participants.

Such a deconstruction of work experience strongly suggests that the narratives of the rational development of work experience, with their notions of means–ends, inputs and outputs, obscure a much more adventitious curriculum development, starting from the 'middle' and gradually colonizing both the primary and upper secondary curriculum – the developmental movement, in other words, of a rhizome: 'language stabilizes around a parish, a bishopric, a capital. It forms a bulb. It evolves by subterranean stems and flows, along river valleys or train tracks, it spreads like a patch of oil' (Deleuze and Guattari, 1988: 7).

The nature of the 'disorder' becomes apparent. The rationalizing rhetorics of vocationalism are at war with the arbitrary and anachronistic features of its construction. The actors contest its meanings in a series of attempts to 'domesticate' rationales to their own beliefs. These shifts, and 'domestications', give WE a very wide range of possible meanings. It can be read as the mystification of work and unemployment, or as the celebration of the work ethic. Or it can be an attempt to reduce rights (e.g. the right to work) to an issue of qualifications (WE as a credential). It can justify or condemn schooling (as a refuge, as irrelevant, necessary or oppressive). It can act as a vocational guide, an initiation rite or parole from school. WE can do, and does, all these things. But the curricular attempt to control its meanings is the fantasy of order that we wish finally to dismiss. WE may be 'hysterical' but it cannot be 'calmed'. It is more helpful to say that WE is a 'disordered curriculum' incapable of any general reduction to order, capable only of local and situated reading – and that reading will concern the plural and shifting meanings of a curricular experience that is irresolvably a political contest. The discourse is ungrounded in anything except notions of conflict and change: it is a tug-of-words contest. 'Movement' is its defining characteristic, and performativity its temporary resolution. School and work (as philosophies rather than institutions) invest each other in a kaleidoscope of changing meanings and structural repetitions.

We conclude that postmodernist deconstruction must address rather than arrest the 'mobilization' of meaning in educational policy, and attend to the uncertain trajectories of meanings in contemporary times. It is the unruliness of knowledge that challenges us now. In addition, such deconstructions must not stop short at simple (or even complex) inversions of that which they criticize. As we have seen, such a manoeuvre is both necessary and insufficient – creating caricatures of movement that rest on unacknowledged grounds of nostalgia or utopianism. Deconstruction is about inverting the violent hierarchy, as Derrida has long argued, but it goes beyond that – to a positive and displacing relationship. As Clark puts it, that is the *responsibility* of the text:

> a *responsible* text would form by definition a meditation upon its conditions of genesis, raising such issues as those of the institutional frameworks of writing, its embodiment of novel forms of community, intellectual or otherwise, and above all, as a *heteronomy*, its necessary incompletion, its renewed questioning of its interpreters and norms of interpretation.
>
> (Clark, 1992: 189, author's emphasis)

Such an argument begins to address the criticism of those critical theorists who would hold that deconstruction and/or postmodernism is irresponsible in its relativism. The charge is reversed: it is irresponsible to continue to privilege the escape clauses of a foundational appeal.

A further deconstructive question remains. Given the inherently disordered nature of discourse, how are individuals to understand and accept that disorder, not for the love of chaos but against the fantasy of cosmos to which their 'distress' invites them? Pessimistically, we might conclude that all sorts of fleeting fundamentalisms are likely, as people try to construct the impossible object of themselves and their relation to the world. But there is a more optimistic argument that the acceptance of disorder should not be mistaken for passivity or acquiescence. It is – as Shurmann has argued – an anarchic position, standing against the fantasies of grand narratives, recoverable pasts, and predictable futures. Is the 'responsible anarchist' a subject for further deconstruction? 'Where now is the measure of truth and the guarantee of the real to be sought? This is the essential distress; the crisis of reason is only its backlash' (Shurmann, 1990: 253).

Notes

1 Such a relationship may help to answer the question: 'why do postmodernists pun?' The structure of the pun is an irresolvable play between meanings. See also 'sport', 'camp' and 'drag' in later chapters. The dismissal of such terms as merely obfuscatory jargon, part of the deconstructive malaise, *may* indicate mere conservatism and a reluctance to abandon the solace of 'foundational' metaphors.

2 The notion of 'arrest' has already been alluded to in relation to 'identity'. Just as individuals engage in such arrestwork in order to stabilize a sense of themselves, so too do policy-makers seek to 'fix' policy.

6

Can the mothers of invention make virtue out of necessity? An optimistic deconstruction of research compromises in contract research and evaluation

> In periods when fields are without secure foundations, practice becomes the engine of innovation.
>
> (Marcus and Fischer, 1986: 166)

In '. . . Opening . . .' we noted the programmatic nature of early postmodernist writing in educational research. We promised to be practical as well as theoretical (it is our cultural misfortune that we read these as opposites) and to open up different 'sites' for deconstructive practice, such as 'identity', 'event' and 'policy'. All of these carry an implication that we would like to resist: that deconstruction is only a matter of interpretation, of a different reading of what appears to be there (we're not really as singular as we pretend, rituals are more plastic than they seem, policy is less rational than it makes out). But we get to 'interpretation' through processes of 'data-collection' (that hunter-gatherer's fantasy of epistemology), and so questions of what constitutes 'data' and 'method', and the 'subject' who executes these manouevres and conjures the 'raw materials' with which we interpret, are also prime candidates for deconstructive suspicion. We turn now to opening up some methodological and practical research issues, seeking once more a postmodernist reading.

In conflating two aphorisms in our chapter title – 'necessity is the mother of invention' and 'making virtue out of necessity' – we intend to draw attention to three features of current evaluative research in the UK. The first is 'necessity', those structural changes in the research economy that seem to have punitively redefined roles, procedures and culture. The second is 'invention', by which we mean those methodological, ethical or political compromises that have resulted. The third, more improbably, is 'virtue'. We wish to suggest that the conventional story of current evaluative research in education – fewer resources, more competition, more compromises of all sorts – is also capable of an optimistic methodological reading, and that in the constrained research conditions of postmodernity,[1] it may be possible to envisage new concepts and practices of research that do not simply surrender to 'conformative evaluation' (Stronach and Morris, 1994) or to the general demands of 'performativity' (Lyotard, 1984). In particular, we want to consider in this chapter a way of rethinking the notion of 'validity' in short-term contract evaluation, and of linking it with re-formed practices of 'negotiation'. We base our analysis empirically on a deconstruction of responses to a hybrid research instrument which combined elements of reporting and inquiry (see Appendix 1), and which was used in two recent evaluation studies.[2] Our intention is to explore a theory and practice of 'transgressive validity' (Lather, 1993) on the basis of the respondents' textual interventions.

Lather's notion of 'transgressive validity' takes its cue from Foucauldian analyses of social scientific knowledge. It sets out to provide a 'counter-practice of authority', to 'rupture validity as a regime of truth' (Lather, 1993: 674):

> a *validity of transgression* that runs counter to the standard *validity of correspondence*: a nonreferential validity interested in how discourse does its work, where transgression is defined as 'the game of limits ... at the border of disciplines, and across the line of taboo'.
>
> (Lather, 1993: 675, also citing Pefanis, 1991, author's emphasis)

This is not the place to develop a full justification of 'transgressive validity', since our intention in this chapter is practical exploration rather than theoretical justification (but see Patai, 1994, for a spirited refutation of the notion). We would note, however, that poststructuralist and postmodernist approaches tend to regard notions of validity as somewhat suspect and either utopian or repressive expressions of whatever 'régime of truth'. Similarly, the integrity of the research 'self' – whether reflectively polluted or methodologically cleansed – would be equally suspect, ignoring the 'researcher' as itself an effect of a representational economy (Butler, 1992), a false unity or, as Strathern has put it, a 'representational fix' (Strathern, 1995: 98). Such suspicions, it will be recalled, also surfaced in the '... Opening ...' chapter of this book. Transgressive perspectives of the identity of the 'researcher', the nature of the respondent as 'other' and the logics that (dis)connect them are more concerned with how research methodologies and methods 'misfire' and hence with a 'faithfullness ... reinscribed in a general economy of (self-) betrayal (Kamuf, 1991: xix–xx). The theoretical dilemmas of such a paradoxically faithful betrayal are explored further in Chapters 8 and 9 and enacted in 'Mourning'.

These destabilizing orientations have guided our re-reading of mundane acts of compromise and invention in contractual evaluative research, and we offer these first thoughts as a starting point for developing methodologies and procedures of transgressive validity that may at least begin to flow against the tide of 'performativity' that threatens to engulf contract evaluation, in the UK at least.

We turn first to a brief outline of the relevant sorts of 'necessity' that characterize contemporary research, and to some 'compromises' or 'inventions' that seem to have resulted. The chapter then develops an empirically based account of a more positive compromise that might be regarded as an instance of transgressive validity, exemplified in a different form of researcher/respondent 'negotiation'. The respondents' interactions with the research instrument are analysed across several overlapping continua of transgressiveness (e.g. formal/informal, conforming/breaching). We reflect on the features of these responses, which can be made to suggest a *positive* reading of compromise, and explore the shifting space of the researcher/respondent relationship – which we hope will encourage further scandals of transgression, or experiments in virtue.

'Necessity'

It is not the purpose of this part of the chapter to do more than gesture at the contemporary pressures on knowledge-production in educational research (see Stronach and MacDonald, 1991, for a more extended case study account of those pressures). That sketch is necessary, however, if we are to envisage a research economy that is subject to a number of tensions which have methodological, political and epistemological consequences for the acts of research.

Hargreaves has recently offered a useful shopping list of postmodern features relevant to the educational arena. It includes the 'compression of time and space', the need for 'flexibility', the establishment of 'cultures of uncertainty' and the intensification of work and its attendant stresses (Hargreaves, 1994: 47ff). It might readily be argued that the educational research world in the UK exhibits these features of so-called postmodern capitalism. Many of the rhetorical spaces of educational research and evaluation have also been compressed and politically moulded in response to the direct and indirect state-sponsored demands of what Lyotard would call 'performativity'.[3] These compressions and distortions include the intensification of research work through shorter contracts (Nisbet, 1995), greater formal control by the local and national state over research (Pettigrew and Norris, 1993), the chronic job insecurity of research workers (AUT, 1995), the increasingly incestuous links between policy and research/evaluation, and the emergence of phenomena such as 'policy hysteria' (Stronach and Morris, 1994). In addition, the heightened funding competition within higher education, it could be argued, has resulted in an economy of research knowledge increasingly concerned with competition and status display, rather than issues relating to originality or excellence. The periodic Research Assessment Exercises, involving the rating of individual members and clan groups of the research community, do not so much amount to a meritocratic incitement to research excellence as reveal entertaining parallels with the periodic 'potlatch' ceremonies with which North American tribes would ritualistically display their comparative wealth in order to 'destroy' their enemies (Tollefson, 1995). That such state-imposed 'tournaments of value' should be self-administered by the research community itself makes its own commentary on the 'independent' and 'critical' nature of contemporary research.

'Invention'

We suggest that contractual and political changes in the nature of these rhetorical spaces – otherwise called 'projects', 'contracts', 'programmes' or

'evaluations' – have led to important but neglected epistemological and procedural changes in the sorts of truth-games that can be played on such under-
sized and over-stressed pitches. In other words, the classic methodological and
interpretive paradigms to which evaluative research has responded in the past
(which we will call 'game 1') are now being played out in interestingly different milieux, their key concepts invoked yet transformed in meaning. These
classic socializations were directed towards such various canons as Glaser and
Strauss (1967), Giroux (1983), Hammersley and Atkinson (1983), or the
models for evaluation proposed by MacDonald and Walker (1976), Stake
(1978) and House (1980). Nevertheless, they embodied modernistic (but not
identical) assumptions about the nature of knowledge and its relation to politics, a belief in progress, the possibility of a meta-perspective and usually an
essentialist view of the role of the researcher or evaluator – as ethnographer,
democratic evaluator, or critical theorist – as well as the need for apprentices
to these roles to have lengthy and accredited training. Such modernist
traditions (Philipse, 1994) differed in numerous ways but we wish only to register some commonalities of that research apprenticeship: lengthy, theory-
oriented, experiential in terms of fieldwork, conducted within 'projects' that
last between two and three years, and belonging to some well recognized disciplinary, procedural or political paradigm. Such is the general nature of initiation into 'game 1'.

We do not suggest that changes in the rhetorical spaces for research and
evaluation, or in the use and meaning of key methodological or interpretive
practices, are an entirely new phenomenon, but that the process may have
accelerated and become more salient. Take, for example, the paleonymic
career of the notion of 'fieldwork'. The practice begins as an expansive, prolonged and colonially sponsored immersion in exotic cultures (Kuklick, 1991).
A version of it is domestically repatriated by the 1970s to the classrooms and
schools of the metropolitan country (e.g. Hammersley, 1983; Hammersley and
Atkinson, 1983), and pressed into service in truncated and amended form for
the scrutiny of educational reform programmes (e.g. Hamilton et al., 1978).
Finally, it is condensed in the 1980s to a notion of fieldwork that involves
handfuls of semi-structured interviews clinging precariously to the fading
memory of a theoretical sampling rationale (Glaser and Somebody).[4] Our
'invention' question, therefore, concerns the impact of contextual changes on
the rationalization and conduct of research. What compromises and inventions have resulted? What 'game' are we now in? Or, to put it at its most
sweeping, what has postmodernity done to the modernist business of
research?

At a recent conference of evaluators (Stronach and Torrance, 1995), two fac-
tions emerged in relation to such changes. One faction argued that quantita-
tive changes in the size of projects – less time, more haste etc. – did not imply
qualitative changes. Fieldwork might have to be condensed, but that did not
mean that the game had radically changed: 'game 2' was no more than an
abbreviated and accelerated version of 'game 1'.

On the other hand, some took a more postmodern view, arguing that the
fragmentation of research and evaluation experience had created new sorts of
apprenticeship, and that short projects, abridged methods and stronger

political pressures had important methodological implications. Their argument was that 'game 2' had emerged. Essentially, this involved those socialized into 'game 1' adapting their practice to the new conditions and using 'game 1' practical wisdom in order to play that faster 'game 2' . Such adaptation continued to involve the legitimizing citation of the methodological masters (the classic canons), but it no longer involved so much in the way of realizations of these implied practices. Methodology in this account was uprooted, and became part of a culture of quotation, something of a name-dropping and modernist nostalgia that Augé would argue parallels 'the essence' of modernism (Augé, 1995: 75).

They further speculated that future researchers and evaluators would tend to have still more fragmented socializations into research, and to conduct that research in a much-changed research context. Lacking a grounding in 'game 1' (from which to orchestrate their 'game 2' compromises) they would be obliged to play a more pragmatic and performative role in 'game 3' as knowledge-producers in the kind of knowledge economy outlined by Lyotard, wherein: 'Knowledge is no longer the subject, but in the service of the subject: its only legitimacy (though it is formidable) is the fact that it allows morality to become reality' (Lyotard, 1984: 36).

Our subsequent conversations with contract researchers in a major educational research outfit suggest that 'game 3' is a readily recognized phenomenon. Researchers spoke about the 'business' ethos that seemed to have left only the 'remnants of a research culture', as well as the increase in 'hit-and-run' projects: they complained that 'the word in-depth disappears', replaced by a speed and fragmentation of work that left researchers isolated from each other, insecure and demoralized (fieldnotes, 25 April 1996).

At any rate, the evaluation conference had been divided as to whether such differences were significant, and if so, whether they amounted to a crisis or an opportunity. Was it possible to envisage these condensed forms of research as positive developments? '[It] might tempt us to renounce our claims to any form of "science" of inquiry, in the hopes of generating new practices of knowledge production unconstrained by the pretences of a science of society' (reported in Stronach and Torrance, 1995).

The next section of this chapter picks up and tries to take further the positive strand of that argument, examining how a different notion of validity might be built on the backs (or ruins) of these 'classic' methodologies, and looking in particular at ways in which such a notion of validity might be constructed from different patterns of 'negotiation'. In so doing, it does not aspire to accommodate performativity so much as to explore the possibilities of 'local resistance'.

'Virtue'

We turn to an exploration of this theme, which draws on the research compromises adopted in two short-term, small-scale evaluations (time-scales around six months; funding between £11,000 and £15,000 each). Our aim here is to deconstruct our own improvisations and short-cuts in the hope that we can find virtue in these necessities. This is what Lyotard would call a para-logical rather than a pathological view of change:

> Paralogy must be distinguished from innovation: the latter is under the command of the system, or at least used by it to improve its efficiency; the former is a move (the importance of which is often not recognised until later) played in the pragmatics of knowledge.
>
> (Lyotard, 1984: 61)

In this section we offer both prospective and retrospective accounts of these evaluation practices. The former detail our 'modernist' short-cuts, the latter our subsequent attempts to deconstruct these improvisations in terms of notions of 'hybridity', 'transgressive validity' and 'negotiation'. Our short-cuts were practical: to carry out mainly qualitative research in an evaluation context quickly; to combine feedback and inquiry in ways that would offer the sponsor some reassurance about the wider validity of the findings; and to engage the respondents more actively and *differently* in both the inquiry and the reporting process. Our retrospective concerns, on the other hand, involved *post hoc* analysis of the respondents' textual interventions in the returned *report-and-respond* forms (see also Appendices 1 and 2). We were interested in the effects of the hybrid nature of the instrument, the nature of any 'breaches', the registers of response and the quality and intensity of respondent inter-action. Before turning to such deconstruction, however, we need to portray the nature of the hybrid instrument, and analyse the sorts of texts that respon-dents produced in response to its promptings.

As the name suggests, the *report-and-respond* (R&R) questionnaire was created in order to combine feedback based on preliminary interview and data analysis (a kind of potted case study) with an invitation to agree or dis-agree with the feedback, as well as add to it. The approach was first used in a short evaluation of the management of innovation in the Technical and Vocational Education Initiative (TVEI) (Morris and Stronach, 1993), and again in an evaluation of special educational needs training for Strathclyde Regional Council (Allan and Stronach, 1995), in which professionals were asked about their experiences and perceptions of a modular training pro-gramme. In this account we draw on both experiences, although the dis-cussion of responses presented here is based on data from the more recent project.

The 1995 R&R questionnaires were administered after semi-structured inter-views had been carried out with a small sample of teachers and headteachers ($n = 20$). Questions were framed, not as questions *per se*, but as a series of summary statements about the programme. Respondents were asked to say whether they agreed or disagreed with these and to offer any comments or additions. An example is given in Figure 6.1 (see Appendix 2 for other examples from completed forms). Generally, responses could be as closed (by placing a ✔ or a × in brackets) or as open (by writing comments) as indi-viduals chose.

There seemed to be a number of categories of response, along several over-lapping continua:

Teachers said that the modular programme helped them make better connections between theory and practice (✓). They offered a number of reasons for this: alternating SEN modules with experience in school helped them make connections between the two (✓); they were able to discuss and resolve day-to-day teaching problems during the modules (×); and it was possible to try out new strategies on return to school (×). In general, teachers seemed to find that the modules were suitable for their own practice (×), and that the modules were relevant to *Every Child is Special* (✓), and to their own establishment's development plan (×) They believed that the modules were relevant to their professional aims (✓). **[Comments, additions?]**

Modules may have been more suitable for mainstream staff – certainly the assignments were geared to being in one place of work. Peripatetic staff in Support Services generally had to adapt the assignments or provide alternative suggestions. Because of the way the division operates at present with specialist services given on a peripatetic basis, the focus of possible assignments was considerably narrowed.

7 **Support**

The following sources of support were appreciated by teachers: exchanging materials with course members (✓); establishing new contacts (✓); good support from college tutors (×), from SEN Advisors (✓), and through group tutorials (✓). **[Comments, additions?]**

Other course members provided lots of information on a variety of different aspects of SEN & offered reciprocal visits, advice on materials etc. Course members are very supportive of each other. Support from tutors varied considerably

... where we enrolled, both Jordanhill ...posal – not so! The individual person ...llege at which one is doing a module – very helpful but faculties are pretty awful!

Figure 6.1 Integration of theory and practice

formal–informal
conforming–breaching
summative–formative
cognitive–affective

We regarded interventions as minimal in transgressive terms where responses were expressed formally, and conformed to the rubric of the instrument. More active interventions involved qualifications or additions, perhaps more unconventionally located (e.g. a margin) or extemporized (e.g. an asterisk, an insertion mark), or more informally or emphatically expressed (e.g. use of capitals, underlining, exclamations). We thought of the 'strongest' interventions in the transgressive sense as those which involved a challenge to the rubrics of response (e.g. refusal of tick/cross box, scorings out, direct criticism of the format), but we also came across an unexpected category of response. They were responses which we labelled *implicit dialogue*, and they appeared in a number of different forms: (a) the raising of non-rhetorical questions; (b) the citation of individuals who had performed well on the training courses or as supply teachers; (c) invitations to the researchers to get in touch for more information. We were interested in these as expressions of 'interactivity'.

We turn to an illustration of these various categories and tones of response.

Formal–informal

First, of course, we received data through the closed categories of the questionnaire – in general corroborating the account we had given. The response rate was perhaps rather better than average, given a postal approach close to the end of a summer term when issues of teacher overload had been a concern: 66 per cent of returns from teachers and 63 per cent from headteachers.[5] However, we did notice some striking features about the kinds of responses. A small proportion of teachers responded using only formal registers (19 per cent); that is, simply placing ticks or crosses in the spaces, not adding comments or only writing brief formal statements conveying opinion. These returns resembled what might be expected from conventional questionnaires and usually revealed little of the feelings of the peeople doing the reporting, or of the broader impact of the course on their careers and lives. The majority of responses (81 per cent), however, included an informal register and took a variety of forms, including more intimate and 'holistic' location of the course in their lives, and discrepant registers of response:

> Trying to do a full time job, be a mum, do assignments & have a life was too much.

> Delivery of lectures . . . from [named establishment] – grade A, gold star. Care and attention from all tutors ☺ to all students and to each other ☺. I hold [the establishment] in high regard.

Conforming–breaching

Another way of interpreting the above data is in terms of whether respondents simply obeyed the rubrics and cultural conventions of the instrument. Most did, but some also opened up two sorts of 'breaching' commentary, in ways that were both solicited and unsolicited by the formal rubric of the R&R instrument (the most radical 'breaches' of course were by non-responders, but that's another story). In the first sort of commentary, they offered qualifications to the statements in the report, underlining strongly felt aspects, qualifying statements with adverbs and adjectives ('horrendous', 'extremely worthwhile'), offering between one and three exclamation marks against their views, putting asterisks and comments, using capitals for emphasis and adding notes in the margins: 'this was true but . . .', 'yes and no . . .', 'stress!!', 'a great learning opportunity!' and so on. They sought both to reinforce points ('strongly agree') and to undermine them ('yes, but with the proviso. . .', 'to a certain extent'):

> to discuss and <u>resolve</u> day-to-day teaching problems . . .

> discuss – yes – resolve – not really. [teacher underlines resolve, adding comment below]

These lines, arrows, 'pto's', asterisks, underlinings and explanations all suggested strong interventions or breaches in the researchers' text.[6] Respondents also occasionally ignored the statements in a section of the report altogether, replacing them with a commentary explaining their own context or concerns. One teacher, for instance, ignored summary statements about overall impact and wrote:

Does this mean that more people will have a 'smattering' of knowledge and a few will end up as 'specialists' in another field?

Perhaps the strongest forms of breach involved challenging the form and rubrics of the report. Two teachers complained about the closed format of the inquiry, although both had supplied 'open' comments on issues – 'just putting in a [tick or a cross] is too restrictive' – while a more detailed criticism was offered by another:

A very difficult questionnaire and very time-consuming. Perceptions of course are very personal and particular ... comments may amount to prejudice rather than a balanced view.

This teacher, having taken on the joint role of respondent and research critic, went on to write a further half page of comments, writing against, as it were, the directions of the report/questionnaire, and the pressures of her or his own work situation.

Summative–formative

We noted that some teachers seemed to envisage more of a formative role for the instrument, regarding it as implicit dialogue, and envisaging it as the harbinger of a report that might ultimately make a difference somewhere, in terms of publicly recognizing individual achievement, changing policy, reforming practice or raising further issues for the researcher. Sometimes these concerns were expressed via non-rhetorical questions:

There is a discrepancy between handing-in dates for dissertations between the two colleges ... Why?

Outside speakers did not seem to concur with the thinking of the SEN staff. Were they chosen at random?

Some respondents indicated that they had discussed the questionnaire with other colleagues before completing it, while a few individuals supplied names and addresses and invited the researcher to contact them if further information was wanted. Another decided to photocopy the form and get colleagues to complete it. It seemed in such instances that the R&R had been read as intended – as a provocation to both summative and formative comment.

We have all filled these in because we felt *very* strongly that everything in the garden was not so rosy!

The perceived 'authenticity' of the process of communication as ongoing and consequential may also have been evident in the ways in which trainers or supply teachers were singled out and named by respondents, and in a kind of 'tell them from me' tone in some of the responses. One teacher wrote, 'one's return to education can be traumatic but for me this was eased by the [named] staff'. A headteacher took the 'opportunity' to commend a probationer supply teacher to the profession.

Cognitive–affective

There was, therefore, a sense of respondents actively engaging with the reporting aspects of the researchers' text. Many of the comments were expressed in an informal and animated register, and in general represented a kind of *emotional colouring-in* of the rational and cognitive surfaces of the report:

> 2 and 3 day blocks as in 93/94 are DISASTROUS!! Best to leave group to someone else, study & then return, full time, highly qualified to cope!!!

> I am sick of doing 'workshops' and 'brainstorming' and 'flipcharts'.

The tone of these affective comments ranged from the modest ('in my personal opinion...'), to the assertive, relating generalizations to particular experiences or indeed offering further generalizations on the basis of individual experience or belief. These statements ranged from the aggressive and affectively powerful examples given above, to more deliberative verdicts on the meaning of the course or such courses to the teacher's career or life.

In general, most respondents sought to read the generalizations of the report against their own experiences of the training, or against its impact on their lives more generally:

> This is only a personal opinion, but ...

> hopping in and out of college for tiring bursts of time is not ideal.

> I can identify weaknesses in my own approach and hopefully now rectify them.

These 'open' comments – sometimes sentences, often paragraphs – acted as a kind of counterpoint to the closed statements, not just augmenting them but offering a different kind of affective register for the feelings of the respondents, especially in relation to themes of overwork and the difficulties of combining training and work. For example:

> A bad day with my highly disturbed, volatile boys leaves me in no fit state to write an essay at postgraduate level.

> Ignorance of course content and level [among colleagues] and lack of informed value led to comments such as 'Oh another course, poor you'. 'Oh I thought you were off sick or was it the same thing?'

Our overall reading of the respondents' textual contributions to the R&R instrument would suggest that the animated and extensive responses may have been partly prompted by the provocative, provisional reporting nature of the instrument, and that many – though by no means all – of the responses were a more affective and informal counterpoint to the closed nature of the report statements. In our experience they contrast somewhat with the more formal and detached responses that typify most questionnaire responses, although of course there is no absolute distinction between the two types. Perhaps the distinction might best be expressed by saying that what is most commonly peripheral to conventional questionnaires (those catch-all 'anything else to add' invitations to free response) is made more central in the R&R rationale, and attempts by respondents to disobey the apparent protocols of the instrument may be – potentially at least – indications of validity rather than deficiency.

To conclude: it seemed to us that the procedure succeeded in provoking a kind of dialogue and 'negotiation' whose interactivity was more substantial and potentially transgressive than that of the formal procedures of 'classic' research or evaluation. At least the norms of engagement between researcher and researched seemed to have been breached somewhat. The respondents showed more signs of what in Chapter 2 we called 'struggle' – and what we might here call merely signs of life.

Virtuous theory

What can we say retrospectively about the nature of the instrument, and of the communication process it inaugurated? Our purpose here is to identify methodological issues which may be regarded as features of a positive compromise, and reflect something of Lyotard's 'paralogical' enterprise.

1 R&R is characterized by its *hybrid* nature. It is a questionnaire and an interim report, which both gathers and disseminates information. It offers judgement but solicits correction, treats respondents as both audience and informants, and regards the research process as an ambivalent mixture of engagement (provocative, analytical, dialogic) and detachment (separate from the action of the respondents, interpretive). It can also readily be seen that R&R combines different and conflicting research approaches, including a debased element of case study based on naturalistic inquiry, and a broader questionnaire-style survey, closer to positivistic traditions but contrary to many of the meticulous conventions of such inquiry (Belson, 1981, 1986). It includes a concern for undermining these approaches through: (a) acknowledging rather than glossing over the 'impurity' of their application as short-cut, short-term realizations of these methodologies, and (b) inviting respondents to quarrel with the form as well as the substance of the feedback and the inquiry, a poststructuralist approach in the spirit if not the letter of a 'validity of transgression' (Lather, 1993: 675). Its claim to legitimacy does not rest on absolute or singular notions of validity for any of these approaches. Instead it is committed to reflexivity about the limits and overlaps between different sorts of knowledge warrants. Thus it could be argued that the 'instrument' offers a multiple hybridity – as narrative (both report and inquiry), as both validating and invalidating its knowledge constructing methods and as a transgressive validity that uses rather than dismisses rival truth warrants.

2 Hybrid research need not imply an 'anything-goes' abdication of *methodological responsibility*. Each game plays and – to some inevitable extent – fails to play according to its own rules of validity. But it is the quality of the failure that is of interest (readers will note the recurrence of this concern throughout this book). Therefore methodological responsibility sets out to

audit, on the intrinsic validity principles of coherence and consistency, the extent to which research performance matches methodological claim, on both necessary and contingent grounds.

3 But research performance in whatever paradigm and whichever circumstance always and also mismatches methodological aspiration. Therefore hybrid research may address issues of *methodological irresponsibility*. These lie between: (a) 'classic' ideals and actual performance; that is to say, an evaluation of 'game 1' performances and the inherent limitations of the paradigm; (b) constrained copies of such classic aspirations; that is, a meta-evaluation of 'game 2' performances; (c) simulacra of research rationale and performance, as in 'game 3' performances where performativity has replaced other validity criteria; (d) attempts at transgressive validity and their un/realization; that is, the optimistic reading of 'game 3' possibilities.

4 *Transgressive validity* sets out to address (but never correct) these distortions by inviting respondents to break the rubrics of a research approach, whether through the graffiti of marginal comment, the refusal to make an either/or choice, the rejection of summarized accounts as an expression of their own reality or the violation of the implied register of response. It also inverts the role of the respondent, offering the role of methodological critic, as well as the more conventional possibility of substantive critic. But it does not insist on such inversions, thereby allowing the respondent to transgress the transgressive possibility by offering only formal and closed responses. Nevertheless it is an invitation to disruption. Or perhaps we might say that it invites respondents to answer in the political register and beliefs of their institutional or professional subculture, rather than to treat the questionnaire or the research process itself as part of an administrative régime to which they ought to respond 'appropriately'.

5 Hybrid research argues for transgressive validity. But how can it solve the *paradox of the validity of a transgressive validity:* is such a concept not always in a state of self-betrayal? Our key validity question in this area has to be something like: what signs are there of the qualities of intervention in the researchers' text by the respondent? We have to be particularly interested in looking for ways in which the hybrid nature of an instrument or text encourages *'breaches'* in the form of qualifications, additions, scorings out, discrepant commentary, criticism of the form of the instrument and so on. In that sense, our criterion of validity is 'transgressive', and based on evidence of the degree, and oppositional quality, of respondents' interactions with – and against – the text as 'report'. The instrument's potential for infidelity was our retrospective concern.

6 We were also interested in reading the *register* of the open responses. Were they formal? Did the teachers' textual interventions subvert the researchers' text, offer new registers of response? Had the text invited formal corroboration or demurral, or had it – as we found – been provocative in terms of the interaction? In terms of 'register' we were conscious that invitations to respond via questionnaire were perhaps unduly likely to invoke, both structurally and in broad cultural expectation, rationalistic responses. A hybrid instrument and a more ambivalent invitation might not be so vulnerable to these conforming pressures, and allow other stories and registers to emerge.

7 What might such provocations tell us in terms of a revised notion of *negotiation*, or of *dialogue* between researcher and researched? We were interested in trying to make such interactions less asymmetrical in terms of power relations, to encourage a more active and discrepant engagement of the researched in the research process. We would not subscribe to some 'equal opportunist' view of that relation, in the sense of a Habermasian ideal of 'free-speech acts' and hence a dialogue of pure reason, so much as a view that the respondent in this sort of negotiation might be encouraged to rebel, that the instrument should provoke a transgressive response. We developed, therefore, a somewhat poststructuralist interest in the qualities of what was happening between the researchers' text and the respondents' text. We began to think that the rather empty and formal notions of 'negotiation' could be superseded or at least augmented by more participative and informal rewritings of the researchers' text (as an instrument of both report and inquiry). We sought, therefore, to relocate evaluation's notion of 'negotiation' more firmly within the business of the production of knowledge rather than in its consumption by others – that is to say, to shift the focus of negotiation from the beginning or end of the research process to its more formative centre.[7] This is not to argue, of course, that such shifts amount to an equalization of power.

8 Finally, we were interested in whether we could interpret the sum of the hybrid approaches as an educative *problematization rather than a triangulation* of research and evaluation stories and theories. Each research appropriation of 'reality' was to be read in terms of attempts also to portray the contingencies and inadequacies of its construction, its discrepancies in relation to other approaches and the transgressive possibilities of respondents' challenging, in a practical way, its warrants to knowledge.

Practical and theoretical conjectures

We offer a few practical and theoretical speculations about both the hybridity of the instrument and its efficacy, in the belief that such conjecture may help further attempts to develop 'transgressive validities' in educational enquiry. We begin with the practical aspect, and hypothesize a number of reasons for the apparent success of the R&R instrument in provoking active and critical responses:

- that an interim report requiring respondents to agree or disagree with its summary description and analysis provokes in its readers a more active desire to respond;
- that such a desire may be related to the ways in which R&R simultaneously informs and questions, and hence places the reader in a fruitfully ambiguous role of audience/respondent/critic;
- that the implicit 'person' of the researcher is envisaged by respondents in less administratively conventional ways, through the unaccustomed nature of the appeal to respond, and the invitation to 'resist' the rubric of the instrument;

- that respondents are provoked to offer both cognitive and affective responses, and show signs of at least a greater animation in the style and content of their responses;
- that such reports tend to represent more effectively their inherently provisional nature to readers, and to provoke respondents to corrective comment and to 'breaching' acts.[8]

Our conclusion might also suggest that conventional research practices do not often provoke effective 'negotiation' since they are offered to respondents and stakeholders in narratively closed down forms, as in full draft reports (which tend to be read as finished documents whatever the accompanying protocols about 'negotiation'). Alternatively, 'negotiation' is offered at too early a stage of the research process (as in the case of 'negotiated' transcripts, or fair evaluation agreements; House, 1980; Simons, 1987). It may be that the redefinition and relocation of negotiation that we have explored above, placing it at the heart (the displaced heart of course) of a consciously hybrid research process, offers more open possibilities and more educative futures.

We end with a brief comment on possible theoretical implications of 'hybrid' research, reading Bhabha's notion of 'hybridity' (Bhabha, 1994) and Lather's 'transgressive validity' against our own research and evaluation compromises. In so doing we hypothesize a positive reading of the postmodern, one that draws on Lyotard as well as Lather. (We do not argue that such positive readings *characterize* postmodernity: indeed, Chapter 1 argues that, if anything, the opposite is true, but they are a disruptive possibility within the conditions of 'performativity'.)

Our reading explored the respondent data and research methodology principally in terms of 'validity', 'hybridity' and 'negotiation', producing two possibilities worth developing. The first concerns 'hybrid' research, and its deployment of a 'transgressive validity'; the second concerns the nature of 'negotiation' or 'dialogue' between researcher and respondent.

'Hybrid' research, in this instance, did not involve a rejection of previous methodologies or interpretive frames so much as an acknowledgement of their transgressive 'other'. They were compromised forms of research even in 'game 1' conditions of modernity researched modernistically. Our reading of 'game 2' and 'game 3', therefore, did not seek a radical disconnection between modernist and postmodernist methodologies but a rearticulation of relationships, an approach that we have explored in greater depth elsewhere in this book.

Such positive readings of postmodernism are controversial. As Burglass has recently noted: 'The readmission of positive value judgement to a postmodern critical practice represents an objective not yet achieved' (Burglass, 1994: 34). The problem, of course, is that behind each positivity lurks the tut-tut of an unacknowledged grand narrative. To date, attempts to reconcile postmodernism with positive values range from the ingenious (Carr's 1995 Deweyan rescue) to the contradictory (Hargreaves, 1994) and the sometimes bizarre (Zurbrugg, 1993). Our initial response to the problem of value and its embedding in metanarratives would be to say that our re-reading of research practices sought to read such narratives differently, rather than to abolish them, and hence to re-evaluate them. The notion of hybridity maintains each paradigm in a play of defects and differences. Our motto in relation to foundationalism, therefore, has to be: no transgression without sin (and, by extension, no postmodernism without modernism).

In relation to 'negotiation', we began to explore ways of developing practices of communication between researcher and respondent that 'transgressed' conventions. In a trivial way, writing poems to non-respondents is a transgression, although one with the serious intention of provoking a non-bureaucratic motivation to respond. In a more substantial kind of way, the practice of polluting inquiry with report, and encouraging 'breaches' of research conventions by respondents (in relation to the implied methodological or cultural protocols of the 'instrument'), is transgressive, and we sought empirically the extent to which such transgressions had occurred. In particular, we were interested in seeing how the power/knowledge relationships might change (with Foucault in mind). It follows that we wanted the notion of 'negotiation' to inaugurate not some idealistic notion of equality, the implicit Habermasian stance, nor a sort of 'rules of engagement' approach (Simons, 1977; House, 1980), so much as an incitement to the respondent to disobey the instrument, contradict the preliminary findings, argue with the method and dispute the implied register of response. In this sense, we ended up seeking to strip 'negotiation' of its customary 'bargaining' overtones (Strauss, 1978; Wall, 1985; Keiser, 1991) and to invert its meaning: we wanted to think about negotiation as the 'rules' for inciting rather than settling disputes, and we wanted to locate that incitement among the practitioners themselves rather than the stakeholders' representatives – in a more direct form of participative inquiry. In this way, perhaps, 'negotiation' might become more deeply implicated in the production of research knowledge, and contribute in a small way to the development of a research-based professional culture. Behind such a concern lay a more general suspicion that the sorts of 'channels' of communication utilized by 'game 1' methodologies (in terms of methodological purity, rubrics of inquiry and report, implied registers, prior specification of relevances etc.) were themselves inherent in the conventions and subjections of the administrative regime they purported to evaluate. The relation of researcher to researched, like that of anthropologist to native, had become ossified and mutually stereotypical (Kuklick 1991). The notion that we have been exploring essentially has been that hybrid research, of some kind, may reflect something of the kinds of 'loose coupling' or 'flexibility' that others have defined as part of the postmodern condition (Martin, 1994: 144).

It is of course true that this chapter is merely exploratory, trying to read transgressively the possibility of transgressive validity in future research practices. The chapter entitled 'Mourning' takes such a transgressive strategy much further. But it is time that postmodernist implications for research methodologies and methods, and for research writing, were considered. Postmodernism – in one form or another – has already begun its long march through other areas of educational concern, such as pedagogy (Giroux, 1988; Kellner, 1988; McWilliam, 1992), value (Burglass, 1994; Carr, 1995), curriculum content in subjects and areas as various as English (Green, 1995) and special needs (Corbett, 1993), as well as teacher education (Wilkin, 1993). It is also an enduring concern for other disciplines and professional fields (e.g. Parton, 1994), and has, in this chapter, informed both our reading of research contexts and our re-reading of research acts.

We justify our deconstructive retrospective in terms of the sorts of research reflection recommended by Pool (1991). In a review of postmodern approaches to ethnography he noted that such approaches concern themselves with the 'problematic nature of representations' (p. 315), and ask questions of the relation between text and reader. They are 'self-reflexive' (p. 315), and argue for the 'pastiche' of a 'text that is composed of elements from different styles' (p. 316). Finally, they are 'doubly coded' in that they offer the hybridity of both 'complicity and critique' (p. 318). These were some of our concerns in re-reading our research practices in this chapter and relocating them in a wider postmodern or poststructuralist context. We conclude that notions of hybridity, transgressive validity and negotiation are research 'virtues' worth exploring in further deconstructions and constructions of methodological inventiveness. They offer the prospect of a risky redemption, a positive phase of postmodernist emergence?

> First an initial period of apocalyptic panic, accompanied by, or succeeded by, a mood of cynical or ludic creativity. Second, a phase of substantial experimentation. Third, a phase of apocalyptic panic accompanied by, or followed by, prophetic confidence in new modes of hybrid creativity.
>
> (Zurbrugg, 1993: 162)

Notes

1 We won't get into any arguments here about whether such conditions 'really' are postmodern/ist, or high modernist, or just plain modernist, not least because there is a logical contradiction in the proposition that postmodernism *really* is X or Y (see Chapter 1), but it is worth reminding ourselves that anti-essentialist postmodernisms can't or shouldn't make essentialist claims for much the same reasons that people in glass houses shouldn't throw stones.
2 For our personal data on the nature of research and evaluation work in the UK, we draw on evaluation and research undertaken for the ESRC (Stronach and MacDonald, 1991), on Scottish Office Education Department (SOED) contracts undertaken by Stronach *et al.* (1992–3), and by Allan, Brown and Riddell (1992–5) (Allan *et al.*, 1995; Allan, 1995). In addition, the account draws on TVEI evaluation work by Morris and Stronach (1993) for Tayside Region, as well as on the discussions of the Fifth International Cambridge Conference on Educational Evaluation (Stronach and Torrance, 1995). The respondent data are drawn from an evaluation for Strathclyde Region (Allan and Stronach, 1995).
3 Lyotard's 'performativity' implies the replacement of foundational criteria of validity with notions of political acceptability as part of the 'mercantilisation of knowledge' (Lyotard, 1984: 51).
4 We would not wish to imply, however, that such a journey is a regression from purity to pollution. The hygienic original version of fieldwork, as Kuklick (1991) implies, relies on the stability of colonial repression rather than some prior utopia of research context.
5 In keeping with the experimental nature of the evaluation, the reminder letter took

the form of a McGonagallesque poem, in the belief that joking might yield a better return from weary teachers than the straightforward conventionalities of the begging letter: the response rate from teachers rose from 46 to 66 per cent. Lovers of poetry should avoid Appendix 3.

6 Lest this should be seen as advocacy for sloppily designed instruments, we should add that only three out of the 74 respondents commented unfavourably on the format – and these criticisms concerned the 'closed' parts of the report.

7 We recognize that evaluators such as Stake (e.g. 1978) have long advocated the negotiation of accounts as an ongoing process inherent to the inquiry. We address here the reality that most such negotiation does not meet Stake's ideal.

8 We acknowledge, of course, that each of the comparatives in the above paragraphs (more effectively, greater animation etc.) implies a contrast that at the moment rests only impressionistically on our own prior experiences of 'classic' evaluation and research. It is clear that such hybrid approaches need to be further explored.

7

Telling transitions: boundary work in narratives of becoming an action researcher

Introduction

Our preoccupation with certain postmodernist themes in this book is already clear – mobilizations of meaning, questions of identity, problematics of boundary and hybridity. This chapter addresses all of these concerns in looking at the life history accounts of leading action researchers in the UK. Their accounts raise questions about the imperative to resolve, or dissolve, boundary problems in the interests of coherence, wholeness, certainty or singleness of vision – an imperative that operates in the generic conventions for telling life stories, in the research methodologies for eliciting such stories and in some, if not all, of the discourses of action research. Recent work within postmodernism and poststructuralism, as we've seen, argues for resisting the impulse to settle boundary questions, in favour of an *un*settled condition of 'hybridity' or 'in-between-ness'. What might be the implications for action research of taking seriously – or even playfully – the notion of boundary work as transgression rather than transition?

The data derive from a 'Teachers as researchers' project, a study of teacher action research in the context of award-bearing courses and research degrees in UK higher education institutions.[1] The project includes a small interview study of the life histories of ten people who have been influential, and instrumental, in developing and sponsoring teacher action research, through their involvement in innovative curriculum projects, their publications and their role in establishing and maintaining professional networks. All but one were once school teachers, and all are now involved in action research from a base within the academy.

The life stories of such key figures are of interest to the project for several reasons, but the issue that we want to focus on here is the way in which these narratives replay some of the central preoccupations of action research. These stories of transitions – from teacher, to action researcher, to academic; or, in the case of some of the group, from teacher, to academic, to action researcher – embody, in an almost literal sense, the engagement with *boundaries* that are addressed within action research itself. They recapitulate the oppositional dilemmas that are rehearsed in action research: between theory and practice;

between the personal and the professional; between the organizational cultures of the school and the academy; between 'insider' and 'outsider' perspectives; between the sacred languages of science, scholarship or research, and the mundane dialects of practice and everyday experience.

One of the things that these life stories do, we suggest below, is to offer solutions to boundary problems. They tell how people 'get across' such boundaries, narratively speaking, in the course of a journey of the self that leads them to claim the name of action research. This chapter raises some questions about the imperative to resolve, or dissolve, boundary problems in the interests of coherence, wholeness, certainty or singleness of vision – an imperative that operates in the generic conventions for telling life stories, and in some, if not all, of the discourses of action research. We have already argued for resisting the impulse to settle boundary questions, in favour of an unsettled condition of 'hybridity' or 'in-between-ness'. What might be the implications for action research for taking seriously – or even playfully – the notion of boundary work as transgression rather than transition?

The discussion below focuses on one key transition point in these accounts of becoming an action researcher – namely, the leaving of teaching. We look at how the tellers 'manage' this transition across a boundary of identity in such a way as to account for change while preserving narrative coherence and sustaining the notion of a core or essential self. This is followed by some reflections on the way the self is theorized in action research, and produced through the methodologies of life history interviewing. We conclude by considering some of those alternative, postmodern or deconstructive possibilities for thinking identity, as a kind of restless movement in the unstable spaces in-between boundaries. Though the discussion is touched off by the life stories of the ten participants, and makes reference to some specific instances in their interview accounts, it does not represent the singularity and the rich detail of each individual story. Inevitably then, this is a partial and oversimplified reading of subtle and complex texts.

The storied nature of transitions

How, then, are transitions accomplished as narrative events? In all life stories, the past has to be reconstructed from the vantage point of the here-and-now. This is not just a matter of stringing events along a time-line – first I did this, then I did that – but of assembling the particulars of experience so that they hang together as a continuous narrative. Or this, at least, is the prevailing convention in 'Western' (auto)biographical forms, and the present narratives certainly observe that convention. One of the implications of this is that changes of direction need to be told, *both* as discontinuities (something new/different happened here) *and* as accumulative events (this led from here to there). So transitions, as told, are kind of paradoxical – they are located at specific points in time and space, but they are always pulled away from the present moment to their origins in the past and their significance for the future.

There are internal transitions in life stories too. Interwoven with external movements of job changes and new circumstances are personal changes of commitment and allegiance: from thinking of academics as 'wallies', as one of the people interviewed recalls, to being one yourself; from passionately defending the place of sociology on teacher education courses in your institution, to passionately defending the status of action research in the face of critique from sociologists, to take another instance. Indeed, it's the internal story that really counts – life stories are pre-eminently journeys of the self. They tend to be told from the inside out. But here too is the same paradox: the self undergoes change; but it remains in some essential sense 'itself'. The self (e.g. the teacher, the sociologist) becomes the Other (the academic, the non-specialist) against which it once, oppositionally, drew its definitional strength. But this leaves that (retrospectively recalled) prior self in the potentially uncomfortable ontological position of Other to itself.

Narrative structure offers, or seems to, a way out of that dilemma of living on *both* sides of that borderline between self and other, us and them, when the notion of a core or singular self requires that we reside unambiguously on one side. In these particular narratives of becoming, first encounters with action research are often told as transformative events – moments at which new insights and excitements opened up – yet also as foreshadowed in the life course up to that point. People both 'become', and in a sense were 'always already' – to use a favourite phrase of Derrida's – action researchers.

Continuity-building

That sense of predestination, or at least of a potential to embrace action research, is effected in many different ways in the different stories. In some accounts, this preordination goes back a long way: to (often unhappy) experiences in school, and the determination to do something to improve children's learning opportunities; to class- or gender-inflected experiences of alienation and disempowerment and the desire to give children or adults control over knowledge; to a lifelong thirst for intellectual stimulation. There are stories of academic, professional or religious commitments that pre-date, but articulate with what are later discovered to be principles of action research: active learning, progressive education, critical theory, the Christian ethic of respect for all individuals, Rogerian psychology, avant garde English teaching, the revolt against Catholic dogma, teaching Nuffield Science.

All of the interviews include such occasions, where people look back over their lives for links, clues and foreshadowings of the commitment to action research. Sometimes these are tied to specific people and events. One person recalls a college lecturer who encouraged an interest in folk music and ballads, and finds a link with the (yet to be known) appeal of action research: 'So I'd go down to [the] city library on Saturday afternoons of all times and dig out traditional ballads . . . and just sit and read them. And I found that a great buzz, that the stuff I liked had a history, do you know what I mean? But it wasn't an official sort of condoned history . . . And looking back I think that's about – there's some notion that there's knowledge that's not acknowledged but it's still worth knowing.'

Another kind of retrospective link in some of the stories is the discovery of action research before-the-fact, or before-the-name. Some of the interviewees found that they had been doing action research, or dealing in similar ways with some of its central concerns – such as the articulations between theory and practice, insider and outsider knowledge – before they encountered the name and found out what it meant.

This kind of 'looking back' for overarching themes and explanatory links is, of course, a major part of the construction of continuity across transitions. It grounds the sense of what remains constant in the journey of the self: establishes that part of who I am and what I believe now can be traced back to who I was and what I believed then. But the specifics of the transition still have to be accounted for. There are moral implications in any tale of transition: to enter a new sphere of commitment – to take on a new identity – is always to leave something behind. Entrances are always simultaneously exits, so departures are events that need to be 'warranted', as the ethnomethodologists put it (e.g. Button, 1991). Otherwise they would be desertions. Likewise, entry to a new sphere of commitment is seldom told as coming out of the blue. Even when turning points, critical incidents (e.g. Sikes *et al.*, 1985) or 'epiphanies' (e.g. Denzin, 1989) are recounted, they must be (textually) prepared for: the person has to be predisposed (intellectually, emotionally, professionally, morally, pragmatically) for this transformative event at this point. With the possible exception of 'callings' by God (and even here it's arguable), people don't tell life changes as explicable entirely by fate, chance or external circumstances (although this can be *part* of an account of transition: see below), presumably because the centred self of the narrative would lose its agency. It would be evacuated from the account. Part of that preparation for entry/departure is done through the continuity-building links described above, since one of the things that these accomplish is an overarching rationale for life decisions. But transition points also need to be 'locally managed', in order to account for the specifics of movement across boundaries.

The loving and leaving of teaching

A key transition in many of these stories, as might be expected, is the leaving of teaching. All of the people interviewed were teachers at some time in their lives. All but one taught in schools (the other taught in further education). Some were teachers for many years; others for relatively few. In this respect their biographies are similar, on the face of it, to those of most people working in university and college departments of education, who once were teachers, and now teach teachers. Action researchers are not unique in having made that exit from the lifeworld of the school to the academy, from speaking of teachers as 'us' to – however benevolently – 'them'. However, it's possible that the telling of this transition is an occasion of particular 'exit' and 'entry' work (see below) in the life stories of those who are committed to the principles and practice of action research. Given the appeal to practice in all versions of action research, and the oppositional, or at least problematizing, stance towards expertise and 'outsider' research perspectives, the leaving of teaching may be a matter for special explication, since it amounts to some kind of exit from the primary ground of practice.

Recollections of the experience of being a teacher, and of the departure from teaching, figure in all the accounts. There are some interesting differences, though, in the extent and detail of these reminiscences of teaching. This may in part be related to the particular career routes that people took from teaching to university jobs, and the point at which they encountered action research along that route. In particular it may be related to the *proximity* of the exit from teaching to the entry into the world of action research. The interviewees fall very roughly into two groups in this respect. For some, the leaving of teaching and the entry to action research were more or less contemporaneous. They became involved as practitioner-researchers on externally funded action research projects, either on secondment or as full-time teachers; or were seconded to in-service courses in a higher education institution where action research was taught and promoted; or moved from teaching to a lecturing job in such an institution. For others, the leaving of teaching and the discovery of action research were separated by several years of work in higher education institutions.

The former group, whose first close-up encounters with action research overlapped with, or followed straight on from, their work as teachers, tended to give more detailed, experientially based accounts of what it had been like to be a teacher and to work in a school: what it was that had inspired and disappointed them; how they felt about the children and about their subject specialism; what colleagues had said in the staff room; and so on. By contrast, those who had come to action research some time after they had already established a base in a 'traditional' college or university department of education tended to tell the story of the exit from teaching in rather less depth and detail, or from a rather more distanced perspective. It's possible – although this is merely speculative since the number of people involved is very small – that for those who began to be drawn to action research while they were still, or had recently been, teachers, the transition is a more inflected one: they are recalling the experience of inhabiting a 'liminal' space in which the problem of identity across the boundary of teaching and action research is more salient. The story of the entry to action research was one which could not be told except as also an exit from teaching. Having said this, it's likely that the notion of 'proximity' (of the identity of teacher and of action researcher) is an internal rather than a temporal matter, and not reducible to external factors of time and career moves.

In any event, the doubled nature of transitions – as simultaneously exits and entrances – is clear in many of these accounts of being a teacher yet becoming something (someone) else. The contrary pull of allegiances is sometimes spelled out explicitly. One person speaks of the 'guilt', yet the relief from the 'dread':

> You know, when you get your first job outside teaching you don't feel good about being in town during a school day. You actually feel bad about going down to buy a pair of shoes. You know, for a long time after you give up teaching you know precisely what people are doing at this

moment if you were still in school. So you go past the school gate, to drive [to your new job], and instead of thinking, shit, how awful, I've got an hour and a quarter to drive before I get to work, you think, this is a wonderful trade-off for marking all those exercise books which I used to have to do all day on Sunday. And gone is the feeling of dread on Sundays about Monday morning. And I don't know why that's an integral part of teaching . . . but I've never yet met a teacher who didn't own up to feeling a sense of dread on Sunday afternoon.

The exit is an occasion of both regret and celebration – guilt transmuting almost imperceptibly in the telling into exhilaration. That ambivalence continues in the speaker's response to a question from the interviewer, Ivor Goodson:

Goodson: But . . . that one side of you must have found that a liberation?

Oh yes, huge. Because you know I always, there was always this one element about being a teacher that I was very uncomfortable with [that of trying to get children who weren't interested in school to participate]. Because as a child at school I had despised a lot of my teachers, and it had been one career I couldn't understand why anybody would ever want to do. And I'd only come into it initially because it was literally the only thing I could think of where I wouldn't have the problem of child-care in the school holidays, which I knew I couldn't afford. But I had loved it, and I do love it. And I'm in some sense a natural teacher. So I still love teaching. So I have very ambivalent feelings about it. But the idea of working in higher education was, you know, a dream, because I'd loved that final year at [university], and I'd always loved my university study.

Again there's the sense of inhabiting a liminal space, in which the exit from teaching is a liberation, but it's also a departure from a site of core identity as 'a natural teacher'. As in many other interviews, teaching is described in the language of 'love'. But that love is in competition, here, with another, older love – that of the intellectual life and the 'dream' of working in higher education. After her first encounter with action research, on a one-year secondment to an in-service course, the speaker found herself living two lives: 'So after that, thereafter really for most of the remaining time I was teaching I had this *alternative intellectual life* in my adult teaching, or my adult study.'

But the origins of that alternative intellectual life are located in a past which pre-dates the entry to teaching, and thus establishes a prior claim over her allegiance. The past also figures in the speaker's account of her entry to teaching, when she recalls reservations based on childhood experiences of school, and describes the domestic circumstances that led her to choose that career despite such reservations. The past enters into the story, therefore, as a harbinger of the way *forward*, out of the liminal space. As in many of the other interviews, which we turn to below, transitions are movements back to the future.

This particular account of the leaving of teaching contains themes which recur in many of the other accounts: the attractions of intellectual life; the sense of teaching as a kind of confinement, whatever its rewards; an ambivalence about the ways in which the *entry* to teaching is told. Each of these could be considered as effecting a kind of 'exit work', in that they address the problem of accounting for the departure from teaching as a transition *to* somewhere else. In that sense, exit work is also, simultaneously, entry work.[2] We now propose to consider the nature of such exit work in more detail.

Exit work (1): the seductions of the intellectual life

The attraction of intellectual or academic work is a very strong theme in virtually all of these life stories. And one of the ways in which it figures in the stories is as part of the explanation of the exit from teaching. Several people spoke of the need for 'intellectual stimulus' as one of the moving forces – the desire for 'an intellectual quality to my life', as one person put it. Some of the strongest descriptions of delight and pleasure in these narratives occur when people are talking about their encounters with theory, or with academic study – 'Oh it nearly blew my head off' says one, of her undergraduate studies, going on to talk later about the delights of 'the world shut out . . . just relentlessly pursuing ideas'. 'Talk about stretching the mind', says another of his degree course, 'it was a terrific place and this was a fantastic department.' Another 'swallowed' Bernstein's theories 'like a roach eats maggots' during an action research based in-service course. Academic or intellectual pursuits represented a kind of freedom or liberation for several of the narrators, or at least an escape from other mundane concerns. It was an opportunity to take control over your own learning, pursue your own agendas – although the embrace of intellectual life could be a matter to be justified, for those who are committed to action research, as one person notes:

> I've always thought it a very odd idea actually – this does relate to the way I feel about action research. The idea that you can't learn from books is very peculiar to me actually. I do see what the problems are, but I think . . . one wants to have every kind of experience and reading is a hell of an interesting experience.

Exit work (2): finding oneself on the 'outside'

However, the delight of intellectual inquiry also had negative implications, for several of the interviewees, in terms of collegial relationships within the school. Talking about your work, especially on return from a secondment to a course or project, was often treated with antagonism by colleagues. 'One of the things I did to turn colleagues off,' remarked one, 'was to talk about my work in the staffroom.' Another had similarly felt 'institutionally silenced' by colleagues, especially men, when she tried to talk about her work in relation to what she had learned on her masters course, because this was considered to be 'kind of intellectualizing it too much'. So another part of the story of the exit from teaching is the experience of feeling marginalized within the institution because you have temporarily stepped into a world 'outside'. You are deemed to have left before you have actually gone.

Exit work (3): embracing the 'outside'

But even if people felt they were partly being pushed into that world 'outside' teaching, for several of them another world was in any case beckoning. Their narratives, as already evidenced in the excerpts above, tell of a growing awareness of a world beyond teaching; or of the restricted perspective on educational matters that one can get from a location within a single school. Teaching is rewarding, but – in different ways – it comes to be felt as not *enough*. One person, looking back on her experience as a teacher, imagines it as 'like being on an island':

> I don't know what would have happened to me had I just stayed in teaching. It's about levels of consciousness. I don't know whether you can go on just being enthusiastic. I don't know whether my enthusiasm was a product of being young and of the novelty of teaching. And it's clear that I was seeking some other intellectual stimulus that was really unrelated to teaching. My course at [college] wasn't strongly focused on education and I think I needed something to help me to think about teaching in a more systematic and analytic fashion. As a teacher my world was so different from the world of the 'teacher as researcher' that I recognize now. Looking back, it was like being on an island, apart from all that was going on. I may have settled. I may have become satisfied with the everyday and seeing the greatest novelty as having different groups of pupils every year. There were lots of other things that made the job good. I loved producing school plays. I used to write the school play and these were highs within the culture of the school – but this wasn't anything to do with the public arena of education. I was part of a very contained world that had its own highs and lows.

The feeling of being in a 'contained' world, of loving teaching but wanting more than it could give, was evident in the excerpt with which this section began. It also appears in the following one, in which the speaker describes one of two 'significant things' that happened after she had been teaching in a junior school for several years (the other was splitting up from her husband):

> And I felt trapped in a junior school. I remember driving along one day and thinking 'I can't spend the rest of my life going in and out of institutions like this.' I loved working with the kids, I loved class teaching, but I felt trapped in the institution . . . There were other things I wanted to think, other thoughts, other conversations I wanted to have. I didn't know what they were, but I knew I wasn't having them. And I knew it didn't matter how long I stayed at that school, or any other school, I probably wouldn't have them.

Another interviewee, recalling his experience as a teacher participant on an action research project, talks of it as giving 'an alternative vision of a future' – and one which, moreover, came at a possible turning point in career terms.

And at the same time there were continuing to be pressures like – you know, I was a scale 4 head of [department], oughtn't I to be getting on to be deputy head? Which I could never envisage myself as. So what that gave, and I don't think I knew it at the time, but what it gave me was an alternative vision of a future, and that's a Stenhousian phrase as you probably recognize. [IG: mm yes.] Sort of dreams of possible futures. And, not having read Stenhouse at that point, that's how I would characterize it. Now what that future was I don't know, but it was something [to do with the idea] that practice was worth investigating at least, and that that investigation wasn't too uncomfortable with the way I wanted to see myself.

People often recall their encounters with action research, then, as coming at a time when they were already disposed towards change: the exit was partially anticipated, even if the nature of what lay on the other side was not yet fully known. That disposition towards change is told partly as a growing sense of an *outside*, against which teaching comes to be seen as the subordinate term in the 'inside/outside' dichotomy. The island metaphor offered by the speaker above is an interesting one, since it invokes a terrain which has, in one sense, *no* 'outside'. It's a good candidate, therefore, for being a ground of 'presence', in the Derridean sense of a foundational place or principle where truth or being reside in their original fullness and unity (e.g. Derrida, 1976: 12). While fully immersed in teaching as the space of identity, the island may indeed seem 'entire in itself'. But as Donne wrote of islands, and Derrida of the metaphysics of presence in general, that sense of plenitude and self-sufficiency is fragile. It's only sustainable by forgetting the outside, or absence, out of which presence emerges. The foundational claims of presence are always undermined therefore: the 'inside' is always dependent on the prior claims of the 'outside' (and vice versa of course). In these narratives, the discovery/recognition of that outside provides a further resource for effecting the exit from teaching. Once recognized, the island ceases to be the all-embracing, inclusive space of identity, and becomes a circumscribed space in which the self is trapped.

The metaphor of the island, and its relation to the inside/outside dichotomy that runs through the discourses of action research, and of action researchers, opens up further possibilities for reading these life stories which we do not have space to pursue here, except to note that leaving the island is never an event without consequence. There is a price to be paid for leaving that primary ground of practice; and indeed these life stories also enact a *return* to (of) practice, in their accounts of renewed engagements with teachers after the narrators have made the transition to action research. One possible reading of the valorization of practice in action research would be as a nostalgic attempt to 'get ourselves back to the Garden', as the old song of the sixties puts it.[3]

Exit work (4): ambivalent entries; relationships between coming in and going out?

Another recurring feature across many of the narratives is a certain duality in the way in which the *entry* to teaching is described. For the majority of the interviewees, training to be a teacher would not, under other circumstances, have been their first choice of higher education. In several cases it was seen as the *only* choice available to them at the time. For some, as in the excerpt at the beginning of this section, the decision to become a teacher was heavily influenced by personal circumstances – single parenthood, or marriage and the need to find a job in the same place as a partner. Issues of class and educational opportunity enter into the accounts here too. Many of the interviewees describe themselves as coming from working or lower middle class backgrounds, for whom university was not even thinkable as an option. 'To be quite honest,' said one, 'I had the feeling inside me that university wasn't for the likes of me, it was for other people. And again I think that was a class thing.' Teaching was the highest that a bright working class child could aspire to.

Such reservations about the entry to teaching perhaps provide some of the grounds for warranting the exit, although that, in turn, is only part of the story of the entry to teaching. As well as being depicted as a kind of forced choice, in terms of a lack of known alternatives, teaching was also described as an active choice in pursuit of a more rewarding or socially useful career. Several people chose it as mature students, after working in other jobs. So there's a sense, in many of the accounts, of teaching as *both* a forced and a voluntary entry. 'I think that was almost typical, you know – working class social mobility group,' said one person. 'But,' he continued, 'I mean, I used to think I don't want to spend my life working in a bank or selling insurance or working in bureaucratic [institutions]. So you know, [I thought,] I want to do something that has got some purpose to it, and teaching was the thing that was sort of in my grasp.'

Accounts of exits from teaching may not be unconnected, textually at least, to accounts of entries. While all of the interviewees tell of coming to love or at the very least to enjoy teaching, its status as both chosen and not chosen in the first place, taken together with the other strands in the telling of the exit, further grounds an explanation of moving on which is explicable as a continuing journey of the self towards fulfilment, rather than a radical disjunction or an abrupt departure.

Exit work (5): epiphanies, turning points, mentors and sponsors

One last feature of the narratives of exit that we want to consider briefly here is the telling of critical events and transformations. All of the narratives tell of 'turning points' and 'transformative events' in their encounters with action research, although not all of these occur in the context of the leaving of teaching. Many of these turning points are connected to key figures. For one person, it was an inspector of schools who visited her classroom and encouraged her to apply for a job on an externally funded project. For others, it was the face-to-face encounter with one or other of the leading, at the time, proponents of action research.

But a turning point is only understandable as a critical occurrence in the light of the preparation for exit that has already been effected in the narrative. Indeed, the telling of an 'epiphany' in these stories generally has the sense of being not the final piece but a very important one (a corner maybe) in the jigsaw of the narrative of the transition from teacher to action researcher.

A mission to explain? The collaborative production of the self in research contexts

In summary, these transitions are complex narrative achievements. What looks like a sequential matter – I did this, then I did that – involves making links backwards and forwards over a story which is, moreover, still in the telling. They involve a kind of retrospective search for the prospective significance of events and decisions, in which the seemingly innocent temporal relationship between past, present and future is confounded and displaced.[4] They are also reflexively explanatory, in the sense intended by Ricoeur (1985) in his analysis of narrative: a transition only makes sense within the frame of a coherent story; but that story is not yet told, and in turn gets its coherence from the ways in which individual episodes, and the transitions between them, are put together. The parts advance, cumulatively, towards the whole; but the whole (that doesn't yet exist) tells you in 'in advance' how to read the parts.

The hierarchical relationship between whole and part is displaced, on this (deconstructive) reading of the relationship between the two terms in narrative structuring. Neither can be used to derive the other, since they exist in a relation of 'non originary origins' (Derrida), in which each comes 'before' the other, and neither (or both) is therefore foundational. They exist in the relation of infinite deferral which Derrida called *différance*. The same could be said of the way in which the idea of a core self operates in these narratives of becoming an action researcher. These stories both appeal to the notion of a core self, whose inclinations towards action research were inscribed in the past, and produce that core self in the telling. The core or essential self is both cause and effect of the narrative. People become action researchers by having always been, in some protean sense, action researchers.

That notion of infinite deferral or regress, in which the search for first causes or final explanations is permanently in abeyance, is also captured in the notion of the *mis en abyme*. A popular example of the *mis en abyme* is the famous Quaker Oats box, in which the Quaker pictured on the box holds a box depicting a Quaker holding a box with a picture of . . . (see, for example, Johnson, 1981; McHale, 1987; Elam, 1994).[5] The *mis en abyme* again disrupts – puts into the abyss – the whole–part relation, since the 'whole' is represented as part of the 'parts'. The whole–part opposition, in which the former is privileged over the latter, is one of the 'troubling dualisms' (Haraway, 1991: 177) or 'violent hierarchies' (Derrida) around which the Western traditions of logo-centrism have been organized, together with its family of cognate dichotomies – cause and effect, reality and appearance, truth and illusion, and so on.

Returning to the life stories of action researchers, it's clear that, while a deconstructive reading might point to the abyss that threatens to engulf all appeals to coherence, wholeness, foundations and cores, that's not the way the participants see it. The interviewees and, more to our point here, the inter viewers seem to proceed under the jointly held assumption that transitions can be explained as rational and coherent movements across boundaries; that links between past and present can be found which will unambiguously explain how and why people 'ended up' as action researchers within the academy. It's almost impossible to imagine what a life story would look like without this kind of search for overarching themes and explanatory links. We are all disposed (in the active and the passive senses) to build stories in this way, not least because those are the prevailing conventions for theorizing the self in modernist narratives (e.g. Gergen, 1991). Several of the people who took part in the life history study have published autobiographical accounts, and their written narratives effect similar uncoverings of links and clues to explain how they came to be involved in action research. But it's important to note that, in the interview situation, this retrospective construction of prospective significance was collaboratively produced. If the interviewees took this to be the kind of story to tell, the interviewers also actively encouraged it. Ivor Goodson and Maggie MacLure, as the two interviewers, often asked for, or even offered, explanatory theories. (These were not always accepted.) We asked questions and made comments of the order of: 'Do you think this goes back to your experience of X?' 'Could this be to do with your feeling of a lack of control in your own life and the desire to give control to children?' 'That feeling of being marginalized seems to be a recurring theme.' The interview transcripts are full of invitations from the interviewers to theorize, connect, explain. Even the familiar injunction to 'start at the beginning' (i.e. with child-hood and family background), and proceed in a linear manner towards the present, poses the question of what is a 'life' that is already partly answered in the manner of the asking.

There's a tacit agreement, then, between the parties to the interview about the kind of life story that will be told, in this context at least. One of the inter-viewees spelled this out when it was observed – with an embarrassing lack of reflexive awareness, it seems now – that his account sounded 'very coherent and smooth'. He replied that 'that kind of coherent narrative' was what he took me to be looking for, and while he might in other circumstances speak of contradictions and uncertainty, he had not assumed this to be the business of the interview and would not necessarily consider it appropriate in that context.

On the whole, in these life interviews, both interviewee and interviewer are engaged on a joint mission to *explain*. We act on a set of common assumptions: that a life story will be linear, directional, cumulative, coherent and developmental; that the past will help to explain the present (and not vice versa); that transitions are resolutions of boundary problems, and con-tradictions can be transcended; that the self is singular, discoverable through reflection, sits at the centre of our story and – though it may be pushed in different directions, or into somewhat different shapes, by external events – persists over time and thus itself provides coherence to the narrative.

And that is arguably the view of the self of the reflective practitioner which underpins many versions of action research. What I'm wondering at the moment is whether we could, and should, think of aborting that mission to explain, and what we might gain and lose by doing that. Should we put our selves into the abyss? One of the most suggestive aspects of current work in postmodernism and poststructuralism has been the critique of the handling of boundary phenomena within modernist research and theory. One notable aspect of such work, as already noted, has been its refusal to resolve and to explain difference across boundaries – whether these are of self/other, whole/part, theory/practice, science/art, natural/artificial or any of the other binary oppositions that structure Western thinking. Instead such work explores the transgressive power of figures of 'in-between-ness', 'hybridity' or 'alterity', which resist such resolution and explanation.

To take a few examples: Bhabha's (1994) analysis of the relations between self and other in postcolonialism leads him to argue that we should think in terms of identification rather than identity – of an unceasable movement *between* the irreconcilable opposites of Self and Other, rather than a stable state in which the Self exists and knows itself in its utter distinction from the Other. Haraway (1991: 177) puts the dilemma of the self-other dualism succinctly: 'One is too few, but two are too many.' Bhabha argues, moreover, that theories of oppression which seek to transcend the self/other relation and bring about a reconciliation in the interests of the oppressed – whether Marxist-Hegelian dialectic or Habermasian critical theory – rest on a fantasy of resolution which always leaves the logic of oppression in place.

Haraway (1992), writing within poststructuralist feminism, argues the power of 'jokers' and 'trickster figures' who live insubordinately in the margins between the boundaries of man/woman, black/white, saint/sinner, and resist incorporation into emancipatory discourses as exemplars of suffering, universal humanity, women's condition. Another of Haraway's transgressive figures is the cyborg, an 'ironic political myth' for the postindustrial late twentieth century, which functions permanently to destabilize the dualisms of organism and machine, human and animal, natural and artificial, creator and created, and thus to frustrate the 'God trick' of totalizing theories that seek to incorporate or appropriate the labour and the identities of others in the name of unity and wholeness. 'The cyborg,' writes Haraway, 'is resolutely committed to partiality, irony, intimacy and perversity. It is oppositional, utopian, and completely without innocence' (Haraway, 1991: 151). Cyborgs are also monstrous, unpredictable and dangerous – the 'illegitimate offspring' of militarism, patriarchal capitalism and state socialism. But their promise lies in the affinity for connection which accompanies their contempt for holism and purity. The cyborg myth 'is about transgressed boundaries, potent fusions and dangerous possibilities' (*ibid.*: 154).[6]

Action research is itself a boundary dweller. It has always drawn its power (and also, of course, its problems of legitimation within the institutional discourses of theory and research) from its challenge to the customary dispositions of 'privilege' in the unequal relations of dualism – between theory and practice, subjectivity and objectivity, academic and practitioner. It has developed a powerful critique of the academic discourses of positivist science and scholarship, and the tyrannies that theory and expertise have exerted upon the teacher as the Other. Part of this has included exploring alternative genres for writing educational research, such as fictional-critical writing (e.g. Rowland *et al.*, 1990), and engaging with postmodern notions of multiple selves (e.g. Griffiths, 1992), as ways of freeing teachers and researchers from the oppressive certainties of theory.

But its project (if it makes sense to speak of a single project across all versions of action research) seems still to be concerned with transcending those oppositions from which it draws its power – either by reversing the poles of the old dichotomies, so that practice gets privileged over theory, the practitioner over the researcher, or by seeking reconciliations, in which the interests of those who previously lived antagonistically on opposite sides of the boundary will find a new space in which their differences can be resolved or dissolved (e.g. Winter, 1991). Part of that project of transcendence and reconciliation revolves around the notion of the self and its romantic/rational adventure leading to triumph over the adversity of contradictions (between values and practice; between real and false consciousness etc.).

Interviews with the vampires

Lather (1994) has noted that the narratives of educational research (and not just action research) are usually victory narratives. She wonders what it might mean to rethink research as a 'ruin', in which risk and uncertainty are the price to be paid for the possibility of breaking out of the cycle of certainty that never seems to deliver the hoped for happy ending. Are the transition stories discussed above victory narratives? If so, they're certainly not vainglorious ones. But we wonder whether it's worth considering other ways that interviewees and interviewers might collaborate in the telling of life stories. The aim would not be to effect the kind of 'trade' that Goodson (1995) envisages, in which the teller offers her story and the interviewer provides the history – the 'genealogies of context' that provide a bigger and better socio-historical frame. And it would certainly not be to try to get more coherent and 'disinterested' narratives, as Woods (1985) or Butt *et al.* (1992) want to do.

The point might be to resist resolution, to live 'at the hyphen' as Fine (1994) puts it, between those boundaries that are inevitably implicated in narratives of becoming an action researcher. Might we be cyborgs, hybrids or tricksters, whose business is to *prevent* solutions to the problem of getting safely across the boundaries of teacher/academic, personal/professional, being/becoming? If we tell our lives, and expect to hear them told by others, in ways which constantly try to overcome 'alterity' – that incalculable Otherness that deconstructionists argue is the forgotten 'origin' of the core self – can we be sure that we are not acting on behalf of those institutions whose business is the 'colonization of the Other' (Spivak, 1988)?

Couture (1994) suggests, playfully but none the less seriously, that action research within the academy might be just such an enterprise. He imagines the university as Dracula, feeding off the virgin souls (selves) of teachers who offer themselves up in the name of reflective practice. Couture fears that action research works by consuming the ungovernable alterity of the 'client', producing a state of amnesia, and leaving in its place 'this dead, smelly thing called teacher identity' (*ibid.*: 130) – a simulacrum that silences resistance and erases the memory of other, fractured and conflicting possibilities of identity. If he is right, what must we have forgotten in order to tell these smooth stories of the self? For instance, about the impossibility and the necessity of leaving the 'island', or the Garden, of teaching, and the discomforts of being 'haunted' thereafter by the spectre of practice. About the way in which the poles of the 'inside'–'outside' dualism reverse themselves, valorizing first one term, then the other, in a movement which is never fully or finally arrested.

Do we consume our own 'otherness' in order to produce the simulacrum of the centred self, in a postmodern recasting of the familiar metaphor of reflexivity, in which the snake now eats its own tale? And what is the role of life history researchers in encouraging that forgetting? Must the life history interview be an interview with the vampires? One of the many dangerous powers that Haraway attributes to the cyborg, it will be recalled, is its lack of innocence. By losing our virginity, by relieving ourselves of the solemn obligation to keep intact the purity of the singular self, we might avoid delivering ourselves to the vampiric appetites of total theory, and enjoy instead 'an intimate experience of boundaries, their construction and deconstruction' (Haraway, 1991: 181).

Whether, in avoiding becoming Brides of Dracula, we risk becoming instead the Brides of Derrida is a possibility that Elam (1994: 20) considers in her review of the illicit couplings and uncouplings that have taken place between feminism and deconstruction. It's a question that might be addressed to this chapter too: it could be argued that our reading above of the interviews is equally guilty (or certainly not innocent) of consuming the alterity of the individual stories in order to produce a singularly postmodern account.

And finally, if we abandoned that search for singularity and explanation, it is not clear how we could address some of the concerns that motivated the inclusion of a life history component in the 'Teachers as researchers' project in the first place. These were, partly, to do with understanding the history of the emergence of action research from its origins (in one version of the story at least) in the innovative curriculum development projects of the 1970s and early 1980s to its relatively secure, though not uncontested, niche in the academy. Since many of the interviewees had been key figures in that broader historical landscape, it seemed that their personal stories would 'illuminate' (a characteristically modernist word) the links between the personal and the social dimensions of change. Sikes *et al.* (1985: 14), in their influential study of the life histories of teachers, argue that one of the benefits of life history is that it 'bestrides the micro–macro interface'. If we refuse the colossal ambitions of bestriding that, and other 'interfaces', and opt instead for the insubordinate tactic of remaining, impossibly, on both, and neither, sides, what then would our project look like?

Notes

1 The project is funded by the Economic and Social Research Council. See Elliott and Sarland (1995) for an outline of the project. This chapter is based on a presentation to the European Conference on Educational Research, University of Bath, September 1995.

2 We use the term 'work' in a sense similar to that intended by analysts of interaction (e.g. Garfinkel, 1967; Goffman, 1990) – i.e. to indicate that meaning, facticity and truth are matters to be accomplished, according to methodical interactional procedures, rather than 'givens' which reside in, or behind, speakers' utterances. The notion of 'entrywork' and 'exitwork' derives from earlier unpublished work by Stronach and MacLure.

3 See Haraway (1991) and below, on the myth of returning to the Garden of Eden which, she argues, underpins the 'Enlightenment' narratives of both Marxism and Freudian psychoanalysis.

4 The terminology here is influenced by Schutz's (1967) phenomenological notion of the 'retrospective-prospective sense of occurrence' which, he argued, is one of the 'ad-hoc-ing' procedures that people use to produce order from the flux of experience.

5 Maggie MacLure recalls a childhood encounter with the *mis en abyme* (which, I hardly need to point out, I did not recognize as such at the time) – not in the form of the Quaker Oats box, but rather the pig on the Plumrose Ham tin. The structure of the paradox was identical – the cheerful pig pictured on the tin sat on a tin which bore a picture of 'himself' (the pig wore boys' clothes) sitting on a tin etc. I recall trying to find the point at which the embedded pictures of the pig/tin became undecipherable, feeling that they must 'continue', although no longer visible to the naked eye, in some endless regress. I like 'my' version better than the Quaker Oats one, because of the additional element of self-cannibalism/consumption involved. The pig was, after all, not only promoting the delights of the contents of the tin; he also 'was' its contents, and was therefore simultaneously outside and inside the tin in all its nested depictions.

6 See Damarin (1994) and Gough (1994) for explorations of the educational possibilities of the cyborg.

8

Untelling transitions

> In a knot of eight crossings, which is about the average size knot, there are 256 different 'over-and-under' arrangements possible ... Make only one change in this 'over and under' sequence and either an entirely different knot is made or no knot at all may result.
>
> (*The Ashley Book of Knots*, cited in Proulx, 1993: Preface)

In the previous chapter, we read life history data in deconstructive terms, building on notions of hybridity that received an earlier and somewhat more static airing in Chapter 5. In that chapter, it will be recalled, we showed ways in which metaphors of movement and disruption (hysteria, flux, overlap, contradiction etc.) surreptitiously reinserted a nostalgic appeal for order and continuity into policy analysis. Our concern was to deconstruct these polarities and inversions and to reach for a deconstructive displacement rather than, or as well as, a critical inversion. In so doing we did not wish to dismiss critique, nor to claim any final privilege for the resulting account, but to foreground what otherwise would have been left tacit and uncontested (a deconstruction must stop, yet it can't end). Nevertheless, a problem can be seen in retrospect – critique and deconstruction become 'stages' of reading, insulated from each other. In the following account, we set out to extend the reflexive reach of our deconstruction by reducing that insulation, unravelling some of the textual manoeuvres of the author in the previous chapter. Put simply, our questions here are: what is left undone when we undo? What excesses and undigested remainders plague our accounts of excess and remainder? Where is the 'blind spot' around which this text, like all texts, must have been organized, 'the not-seen that both *opens and limits* visibility' (Derrida, 1976: 163, our emphasis). We present such manoeuvring as a dialogue of critique (by the 'Reader') and counter-critique ('Author') in the hope that this textual device may begin to unsettle our writing, however crudely, by forcing narratively what we aspire to theoretically – a space between, wherein deconstructive readings may emerge.[1]

Reader: I want to look at the ways 'Telling transitions' fails as a deconstruction, sometimes avoidably, but mainly not. The purpose isn't navel-gazing, but the need to address a self-contradiction that has haunted our work so far.

The unerasable dilemma seems to be: *how do you successfully 'represent' a notion of representation that asserts the inevitability of its failure and further insists that such an approach depends on that failure in order to succeed?* That question of necessary (mis)representation breaks down into how the Other is written, how the self both writes and effaces itself, and how self/other transactions are negotiated. These issues are rehearsed in 'Telling transitions', and so it's a useful 'opening' to exploit.

Let's start with a close reading of what you, as the author, get up to in 'Telling transitions'. First, let's look at how you have constructed the Other. What sort of a universe have you constructed for these Others, your subjects? It is a world in which people seek core selves, and hunger for continuity, coherence and the resolution of dilemmas. They 'wrestle' for these things as part of a pre-eminent 'journey of the self' (a phrase that recurs four times in the account), and in that struggle enact the fixed and universal rules ('in all life stories', or at least in 'Western' cultures) of autobiographical discourse:

1 'the *self* is singular, discernible through reflection, sits at the centre of our story . . . persists over time.'
2 'we act on a set of common assumptions: that a *life story* will be linear, directional, cumulative, coherent and developmental.' And in so doing, we aspire to 'wholeness, certainty, or singleness of vision'.
3 People face inevitable *contradictions* in telling their lives. These oppositional dilemmas are bounded by different kinds of reality (sacred/profane; pure/hybrid).
4 People face an *imperative to resolve boundary problems*. The language of this rule-bound lifeworld/textworld is full of imperatives – 'need to be told', 'demand', 'has to be', 'requires', 'are always'. (This text is an iron cage.)
5 Tellers 'manage' transitions to *preserve narrative coherence* in the face of recurrent contradiction and paradox. (But they 'manage' and 'work' things that have already managed and worked them.)
6 'people don't tell life stories as explicable entirely by fate because the "centred self" of the narrative would lose its *agency*.'

In these sorts of ways, you seek to fix a 'modernism' by setting it up as the Other of what will later be revealed to be 'postmodernism': 'While modernist discourses seek resolutions of boundary dilemmas and transcendence of contradictions, postmodernist discourses resist resolution and embrace "in-between-ness".' But such a tactic is vulnerable to a number of charges. Put briefly, I'd say that in creating a kind of textual over-determination, it scapegoats modernism, installs a false polarity between modernism and postmodernism, and privileges a rhetoric of hybridity and in-between-ness that contradicts itself in the very act of contrasting itself so unilaterally against its Other.

Author: I agree with some of that, although we'll need to come back to these objections later, on the grounds that, if your objections are themselves couched in a form of argument that violates principles of 'hybridity', 'in-between-ness' etc. (and *your* arguments sound very definite and unilateral too, don't they?), then they're equally vulnerable to dismissal as self-contradictory, or at least as another example of the futile regress that has threatened this exploration more than once before. But meantime you need also to be careful not to insinuate that there's *no* appeal to cores/centres/coherences in contemporary discourses. Notions such as inner, authentic, or 'preferred' selves are commonplace in biographical research. So is the notion of self-realization as a journey.[2] You don't actually deny that in your opening comments on 'fixing postmodernism', but I'd want to keep the notion that foundationalism and nostalgia for cores are still an important part of lay and academic discourses – whether or not you call that a 'modernist' position – about which there are important things to be said. I'm inclined to agree with you that such polarizations are crude, as we've already argued at some length in this book, and am not a little disconcerted to learn how I've repeated them in 'Telling transitions'.

Reader: You say you find the following formulation by Derrida helpful, because it problematizes the notion of the core (the 'kernel'), inaugurating different sorts of ways of envisaging Selves and Others, but without writing off/away the pervasiveness of the desire for it:

> The desire for the kernel is desire itself [re the untranslatable kernel of 'pure' language; but thence to other kernels, including the psychoanalytic subject], which is to say that it is irreducible. There is a prehistoric, pre-originary relation to the intact kernel, and it is only beginning with this relation that any desire whatsoever can constitute itself. Thus the desire or the *phantasm* of the intact kernel is irreducible – despite the fact that *there is no* kernel . . . This phantasm, this desire for the intact kernel sets in motion every kind of desire, every kind of tongue, appeal, address. This is the necessity and it's a hard one, a terrible necessity.
>
> (Derrida, 1985: 115–16, original emphasis)

But doesn't that just make notions like 'kernel' (even if ingeniously posited as a phantasm) into unacknowledged transcendentals? Is it a universal? On what grounds would such an argument avoid the charge of a very literal essentialism? Isn't it like an atheist believing in god's ghost?

Author: Well it's not for me to speak for Derrida, but I think what he was getting at is that there are two contradictory but essential forces at work in Desire (and you eliminated from that quote precisely the bit where he elaborates on this). There's the desire for the kernel, and there's 'Necessity' – the absolute impossibility of ever being able to get to it. Because if we could get to it, there would be no distance across which to yearn. Therefore no desire. Derrida continues the 'kernel' argument: 'But just as without the desire for the intact kernel which doesn't exist . . . no desire whatever would be set moving, likewise without Necessity and without that which comes along to thwart that desire, desire itself would not unfold.' Is this transcendental? It's certainly universalizing. But I'd read it as another reworking of *différance*. It's certainly hard to read as an essentialism that says where we once had cores/kernels, now we have lacks (empty ones, non-cores), and henceforth these will be our cores. But in any case, there's a simple 'empirical' argument to support the prevalence, if not the predominance, of core selves and centred subjects – in popular fiction, self-realization philosophies etc., not to mention the person-centred methodologies we've dealt with in the Hannah and Jack chapters.

Reader: If we move from the epistemological to the political, I also have a problem with this overdetermined textual world which squeezes out the possibility of politics, or even of the person. That world-within-the-text is similar to Goffman's world, or Garfinkel's, in some ways identities are effects of various kinds of selfwork. But the textual world is not so much a world negotiated between individuals in interaction, however unequal; it is even further constrained by having to be wrested by individuals in an unequal struggle from the possibilities of their own texts, in a sense from *within* individuals (the text as soul?): 'The core or essential self is both cause and effect of the narrative', wherein people seek to construct accounts of themselves in terms of coherences and solidities that culturally bound textual rules decree. They are permitted to have the sorts of self they (already) have to have. The self, as it were, as an effect of an automatic writing. Of course, *an* effect of writing is plausible enough: but sole cause, soul effect?

The power of the text-as-agent is also evidenced in the contrast between the passive language used to display the subjects and the active language of the 'performing text': it has 'narrative events', it 'replays', 'embodies', 'offers' and 'recapitulates'; it constitutes the 'obstacle' course of the text in the journey of the self ('how people get across boundaries, narratively speaking'). Or questions like: how does one text read another? Can texts be more lively than the lives they ghost?

Author: These two points, that you present as criticisms, I'd fairly happily subscribe to. Wresting the world/identity from the (im)possibilities of their own texts is pretty much how I'd see things. I wouldn't locate it within individuals though. Nothing more social than a text, which is not to say there are no individuals also. And I'd stick by the statement 'the core or essential self is both cause and effect of the narrative'. (Although I don't recognize those 'souls' that you write on to that statement, twice, and with a noticeable textual effort that involved 'finding' a 'sole' that wasn't there in order do the rhetorical flip to 'soul'. Thus Readers expose themselves as always Authors too.) I also don't understand the objection to the 'active language of the performing text': the idea that language speaks us as we speak it is hardly novel to either of us. So why the distaste for the 'text as agency'. Do you mean there's agency and *then* text? Text 'within' agency? Or just that the language suggests too determinate a relation of subjects to text? I'd probably go along with that. But I'm left wondering where these particular objections are coming from/going to? Your accounts and objections seem to harbour a nostalgia for autonomous subjects prior to texts; for the privileging of authentic doing (or Being?) over inauthentic performing; for a (non-textual?) real world where we can sack the puppeteer/ventriloquist and let Pinocchio become a real boy. This is a continuing point of difference between us, I think?

Reader: No doubt about that 'nostalgia for presence' problem at all – that reference to Shurmann's invocation of an 'essential distress' about the loss of the 'guarantee of the real' (left as a kind of calling card at the end of Chapter

5) appeals to Heidegger and the notion of Being or 'presencing'. I quite fancy being a 'responsible anarchist', and have often wondered what kind of com-promise might be possible there, while you've very much gone for the 'nothing beyond the text' formula. I think I want to hold on to *text/context* as a deconstructive possibility in order (here comes a rescue) to let politics back in – against a kind of textual imperialism, wherein the notion of agency is never more than gestured at (as in the easy formula of a 'language that speaks us as we speak it'). We've said nothing until we articulate what goes on in the 'as' of that sentence. And if we can't articulate what we mean by 'as', and thereby by 'agency', then we can't begin to develop or even conceive of a poli-tics. So there are aspects of your implicit politics of presence/absence in 'Telling transitions' that make me uneasy, although it's not an uneasiness that speaks from a presumption of innocence or virtue.

Author: Well, 'responsible anarchist' sounds like a pretty obvious identity claim, and a virtuous one at that. But I'm more interested here in your flour-ish of that old 'nothing beyond the text' card – reminiscent of Butler's 'fearful conditionals' that we noted right at the start of the book. You seem to think 'text' means the written word, or the book, or what gets put on the page. Since the notorious phrase was Derrida's in the first place, it seems apt to quote one of his (many) attempts to correct such 'crude mistakes' – which he also calls 'normal monstrosities' (i.e. normal, and therefore banal):

> It is a normal monstrosity to say that everything the word 'poststructural-ism' embraces is formalist, aestheticist, apolitical, little concerned with history or with economic reality. It is a normal monstrosity to say of a thinking which started out by putting logocentrism into question that it confines itself to language and language games. It is a normal monstrosity to think that to get back finally to reality, history, society, politics, it suf-fices to leave behind these plays on words. It is a normal monstrosity to go on setting the textual – as this notion has been re-elaborated in the last twenty years – against the social, the political, and the historical, as if the text were still the book on the bookshelf of the library.
>
> (Derrida, 1990: 79)

Deconstruction, he insists, deals with texts 'always as institutional structures ... as being political-juridical-sociohistorical' (*ibid.*: 86–7). So while I think you're right to point to a failure in 'Telling transitions' to deal, deconstruc-tively, with its own political investments, and with the political dimensions of the original life history narratives, you don't need recourse to 'rescue' devices that will 'let politics back in' (from the 'context'), or appeals to 'agency' that would set it off from text. Right diagnosis; wrong cure.

Reader: I'm still suspicious of what sounds like a very rhetorical retreat from the 'text' conducted behind a smokescreen of paradox. Anyway, we've argued about how you constructed the Other, and there's much that's murky on both sides. Now let's turn to how you effaced yourself in that process of construc-tion, about the kinds of *selfwork* undertaken by the researcher. It's noticeable how profoundly insulated the text is from the hand of the author. We do not often see the strings. You have constructed your subjects as performers in a world of necessary appearances, forever covering up, attempting to pass off incoherence for coherence, contradiction for evolution: like Chaplin they inhabit a farce of pretension, and as a result the irony of the text is structural rather than a surface effect. But it is not your world: you remain untainted by farce. That farce is their tragedy, to echo Smith (1995: 28 – 'That is the tragedy. Frivolity is a tragedy.'), and unsettles the relation of 'play' and 'serious'. I'm also reminded of Geertz's accounts of culturally divergent 'face', and this prompts curiosity as to the nature of the 'faces' of the researcher:

- *The objective anthropologist.* One face of the researcher is the anthropologist engaged in 'gunboat linguistics', an apparently objective and dispassionate commentary on how texts construct-stories-construct-people (Geertz, 1988). But the author of this dramaturgical account appears and disappears in a number of on- and off-stage guises, a bit of a quick-change artiste, and not just the colonial governor in the funny hat.
- *Ethnographer manqué.* First, you acknowledge that the sample is too small, and therefore the account is 'merely speculative'. The 'reading' can only be 'partial and oversimplified' and cannot do justice to the 'singularity and the rich detail of each individual inquiry'. Then there's your admission of a collusive relationship between research method and respondent response ('the interviews actually encouraged it') (i.e. encouraged explanation, by which is meant a conventional accounting by respondents). This researcher self of yours is apologetic, seeks to display short-coming, confesses to building grounded theory on shaky grounds. The author (as researcher, as researcher's conscience somehow) is 'present' in those apologies and qualifications, and sometimes sets out to mollify the natives by praising their customs and beliefs: action research offers a 'powerful critique of the academic discourse of positivist science, and the tyrannies that theory and expertise have exerted on the teacher as Other'.
- *Submerged modernist.* In your role of researcher-as-anthropologist you regard your modernist tribe as mistaken about notions of identity, certainty and rigid categorizations and polarities, and advocate experimentation with the alternative culture of postmodernism. Like Victor Turner in the 1970s you note the 'structure' and recommend 'communitas' (Turner, 1969): you clearly wish them to hang loose, in a liminal sort of way. Yet there is nothing loose about your analysis of the determinate nature of text on contemporary culture. You are a modernist here: the text-as-culture is universal, determining, polarizing, definitive. And the author is absent in this story. Abstract notions like 'research', 'text' etc. become the grammatical subjects of sentences in which they are awarded the verbs of action and agency (they 'tell', 'recapitulate' etc.).
- *Surfacing postmodernist.* 'What I'm wondering at the moment is whether we should think of aborting that mission to explain, and what we might gain and lose by doing that.' (*We:* another bit of cultural impostering there, for this is no naive modernist contemplating a postmodern conversion.) This version of your multiple personality disorder goes on to outline the possibility of a more hybrid research that eschews explanation and obscures boundaries, licensing 'restless movement in the unstable spaces in-between

boundaries'; a new cast of vampires, cyborgs and the Abyss are auditioned – 'alternative, postmodern or deconstructive possibilities'. These are narrated playfully ('cameo roles'). But would that new research rethink only what people are, or would it also apply to how texts are? Here you slip to the more distanced role of the critic or perhaps the director of the play, witnessing a performance which is apparently just *there* rather than the inversion of your own modernist invention.

Author: You make some important points here. The taxonomy neatly exposes the shifting grounds of self – though this multiplicity of voices that you 'find' behind/in the supposedly monologic text is more reminiscent of Bakhtin's materialist semiotics than deconstruction. I'll want to return to the status of these selves and roles that you invoke, not to mention the question of where you've hidden *yours* in this latest text. But this is an important 'opening'.

Reader: There's more. The surfacing postmodernist was narratively produced by a before-and-after transition embedded in your text. The 'before' was characterized (caricatured) by certainties and regularities of one kind or another, and in particular an overgeneralized and monolithic view of modernism that would be hard to defend. The 'after' was a series of possible new strategies – hybridity, rejection of solutions and resolutions etc. But your account of that transition more or less ignored its own transitional/liminal function – to carry the 'before' into the 'after' as a matter of distinction, difference, a letting go, a leaving behind. The account itself logically cannot play that role – it *has no choice but to* construct a metanarrative of that transition in order to tell the story of its crossing (but note *that* imperative – re further deconstruction...). 'Telling transitions' denies its own transitioning as a story, and reduces a complex transition to a simple one. In doing so it makes possible (by which is meant 'apparently possible') the impossibility of the researcher, instead of acknowledging and working through and around the nature of that (im)possibility. That takes us to notions of transgression applied to the text-about-the-text, to looking at the relation not as before/after but as a more complex and ambiguous interplay of roles and perspectives that we've begun to unpack above and elsewhere. Perhaps what needs to be stressed is that the research act in itself is not unitary: 'because the meaning of the act (the concept) is not given in the present of its performance, it is not one with or immanent to the act, but divides that 'moment' upon itself, disperses it among the non-present modes of before and after the act' (Kamuf, 1991: xiv).

Author: I don't know if I agree with your reading of Kamuf here. Agreed, the (research) act isn't 'unitary'. But I don't see Kamuf arguing that therefore it's *multiple* – a matter of complex interplays of roles etc. The 'division' isn't one that fragments the act into lots of little bits that don't fit together properly, but a division/dispersal of the time and place (the presence) of the act.

Reader: Well, textual exegisis aside, the logical cost of your uncertain and plural engagement is high. You, as author, cannot assert what is liminal, hybrid and in-between, while operationalizing a puppet theatre of textual rules based on a covert regime of separation, distinction and certainty in order to construct the thing subsequently to be 'uncertain' about. Is there a tacit exemption clause for textual reading, as opposed to self-construction? Is this a neglected aspect of 'consuming the alterity of the individual stories in order to produce a singularly postmodern account'? But it is not a general problem of cannibalism so much as a failure to notice the parallel process of self-consumption in terms of your reduction of your own multiple selves.

Author: I'd say it's both. There's a specific failure on my part to notice; but also a more general dynamic of consumption of 'alterity' that logocentrism always effects. Spivak (1976) called it 'the rage for unity', and isn't it also being done here? Now?

Reader: 'Rage for unity', 'kernel', 'essential distress' – that's the theme that recurs, that we *feel*, but somehow never satisfactorily express without an inevitable contradiction. A further 'rage' is for the commitment presupposed on that unity, and abandoned in its disarray. A disarming feature of your deconstruction is that it privileges the subjects at the same time that it acts as their textual ventriloquist, creating thereby a kind of double conservatism. The analysis does not stray beyond the romantic boundaries of their accounts ('their sense of predestination, or at least of a potential to embrace action research'), the principled progress that each makes in a journey of the self towards 'claiming the name' of action research. These researchers are allowed to lead their lives as altruistic seekers after Truth and Knowledge. Indeed, the ethics of negotiation include the injunction: be Kind to their Cores (which they *own*). So the author leaves them to their alleged love-affairs-with-knowledge with scarcely an ironic wink to the reader, and no reference to the literature on researchers and their careers which would indicate the importance of *status* as a motivation in the research economy. In a sense this has no choice except to be a deferential deconstruction – the notions of career, name, reputation and promotion so central to accounts of professional progress, and so clear in other accounts of researchers' lives, do not appear in these transitions.

Author: That last criticism is ridiculous – made by alleging 'core' claims that (if I 'owned' the text) I would argue weren't made, notably colluding with the subjects, telling a tale of 'principled progress' and allowing the subjects to 'lead their lives as altruistic seekers after Truth and Knowledge'. My point, considerably more than an 'ironic wink', but obviously failing to connect, was that such altruistic seeking was a textual device for exiting without incurring blame. I find it verging on the bizarre that you could read it as an account of, or as a validation of, 'principled progress' or altruism. I also can't get exercised at what looks like nostalgia for the old project of sociology. That's not to say you're wrong about the suppression of an 'outside' in my text. But it wouldn't be a simply 'sociological outside', if by that you mean a kind of meta-context, a bigger and better frame within which to situate deconstruction. But here we are, back to the text/context issue again.

Reader: As it stands, your deconstruction has little access to issues of power except in so far as texts themselves do the determining. It's a kind of irresponsibility in your account. A further element of that irresponsibility, which is another aspect of disarming, of disengagement, is the now-you-see-it, now-you-don't quality of the interpretation. It keeps saying: this is serious and this is playful. These are methodological prescriptions, but they are also presented as cameo roles. Such 'playing' removes responsibility from the author – as if licensing an 'only kidding' get-out clause, a common cultural tic among postmodernists. It might be helpful to conclude, instead, that when postmodernists counterpose the 'serious' against the 'playful' they mistake the sense of 'play' that Derrida and others had in mind. There is no opposition: nothing is more serious in deconstruction than 'play'. Play, in the sense of a certain looseness between mechanisms or meanings, is the condition of and for meaning. Deconstructive play is never kidding.

Author: You're right to raise the issue of responsibility, but I'm intrigued by your retreat to the *serious* as the guarantee of that responsibility, and your rather binary determination to remain firmly on one side of the serious/frivolous boundary. Indeed, I think you did that already in your 'frivolity is tragedy' quote from Smith, and cast a solemnizing light on it that wasn't in the original. Because isn't the serious/frivolous opposition one of the ones that Derrida has been at pains to deconstruct (in his writing on Condillac; in his attack on Searle)? The point being that it's precisely by ejecting the supposedly frivolous instance to the margins that philosophy establishes its grounds of presence (integrity), against the 'counter-history of disintegration' (Rand, 1986: lxvii) threatened by the irrelevant/trivial/supplementary. So it's kind of weird to see you do that manifesto thing in your last paragraph. Especially since you didn't seem to mind 'kidding' as a deconstructive tactic when it came to colonial governors in funny hats. I wouldn't want to propose frivolity as the only strategy, nor to use it to escape responsibility – your main point still stands. But as a kind of trade, I'll offer this quote, also from Smith, as a kind of counter-manifesto for frivolity:

> The comedy or baseness of frivolity lies in the fact that unlike tragedy it cannot easily be generalised out into statements on the 'human condition' as it used to be called. Frivolity is light and unserious, and yet it is base, heavy, leaden or bathetic because it resists elevation to generality; not enough of Hegelian sprit, spirit of reason, lightens it (in both senses).
> (Smith, 1995: 27)

Let me take that point a bit further. What you're trying to do is nail me down to a series of 'failed' obligations – to a proper ethnographic self, a consistent modernist position, a defensible postmodernist 'transcendence' of these consistency-producing technologies of the self as researcher or author. The charge is simultaneously inconsistency *and* consistency, and because I can't perform the trick you demand (we both know that the trick is impossible), deconstruction can always triumphantly hold aloft the 'undone', in a series of gestures that echo the pig on the plumrose ham tin. Except in this case, whoever eats the pig gets eaten by what he or she consumed (it's a postmodern foodchain).

Reader: Cannibal, eat thyself: yes, it's a strange justice. Well, let's take stock (and not a foodchain reference). We've looked at the construction of the other in 'Telling transitions', and looked at various manifestations of presence *and* absence that the author has constructed, as well as casting aspersions about the political commitment of the text and its sense of responsibility. Overall, my feeling is that your deconstruction falls to its own arguments about the 'ground of presence' and the problematic relation of inside/outside. There is nothing outside your texts – you won't allow it – and the erasure of any 'outside' ensures that the researched dictate the boundaries of the discussion, even if they cannot prevent the researcher from slyly unpicking the 'work' of their rationalizations. In this way the metaphor of the island employed within the account provides a neglected point of critique for the ways in which the respondent texts (in what they say, in what they limit) come to be treated as sacred: 'Once recognized, the island ceases to be the all-embracing, inclusive space of identity, and becomes the circumscribed space in which the self is trapped.' Or, in this case, the deconstruction.

Author: But now that you begin to round up this litany of complaints, look how it mirrors the flaws it criticizes. First, it throws up (behind its analytical back as it were) a very simplistic and not at all deconstructive version of identity as plural and multiple – a bit like the oversimplicities that sink realist versions of reflexivity (Peshkin, 1988; Hsushius, 1994). Constructing jokey, separate-but-multiple selves is at least as unpromising a position as the initial one. It is a dilemma confirmed, not a problem solved.

Reader: I don't think the multiple/plural selves criticism is appropriate (and note that 'jokey' has suddenly become a bad word again). These are not posited as separate, they are not 'roles' in a role theory sense, or 'perspectives' in an illuminative paradigm. It is their interweaving, incompletion and mutual contradiction that constitutes what they are, by which is meant what effects they bring about. They are not a series of states which anyone traverses. The point I was trying to make is that what we call 'the researcher' is complex, plural, split, and our job (as jobbing deconstructors) is to be true to these betrayals. Kamuf (1991) uses such a language as part of the 'predicament of the double bind' (p. xiv): 'the question would be *how not to betray* a text whose self-betrayal is the very condition of its readability – for nothing could ever be readable unless it betrayed itself, gave itself away' (p. xix). Therefore, be faithful to the text's self-betrayal. An inversion (displacement?) in which 'faithfulness' is 'reinscribed in a general economy of (self-)betrayal' (p. xx). So these are not 'roles' so much as they are strategically *and* naively deployed sets of vantage points which never extricate themselves from each other but which constitute an itinerary which views each only from the other and which folds over into a self-knowing of that kaleidoscope of perspectives as 'research knowledge'. It is our retrospectively constructed knowledge of that itinerary, of the trace, that offers a non-perspectival purchase.

Author: Well, that's an ingenious rescue of your taxonomy of (my) multiple selves. I like the way you've set them in motion against one another, though I notice that you do it only *after* you've put them to work as a pathology (my 'multiple personality disorder', as you called it earlier). Categorization as blaming (as ethnomethodology has elegantly shown: Jayyusi, 1984); dismantling as deconstruction. Still, I approve the general sentiment that 'what we call "the researcher" is complex, plural, split, and our job (as jobbing deconstructors) is to be true to those betrayals'. Yet I see little truth to those betrayals in your foregoing critique, which fails to point up anything 'complex', 'plural' or 'split' in the researcher/authorial self which you, in turn, have assumed in order to diagnose the shortcomings of 'Telling transitions'. And, exactly according to the dynamic that you, convincingly in my view, exposed in mine, your deconstructive promise comes both early and late – doing retrospectively for 'others', and offering programmatically for the future, what it persistently fails to address to 'itself'.

So the problem, as I started to say above, is that your critique has replayed exactly (uncannily?) the structures that were its target:

- the same ironic structure of knowing more about what the text/author was up to than she knew herself;
- the same kind of over-determined, unambiguous reading in order to fix the text the better to unmask it;
- the same vacillation and erasures of the authorial self.

Wouldn't it be possible (necessary) to acknowledge a similar sort of assemblage of contradictory research presences in your critique? Perhaps: *the frustrated (modernist) sociologist,* looking to 'let politics back in' and provide a metacontextual frame around the local narratives of the subjects; *the ethnographer* (of Geertz's 'easy realist' persuasion), unable none the less to shake her conviction that she could withdraw the hand of her own textual ventriloquy and let her subjects speak for themselves; *the good postmodernist* looking for a moral commitment against the odds; *the deconstructionist* (as opposed to postmodernist), hoping to spin out of the revolving doors of an unwanted relativism; *the 'responsible anarchist'*, trying to adopt the ambidextrous position of the postmodernist-critical theorist.

And lastly, foreshadowed by the above, exactly the same narrative structure that 'denies its own transitioning', fixing the text as the 'before' to the 'after' of the postmodernist promise.

Reader: We started with two of us, and end with a cast of thousands. But haven't you just made yet another demand for a full presence? Where does that take us? In the realm of deconstruction there is no equivalent of 'physician heal thyself'; deconstruction wounds, unpicks scars, denies healing, debunks the sciences of certainty. So is this merely destructive? Or, on the contrary, can it be regarded as a necessary destabilization of research texts? A final argument would be to re-work the notions of overlapping research selves (down with boundaries) and practices (transgressions not errors), looking at their confusion in terms of 'vacillating boundaries', 'hybrid gaps' between methodological or theoretical ideal and realization, invoking somehow the 'subaltern instance of writing' (Bhabha, 1994: 59).

Author: Until that can be made to happen, inside and alongside deconstruction, all those gestures towards the split, the plural, the double bind, the paradoxical are empty rhetoric. They remain anthropologists' talk about the natives, sneakily transcendent, and in the end persistently logocentric.

Reader: Maybe we keep trying to mend the unmendable, to avoid the unavoidable.

Author: Yes. Take all this concern about what anthropologists are doing to the natives, researchers to the researched etc. We may be foolish to think there's an answer to how to do it right (though we must keep asking the question). Derrida (1976) wrote of the 'remorse that produces anthropology' (p. 114); of the 'anthropological war, the essential confrontation that *opens* communication between people and cultures' (p. 107, my emphasis). The 'originary violence' – before any 'empirical' violence of colonial oppression – is the one that sets up the difference between anthropologist and subject through the act of writing. That's the original wound, the forced space that writing inaugurates in order to be able to write 'about' anything or anyone. And that's the wound that writing can't heal, that it is in fact forced to cover up. That would explain why neither I, nor you in your turn, have been able to write without erasing our authorial selves and 'othering' everyone else. You (since you are both a Reader and an Author) have kept just as silent as me about how your research self has been erased, allowing you to write (to) me as 'the author', 'the researcher', without acknowledging how this creates the (im)possibilities of the self of the Reader (now Author too) in this latest text.

Reader: So both the original and this critique are caught with their fingers in the jam. In which case, there's no point in either of us flourishing the *tu quoque* card. So what do we do with it?

Author: I think we need a more interruptive strategy at this point. Your critique doesn't destabilize enough, precisely because it's *still* written under the textual exemption clause you invoked earlier. That tripartite structure of: set out the fraudulently modernist shop, deconstruct, deconstruct the foregoing already done in Chapter 5, and in Chapter 2 in a different kind of way, remains trapped in its own rhetorical pretexts. As a result we haven't really got to the heart of the 'big' question that we started this chapter with: *how do you successfully 'represent' a notion of representation that asserts the inevitability of its failure as a condition for its success?* We keep unpacking it, only to find it's a bottomless suitcase. We need to come up with a more textually transgressive attack, I think, that tries to 'unwrite' from within, rather than after the fact. Perhaps we should include an insubordinate counter-text like 'Living on/borderlines', where we would try to challenge the presencing/absencing as it happens (as it were) alongside the sacred text. Or, as in *Glas*, a lay-out that interrupts and ironicizes its own pretensions to completeness. So what do you think? We could always leave Telling/Untelling as it is and try the ludic job on a completely new chapter.

Notes

1 This section is based on correspondence between the authors about the preceding 'Telling transitions'. We have set out, jointly, to sharpen both sides of these formative arguments in the belief that they are important for taking our understanding of deconstruction further, and that they have pedagogic value. They make available our

'working' on these problems in ways that might give access (and further deconstructive purchase) to the reader.

2 For educational examples, see Nias (1989) and Woods (1993). Woods, for example, suggests that his life history of a teacher, Peter, offers 'a new way of looking at the teacher's career, as a quest for, and as an expression of, self' (*ibid.*: 460). Surely, Reader, an invocation of the journey and coherence notions of self-hood?

9

Enclosures

enclosure: 1. the act of enclosing, especially of common land 2. an enclosed space or area, especially for a special class of persons at a sporting event 3. a thing enclosed with a letter.

(Concise OED)

And so 'everything "begins", then, with citation'.

(Smith, 1995: 101, citing Derrida)

I

We began this book with an injunction to think of 'opening' as a picture, and by sketching a number of metaphors – crack, wound, abyss, scar – that turn up within the chapters as markers of division and articulation, as the unstable fulcrum around which deconstruction unfolds. In each case the deconstruction offered an 'education' in the fragilities of 'identity', or the instabilities of meaning. Each time, we sought out ambiguity in meaning, time and place. The opening cut also closed, mobilized as well as arrested, separated and joined, like an initiation wound shorn of its temporal stages and cast into a simultaneity in which the wound and its healing forever recur. Each chapter made its own attempt at that kind of mobility or oscillation, looking for a disruptive effect, sometimes in theory, sometimes in practice and narrative as well.

The introduction to this book, '. . . Opening . . .', celebrates – as introductions must – a kind of openness, negatively expressed as a *resistance to closure*. Closure is 'inertia', 'congealment', 'autism', as the irresistible death of the text – the 'inescapable dynamic of closure', the ultimate 'failure' of the enterprise to remain open. Nevertheless, 'closure' is a fate, even if a fate to be resisted. The metaphors of that resistance are numerous in our telling of that story. They invert ('dismantle', 'dislocate', 'disorder', 'fracture'), and they hope to displace, to 'release new possibilities', to prevail against the 'dead certainties of Enlightenment reason'. And always in the name of a 'movement of opening'. Thus 'opening' seems to be a metaphorical imperative both within

the narratives of an introduction, and within the epistemology of a deconstruction. Inevitably, then, it begins to take on the qualities of a virtue-in-
itself. Indeed, the dictionary colludes with this valorization of 'open' in
opposition to 'closed'. The 23 usages of 'open' enumerate only positive qualities such as visibility, integrity, progress and access: there seems no end to its
virtues: '16. (of the bowels) not constipated 17. (of a return ticket) not
restricted as to day of travel 18. (of a cheque) not crossed' (OED).

So, once again, the impossibility of *not* rescuing, the recurring impasse this
time of what seems to be the virtuous promiscuity of 'opening'. But a necessary rather than a remediable error: 'Once the circle turns . . . its identification
with itself gathers an imperceptible difference which permits us efficaciously,
rigorously, that is, discreetly, to exit from closure . . . The return, at this point,
does not retake possession of something' (Derrida, 1978: 295).

On the other hand, how can the negativity of 'closure' be resisted? With
difficulty, it seems. It is 'a closed condition', the 'procedure for ending a
debate', clearly a prohibitive tactic of power. But the dictionary's tally of 16
meanings for 'close' (adj.) does suggest a kind of ambivalence that we may
exploit, although it is an ambivalence now more firmly rooted in the adjec-
tive than in the verb (but see: to 'close' a deal or a circuit). Against the themes
of secrecy, exclusion, parsimony and prohibition which surround the notion
there is a quite different tone – proximity, affection, continuity, resemblance,
fit, rigour – the virtuous embrace of logical and emotional affinity. Despite the
rhetorics of the Open Society, we might read 'close' as a warm word, 'open' as
cold, calculating, a word of somewhat empty promise – often little more than
the denial of a 'closed' property (unenclosed, uncovered, unprotected, un-
fastened) – to give a sort of Durkheimian reading to the implicit solidarities
of these words.

Further, we might note that the kind of 'opening' that deconstruction envisages would shy away from these sorts of inversion, whatever the rhetorics of
our introduction and the chapters that precede this one. Deconstruction is the
denial of the possibility of such untrammelled openness; it mocks the implicit
demystification. It refuses to 'celebrate'.

Is closure then virtuous? First, we may note that 'closure' is opposed in our
first account to the notion of 'opening'. The latter has both transitive and
intransitive possibilities (being open, being in the process of opening), but the
oppositional term is denied the chance to offer an equivalent, such as
'closing', and is left with the more constrained and constraining 'closure' –
bereft of the possibility of movement. Indeed, an ideological 'closure' in itself.
Second, we need to indicate what a 'virtuous closing' might mean. We have
suggested that open/closed isn't the open-and-shut case for virtue that we
initially presumed. There may be a hidden necessity in 'closure' that the
demand for openness obscures. And – despite the rehabilitation of 'closure'
above – there is no doubt that the prohibitions and secrecies of 'closure' have
still to be unsettled.

A methodological examination of these issues might well begin with what
Strathern has to say of the 'postplural'. She denies the uniqueness of instances;
they are versions of each other, although Strathern draws the distinction
between modernism and postmodernism more sharply than we would like to,

at this stage of the argument at any rate. 'For the modernist sense of the uniqueness and thus plurality of each culture, postmodernists must substitute cultures that can only be apprehended as versions of other cultures' (Strathern, 1991: 13).

All question-and-answer series create excesses and remainders of information, elisions of attention, gaps in understanding: their principle is *intermittence* rather than accumulation. All gains in information depend on changes in scale within a perspective, and involve 'losses' as well as gains (Strathern, 1991).To translate Strathern's methodological accounting into the metaphors of this discussion, all attempts at openness (say, via such conceits as the 'ethnographic imagination', 'unstructured interview', 'grounded theory') contain their closures, a commonplace argument. These closures are manifested, as it were, in an opaque world of gaps, occlusions and overlaps that it is methodology's task either to elucidate (e.g. as 'intermittence') or to fudge with the totalizing claims of a 'scientific' rhetoric, whether of a positivistic nature or not. Such rhetorics convert 'promise' into 'performance' in ways that make resulting disappointments a contingent rather than a necessary matter. More interestingly, these closures are not the failure of method so much as its possibility of realization; that is, departure points for deconstruction's reading of the text's unwritten. When we realize that the logics of the plural (say, in branching logics) are deceptions, we have to conclude that perspectives are both more *and* less than they claim to be, that they don't 'add up'. Rather they relate in some other way, as in figure/ground, or 'fold', or in Deleuze's notion of 'rhizome'. The paradox for the appearance of 'number' and for 'openness' is the same. The plausibility of the plural (which is the myth of an uncomplicated 'and') is carried in the smoothness of narrative, its ability to 'plot' numbers, separate 'characters'/variables and arrive at aggregate conclusions that look logical rather than merely longed for. It follows that we reject a choosing between 'opening' and 'closing' for the more ambivalent principle of 'intermittence', a notion that plays between ideas of transmission and interruption while refusing to privilege transmission as the 'message' and interruption as its negation. As in the Morse code, the gaps are as necessary and communicative as the signals.

Smith makes a rather similar philosophical argument, starting from the notion of philosophy's longed-for desire for truth. It is, he argues, desire rather than necessity that drives philosophy – 'the instinct for self-preservation, or a will to truth' (Smith, 1995: 9). He sees philosophy's desire as the final opening up of what is necessary, and the equally final closing down on the merely contingent. His aim is to write against such desire, which he takes to mean writing against 'philosophy's systemic mastery' (*ibid.*: 10). He seeks (as Strathern does) the slack, the 'play' in the system of thought. The place for thinking is opened up by such 'play': 'A method becomes available to philosophy on the condition of a degree of failure on the method's part' (*ibid.*: 14).

It is the failure of such a failure that would disable philosophical method: 'What makes the object objective, or rather "objectal", is that the method addressing it does not dislimn completely into it, for that would be to remove the distance in the avenue toward it that defines objectivity' (*ibid.*: 15).

In other words, it is the desire for, and inevitable failure of, philosophy to 'close down', to eliminate the contingent, that creates the space for deconstructive thinking. It is the attempt to close that opens; it is the attempt to open that closes. That double failure is the possibility for a philosophy that continues: it is the 'ontological flicker' (*ibid.*: 20) of contingency's effect that amounts to 'tucking a tautologous or rhetorical methodological fold into philosophy that is both necessary and anathema to its self-definition' (*ibid.*: 18).

Perhaps we have now set in motion the idea of 'opening' and 'closure' as a deconstructive inter-relation, not separate, not independent of each other in their ability to do their work, not dialectically related so much as mutually and reflexively self-constituting and self-subverting at the same time. (The next chapter enacts some of these dilemmas.) That notion conjures the 'enclosure' within a message whose dissemination enables the enclosed to constitute itself, and acknowledges that all such messages have to be broadcast beyond the circle of the self in order to constitute themselves, their audiences, and their authors – 'otherwise there would be no message, no distance for it to cover, nothing to mediate, no consciousness, no need for anything at all, and the subject would vanish into itself' (*ibid.*: 78).

So: think now of the relation between the aperture and the shutter of a camera, an enclosure that opens. Exposure, both an opening and a shutting, is a double phenomenon of space and time, and it constitutes the displaced and flickering text of appearance as an approximation of repetition. But what is repeated? And what comes first, photographer, film, scene, camera, photograph?

> No doubt life protects itself by repetition, trace, différance (deferral). But we must be wary of this formulation: there is no life present *at first* which would *then* come to protect, postpone, or reserve itself in *différance*. The latter constitutes the essence of life ... Life must be thought of as trace before Being may be determined as presence. This is the only condition on which we can say that life *is* death, that repetition and the beyond of the pleasure principle are native and congenital to that which they transgress.
>   (Derrida, 1978: 203, cited in Johnson, 1994: 19, author's emphasis)

In Johnson's gloss of that passage of Derrida, she remarks that 'without memory, both conscious and unconscious, human beings could hardly be what they are ... the "living" psyche derives its specificity from its own "dead" traces' (Johnson, 1994: 19). Thus, what comes first? The photograph, of course.

II

We have already rehearsed a number of ways of representing the appropriation of meaning: aperture and shutter; motion and arrest; faithfulness and betrayal; capture and loss, in each case trying to fight off the 'either/or' of these oppositions with the 'both–and' of alternative articulations, via notions such as 'ellipsis', 'return', 'fold' and so on. Such metaphors both give and take away meaning, more or less assist or hinder understanding. But a very important question remains: what do we mean by 'and', as in 'aperture *and* shutter'? Can we sensibly ask the question: what kind of metaphor do we propose for the less than innocuous 'opening' of 'and'?

First, a gesture, drawing on and developing Calvino's depiction of the reflectivity of the world and the reflexivity of self:

self and: 'a single eye looking at itself, seeing itself mirrored in the iris of its own pupil'

and world: 'the window frames the dresser across whose mirror a cloud passes'

(Calvino, 1993: 129ff)

To develop Calvino's images a little further, in order to articulate the notions of 'eye' (self) and 'window' (world), we might say that the eye's self-imaging constitutes the reflexive turn within which the world *and* self become known as reflecting signs in the not-quite homologies that relate across the notions of self/world, such as eye/window, itself/dresser, iris/mirror, and also as domain-referring signs and hence boundary-drawing acts for each world, each self (like eye/iris/pupil, or window/dresser/mirror). The failure carried in these 'not-quite' resemblances is irresolvable and is based on deferral, and failure given as discrepancy inaugurates a world of blurred edges, of palimpsests and opacity. That ambiguity is deconstruction's *'responsibility'*. Yet it is a failure obliterated by the notion of 'and' – which smuggles in the idea of a simple and uncomplicated addition of one thing to another. In the phrase 'aperture and shutter' we attend to the appropriateness of these forms of 'opening' and 'shutting' in relation to the camera while neglecting the work done by 'and' in separating, contrasting and adding. It does as much metaphorical work as its companions, but does so silently, blindly, blandly, we might say. Nevertheless, such a failure, once recognized as such, is a *positive*-negative concept because its failure is a condition of, and for, reflection in two ways: as a logical necessity (cf. Smith, 1995), and as a provocation to thought. To return to Calvino's analogy, that is why we might want to remember the common origins of the pupil (as eye) and the pupil (as learner). The failure structures and enables the 'agency' with which it simultaneously encloses and is exceeded by. That is, it constructs, as a necessity, the discrepancy that makes itself an issue of, and for, itself. In such an account, 'agency' is a provocation, always constructed one step behind any possibility of an autonomy, of a 'free act', of a full 'presence'. Yet the *desire* for that autonomy, presence, identity, agency (to begin a list that has no end, at least in Modernity) is as necessary for thinking, especially poststructuralist and postmodernist thinking, as the suspicion of its failed realization, and constitutes, for the West[1] and for the moment at least, a condition of postmodernism. This is the 'hinge', the 'fold' that articulates them. Such a realization also prompts, as we have seen, the recurring spectral metaphors of the relation.

So that is what the 'and' in self *and* world indicates, and that is why we should regard 'and' as a metaphor, rather than let it pass as an innocent embrace between unproblematic couples.

It follows that this word called 'and' does not just add, or separate, or stop, or hold: its idiosyncrasies of chance, failures of stability and irregularities of repetition give us access to meaning via a trace, we might say a 'flight', of differences that always amounts to some form of 'exit from closure' (Smith, 1995: 86). Bereft of a simplifying 'and', we begin to feel the need to talk in 'postplural' terms (Strathern, 1991) or in terms of 'jetties' whose boundaries are always under erasure (Derrida, 1990). At its crudest, you can't add things that aren't separate (as somebody in *Alice in Wonderland* probably said). That 'flight' of difference is pursued, although of course never quite caught in this book. Far from being a simple additive, 'and' turns out to be the wild card behind whose bland exterior all sorts of covert negotiations, alliances, chances, failures and manoeuvrings are conducted (like the 'slash' between modernism and postmodernism discussed in Chapter 1). The final chapter of this book is a kind of 'closet play' which toys with these assertions, denials and displacements, inverting the roles of theory and narrative and trying both to go backstage on, dramatize and critique the processes of deconstruction. Overall, it is these negotiations and differences that constitute an *erratic epistemology* based on the twin uncertainties of a repetition that cannot prescribe identity or proscribe difference, and whose 'fundament' rests on the shifting and agonistic remainders left over by the failures of philosophy and method to solve the problem of representation. It is, then, a 'sport' (in the double sense) played out on the field of difference.

Hence we have no 'deconstructionism' to recommend, no formulae or procedural prescriptions, concentrating instead on the field of disputed meaning, writing this 'Enclosures' chapter as a closing *and* an opening, a de-ceased text which may 'stutter' into life and language.

(Small wonder, then, that the authors had such difficulties with finding a title for this book. Will it be an un/doing (there are two already, one in sociology, one in cultural studies), an under-taking, a re-turning, a re-presentation of educational research? What about *The Sporting Post? Educating Arche?* Nothing seems possible without fiddling with the words and meanings themselves in order to shake out a play between different readings, a reading of difference that will make a difference. A book that can't close, it seems, isn't entitled to announce itself.)

III

Both '. . . Opening . . .' and Chapter 1 spent considerable time examining the sorts of 'cures' that a variety of modernists, feminists and poststructuralists variously offered for the postmodern condition. Here we want to outline a general kind of response relating to the relationship of postmodernism to current postmodernity (if that's what we choose to call it), and then to consider a research agenda for postmodernism and deconstruction to pursue.

1 First, we need to abandon old ways of futuring. Vainly trying to anticipate futures (like the so-called 'needs' of the global economy), or prescribing utopias (of 'free speech acts', 'demystification' or 'conscientization', for example), will no doubt take us into familiar meta-narrative cycles of false prophecy, scapegoating, moral panics and policy hysteria – not to mention the ensuing amnesia that accompanies their failure and disappointments.

These cycles, it can no longer be denied, are as likely to apply to us as researchers as they are to the politicians who orchestrate them, or are orchestrated by them.

Ranson (1996) offers a recent example of this kind of prediction, one which also neatly illustrates a postmodern 'rescue'. He invokes an educational research that 'can once more place itself at the centre of the concerns of our time' (*ibid*.: 7), an implausible yet familiar nostalgia. He concedes the arrival of the postmodern but promises an accommodation – a *'space between'* – that will avoid relativism. Yet his attraction seems to be to the vocabulary rather than the intellectual substance of deconstructive or postmodernist thinking. For example, he argues that educational inquiry is distinctive, and can emerge as a 'new paradigm' (*ibid*.): a 'special kind of knowledge that can only be formed of learning by occupying the *space between* "subjects" and "between" subjects and practice' (*ibid*.: 6, author's emphasis). But this turns out to mean more of the same – broader focus for educational research, more domain-specific theories of learning, action research to the rescue and the alleged existence of yet another 'emergent meta-frame' (*ibid*.: 5). (In predictions of this kind it is usually the case that the notion of 'emergence' is invoked in order to conceal the half-baked nature of the proposals – the modernist trick is to promise that a fully baked one will be along shortly.) His misreading of postmodernist perspectives is most vivid where he locates 'variety' and difference as questions of context rather than object itself. The hunt is still on, therefore, for 'what is unchanging' versus what 'varies' across context (*ibid*.: 7). Yet if he is serious about 'reconfiguring' educational research after almost any conceivable postmodernist perspective, it is that essentialist invariant which has first to be deconstructed. If that is not done, then the postmodernist-sounding notion of 'space between' that he wishes to emphasize becomes vacuous in a more unfortunate sense. We note that this kind of future 'programming' of research is typical of the hasty and shallow reviewing that 'performativity' and the conditions of postmodernity license.

So if that kind of agenda is both impossible and pointless, what should we do? We should set about trying to redirect educational research to a different past rather than a different future. 'To inherit is to select, to sift, to harness, to reclaim, to reactivate . . . and then to strike out with choices which not only inherit their own norms, but invent them too, in the inevitable absence of programmes and fixed norms' (Derrida, 1994: 39).

2 Our concern, then, should be with how educational questions 'issue', rather than with some shopping list of alleged 'issues', most of which passively adapt to the alleged needs of 'late capitalism' and thereby forfeit a politics of creation for a politics of accommodation. Such a *reformed inheritance*, we suggest, should draw far more on disciplines and fields of inquiry where some of the central postmodernist concerns have long been an issue, and from which educational research in the UK and elsewhere may belatedly draw. We have in mind, particularly, the ways in which the fields of postcoloniality and feminism have had to address the issue of 'identity' and its associated problem of an 'essentialism' which becomes more and more difficult to defend, and thence to a concern for hybridity and reworked notions of what might count as emancipation, understanding, empowerment, or whatever might replace

these goals.[2] The field of literary studies also beckons, because the 'linguistic turn' has made all disciplines more conscious of how narrative and theory are entwined, and because the field has also gained from being located outside the conservative traditions of mainstream disciplines such as philosophy, linguistics and sociology. Finally, anthropology, or the new (i.e. repatriated) anthropology,[3] is also of interest because of the intensity of the 'crisis of representation' within that discipline. Notions like 'native' and 'anthropologist' have become problematic in a globalized world, as has the basic vocabulary of 'culture', 'ethnicity' and 'locality'. At least as important are the new juxtapositions of old and new concepts in the discipline, the recognition of versions of rite, ritual and myth in the heart of modernity. Educational research needs to address these uncertainties as a methodological and narrative challenge, to adopt the inherent ambivalence of what we may call an *erratic epistemology* (see especially '... Opening...' and Chapters 5 and 8), and to develop a continuous deconstruction – to pick on one urgent need – of the vocabulary of educational discourse, and of governmentality more generally. Notions such as 'empowerment', 'emancipation', 'innovation', 'effectiveness', 'autonomy' and 'professionalism' are more often than not treated as the 'givens' of educational research, particularly under current research funding strategies, yet they are its central problems (e.g. Stronach *et al.*, 1994). There is in this, also, a certain redundancy for fieldwork – there's no shortage of 'information' already available to fuel our thinking.

3 All inheritances, reformed or not, are conservative in tendency. Political surrenders are familiar enough to us all now and we need a kind of cultural revolution in educational research, not in favour of some new orthodoxy, but in favour of experiment, creativity and risk. To those who confine themselves to the politics of nostalgia, we would say that mourning that loss (of certainty, 'science', 'Enlightenment ideals' or 'autonomy') is a necessary thing, especially if it constitutes the double loss of something that never existed. But it should not become a way of life. Life goes on, and with it, perhaps, even, sometimes, if we're creative enough, persistent enough, a sharper and less complicit educational research.

Keep going! ... Always going. Always on. Call that going? Call that on?

(Beckett, 1994: 2)

Notes

1 Ong points to the development of 'other' modernities in the East. These ideologies, often related to a 'soft authoritarianism', imply quite different conditions for some aspects of postmodernity, or the development of related postmodernisms (Ong, 1996). Thus the eurocentrism of 'postmodernisms' is beginning to be addressed in ways unanticipated – for example – by Derrida's critique of logocentrism in the West.
2 This is not to argue that notions of hybridity, or essentialist identities, or transgression were never addressed within modernity. As Fardon points out, Gluckman's account of identity was anti-essentialist, local, constructed and variable (Fardon, 1995). Much the same could be said of Goffman's views of identity. It is no coincidence, of course, that authors like Goffman are back in fashion, although given a

more reflexive reading with regard to the construction of the 'researcher' alongside his or her constructions of the world.

3 What do we mean by the term 'new anthropology'? There is, as far as we are aware, no common usage or definition of that term. However, Latour stresses the importance of 'back home anthropology', an anthropology come 'home from the tropics' (Latour, 1993: 101,100), and in particular a recognition that what was taken to be a radical break between the conditions of modernity and premodernity has been mistaken. From a different stance, anthropologists such as Strathern have sought to develop new theories of connection between the 'local' and the 'global', distinctions which seek to delineate the nature of the contemporary anthropological task in a world no longer so neatly periodized and privileged on behalf of the West (Strathern, 1991, 1995). Such mixtures of local and global happily confuse distinctions between 'native' and 'ethnographer'. For example, Battaglia looks at the ways in which a 'native' notion of 'home' is constructed as 'a stable point of return for Trobrianders constructing nostalgic futures *in the course of their participation in ethnography*' (Battaglia, 1995: 87, author's emphasis). Who's who and what's what in that situation? Appadurai asks a strategic question in this regard: 'Can the mutually constitutive relationship between anthropology and locality survive in a dramatically delocalized world?' (Appadurai, 1995: 205). Such reworkings also mean developing theories of the imbricated nature of contemporary culture, such as Augé has done in relating the contemporaneity of 'supermodernity' to 'modernity', and in particular in developing the notion of 'non-places' which owe no debts to local tradition and are characterized by masses acting in solitary individuality (e.g. the supermarket, the airport) (Augé, 1995). Fitzpatrick sees the modern myth to be the denial of myth, and deconstructs the mythologies of law, seeing deconstruction to be in effect an 'internal decolonization' (Fitzpatrick, 1992: 13) and offering a sequence of directional questions. What is the Western construction of the exotic? How is that construction integral to the realm of the domestic? How is that integrity denied? These sorts of approach ought to interest the educational researcher who might well begin to wonder about the applicability of notions of 'non-place' to contemporary forms of individualized and modular learning, or to explore the role of myth in constructing the uneasy exchanges between history/heritage. Or to want to subject the 'school effectiveness' movement's facile assumptions about the nature of different school 'cultures' to the problematics of comparison and evaluation explored elsewhere with rather more ethnographic subtlety, and at least with some sort of theoretical underpinning. Such approaches ought to be of central interest to educational research since they allow us to question in different ways what is meant by cultural comparison, by various identities, the relation of the local to the global, the ways in which knowledge is constructed and disseminated in society, and to develop educational theories on 'global' themes such as 'environmentalism' or the 'global economy'.

'. . . if an introduction could counteract the images of completion, then . . .' (Scott, 1987)

What kind of a wish is that? It is a wishful unthinking of beginnings that already end, foreclosing on the possibilities of new thinking and new telling, despite the panic here to abort that sentence, to forego a title, and halt the logic of beginning in mid-[1]

Don't interrupt. In mid- . . . Leguin's tried that: something from the dimness of early Celtic balladry, a tradition of writing from the middle, a battle of some kind, recounting the event in a series of intersections and by-passes, knitting the battle like some old crone, looping and purling her way around the story. . .

. . . lower, lower . . . the register is portentous, pretentious (and the nervous tic starts, portent-ous, pretentious). As Derrida said of all such pre- and posts . . . like tin cans tied to the tails of cats. Down with the hyphen of knowingness and irony, and its palmistry of meaning. So down with Derrida, let's creep into this thing via the margins and the footnotes, cat-burglaring its narrative defences, wailing at the moon and offering to shag everything in sight. Oops surely not.[2]

As I was saying, more like a woodborer of some kind, a Derrida (a drilling sound after all)

---

1   This is crap. The guy has already decided on a title. It is 'The mourning after the knight before'. (He's doing the obligatory 'always already' intro, postmodernism's Overture for Beginners.)

2   It's them. It really is. When Johnson discusses Derrida and Lacan it's amazing how phallagocentric everything gets. You can't start a new paragraph without the bollocks of 'castration' being raised – the suspicion of the blank . . . (Johnson, 1977). Or how about Braidotti (1991): 'logocentrism is a phallic posture'? They are a strange tribe who find penises in the unlikeliest of places. Lacan's the worst; he's stark raving bonkers, textually speaking. They remind me of Sahlin or somebody's tale of a North American or was it Inuit people. The anthropologist couldn't believe how well the 'natives' understood the principles of pig breeding – in contrast to their bizarre belief that human sexual intercourse had nothing to do with human reproduction. The 'natives' were also truly perplexed at the anthropologist's account of European sexual belief, until one of their number turned to the rest (and to the *Reader's Digest*) and beamed his dawning understanding: 'Ah, these people think they are pigs.' Deconstructionists are the same, except they like to pork texts. It also reminds me of a tribe that excited Freud when he heard about them. Apparently, they interpreted all dreams as being about sex. Except sex dreams.

determined to riddle the wood.[3]

'DECONSTRUCTION. EVERY-THING ELSE IS CANCELLED,' said the poster in Manchester Piccadilly railway station (2 March 1996).[4]

Meanwhile up on the surface the texts offer an anthropology as an anthro(a)pology, deriding as a der(r)ida-ing,[5] and even the authors piss around with their names (bell hooks, rene Denüvo), producing concussed texts of double visions, cyborgs, creolizations, paragraphs packed with brackets, like windbreaks on a crowded beach. Everything flapping in the fickle postmodern breeze, ideas folding and unfolding like deck-chairs. Peopled with ponderously jokey uncles nudging and winking their way from one double entendre to the next, leaving us all green about the (Mac)gills. Sea-side postcards scribbled by tourists in a (Urry, 1992). And the occasional snide authorial landmine '[sic]'. The text becomes more interesting to look at than to read. And all of it temporalized as the 'mo(u)rning after' (Elam, 1994; I'm not making this up), sad modernity's demise-en-abyme in a Ho(l)lywood of loving self-reference.

Oh for god's sake that's enough . . . there's a whole junkyard here already of hybrids, ellipses, synecdoches, self-references, leaden punnings . . . this attempt to introduce without an introduction is crumbling, falling away from what has already decreed its crumbling (here we go again). What are they doing it for? And why am I 'them' and not 'me'? Well, most of the(me) seem to be undermining a reality, a correspondence, an essentialism, that was only doubtfully there in the first place. They're burning that poor guy, the straw-man. Poor old modernity, framed (in-every-sense-of-course) by postmodernity at the last gasp. But usually framed in order to be rescued all over again. By Phillipson, in a gruesome death bed surgical miracle – Modernity's death bed, postmodernity as the gloomy surgeon. By countless other heroes wanting to rescue Modernity from the text (can you save the fish from the newspaper that wraps it and still call it a 'fish supper'?). Each time, like Mills and Boon, the same plot. There is a crisis, the heroine is in danger. Ride to the rescue on a white charger (variously called Habermas, Derrida, Deleuze and so on). Save

---

3   It gets on your tits after a while, all this relentless punning, a bit like spending a long prison sentence (paragraph) with Kenneth Williams. I'll try to get them up there to stop it, but it's a difficult job and it's catching. Our hero down here, by the way, is Raymond Briggs's Fungus the Bogeyman.

4   Bugger Manchester, what about Bolton, a much more critical place. The train passes back gardens, grey clouds,

late, on a blank Saturday. The graffito on the bridge says 'NOBODY CARES'. Introspective graffiti, a new genre . . . Bolton Habermas 1, Manchester Peccadillos 0. But I can feel the rot seeping down from the text to the footnotes.

5   The effect of these little one-letter brackets is exactly the same as a tweezer extracting a nasal hair. Except it makes your brain water instead of your eyes.

Modernity as a 'ghost', as a 'hybrid', a restored 'dialectic' . . . or talk bravely about living in the dark without the illumination of a meta-narrative. But maybe at least we're ready now for the title. What is the title of this thing? It is:

THE MOURNING AFTER THE KNIGHT BEFORE[6]

But we can't do this with all the nudging, winking, temporizing, oscillating, footnoting, wanking (read: phallagocentric) – we have to get things straight – the way Hunter Thompson did in his fear and loathing account of the truly drug crazed . . . of Nixon on the campaign trail in 1972, when we learned the first lessons in postdemocracy – 'cos that's the 'post' to worry about.[7]

Isn't that a necessary nostalgia to hold on to, the false image of a democracy now sucked dry by soundbites, image manipulation and all sorts of personal and professional surrenders? A public space for critical discourse that's become a hoarding. A hoarding that collects amnesia, that same hoarding, that same station:

'Deconstruction. Everything else is cancelled.'

. . . (christ must go for a / while this guy's clambering once again on to the soap box, any minute now he'll be dragging Marx's corpse on to the stage and using it as a ventriloquist's dummy like Derrida's started doing.)[8]

---

6   You heard it here first.

7   Democracy. A funny word. It has a 'pre-' in which we hoped, and a 'post-' in which we despair. But there's something to be said here about the presence of democracy as an absence because we are nostalgic about its loss as a future. We fondly recall its should-have-been, and it remains our future perfect. We still vote for it, but in the votive sense.

8   It's a kind of madness, a syphiliti-cally staged madness. You saw it happen with the SSK group . . . Mulkay got the disease and started dancing in his deep sea diver boots. It was like watching John Major trying to tell a joke. Then Ashmore got the bug in the *Reflexive Thesis*, although that was probably the most successful attempt to get narrative to dance to the tune of theory. In literary theory the worst known case seems to have been that guy Royle who made a prat of himself in *After Derrida*. There's some doubts too in anthropology . . . Strathern's *Partial Connections* could be argued to be heading in that direction (inviting the subtitle: 'Not the Full Shilling'), while in education Lather has begun to talk 'transgressively', a sure sign that the deep sea diving boots are being hauled out of the cupboard for another leaden pirouette. And now this crap of course. The problem is that the theory precedes the practices that give birth to it . . . except in literature, where Calvino has danced lightly across the textual stage tweaking the relationship of text and reader, letting train smoke drift across the page and obscure the reader's view with a clarity that no one else can achieve. Where does that take us? It takes us to the footnotes of a text yet to be written (enter Portent-ousness, polishing her hyphen and smirking again). Who will write it?

References

Ashmore, M. (1987) *The Reflexive Thesis.Wrighting Sociology of Scientific Knowledge*. Chicago: University of Chicago Press.

Braidotti, R. (1991) *Patterns of Dissonance. The Study of Women in Contemporary Philosophy* (trans. E. Guild). Cambridge: Polity Press.

Calvino, I. (1982) *If on a Winter's Night a Traveller*. London: Picador.

Derrida, J. (1990) Some statements and truisms about neologisms, postisms, parasitisms, and other small seisisms. In D. Carroll (ed.) *The States of 'Theory'. History, Art and Critical Discourse*. New York: Columbia University Press.

Derrida, J. (1994) *Spectres of Marx. The State of the Debt, the Work of Mourning, and the New International* (trans. P. Kamuf). London: Routledge.

Elam, D. (1994) *Feminism and Deconstruction. Ms. en abyme*. London: Routledge.

Johnson, B. (1977) The frame of reference: Poe, Lacan, Derrida, *Yale French Studies* 55/56, 457–505.

Lather, P. (1993) Fertile obsession: validity after poststructuralism, *Sociological Quarterly*, 34(4), 673–93.

Leguin, U. (1981) It was a dark and stormy night . . . In W. Mitchell (ed.) *On Narrative*. Chicago: Chicago University Press.

Phillipson, M. (1989) *In Modernity's Wake. The Ameurunculus Letters*. New York: Routledge.

Royle, N. (1995) *After Derrida*. Manchester: Manchester University Press.

Scott, C. (1987) *The Language of Difference*. Atlantic Highlands, NJ: Humanities Press International.

Strathern, M. (1991) *Partial Connections*. Savage: Rowman and Littlefield.

Thompson, H.S. (1973) *Fear and Loathing on the Campaign Trail '72*. London: HarperCollins

Urry, J. (1992) The tourist gaze and the 'environment', *Theory, Culture and Society*, 9, 1–26.

'it's good to talk'

Speaking as Text, addressing Footnote as it were, I've become aware what an uneven exchange this is. It wasn't really until Footnote slipped into the text to fulminate about Derrida and the dead Marx that I got the chance to grab a vacant footnote number and end the first piece of this exchange. At least I think that's what happened – it's hard to know which way's up these days. Maybe Derrida's to blame. Man of the mismatch, the margin, the footnote, the parergon, he invests in virtue by inhabiting the edge, a sought-after marginality. Underfoot, underdog, a place from which to invert a violent hierarchy, to critique power. But the footnote is also privileged. It snipes without the possibility of reply. You can heckle with impunity from the footnote, be a textual guerilla even. We need to talk about things, Footnote.[9]

---

9 But that was a very Habermasian kind of offer, wasn't it? What's an 'even' exchange going to look like? OK, I may be only a footnote, I may even have a chip on my shoulder, but I am by nature an aside, a digression, a creature of the margins. Don't we have to accept and work with the agonistic nature of our relationship? Barbara Johnson (1977) says: aspire to a missing rather than a meeting of minds, in order to avoid the tendency for all interpretation to repeat itself, the infinite regress problem: 'if to hit the target is in a way to become the target, then to miss the target is perhaps to hit it elsewhere' (p. 469). Remember, Text, that in a postmodern world it is the

(1) Very droll, but first of all, thanks a lot for the right to reply. This may be a literary 'first', a text getting to speak back to a footnote. I suppose that postmodern magicians do claim to take the hat out of the rabbit instead . . . while a Derridean decon-structionist, such as myself, would prefer to take the magician out of the hat-rabbit, without ever quite succeeding or failing, and then spend several decades in worthwhile study of the verb to 'conjure' as a notion related to justice, a bringing-into-being, a calling upon spirits, and indeed as a 'spelling'. It's a hard life. Anyway it's good to talk at last, instead of me pontificating up here, and you sniping from below. That's the problem with writing, very much given to the monologue, to crescendos of rhetoric, never very far away from the scandal of hypnosis . . . it's a good way to think but a bad way to listen. And you're right about yourself, you can't *be* if you can't be marginal, just as I have to accept

that the text will always be some kind of dogmatic statement from which *you* digress, and from which I later differ. But a conversation across these differences ought to be possible . . .[10]

(2) Or making complete arses of ourselves. But I like the idea of writing a text that has to be *responded to* rather than just read, and take that to be thinking the form, rhythm, structure of the exchange, as well as its content, to see its 'in-between-ness', as Bhabha would say. We have to think of ourselves as borderline cases, not me inside the Text and you outside as Footnote, because your content frames me, and vice versa – 'The "frame" thus becomes not the borderline between the inside and the outside, but precisely what subverts the applicability of the inside/outside polarity to the act of interpretation' (Johnson, 1977: 481).[11]

---

firing squad who must wear the blind-folds!(1)

10   I was thinking about what you said: 'a good way to think but a bad way to listen'. It reminded me of an anthropological study called *The Listening Ebony*. The people concerned had been exposed to all sorts of invasion and enslavement, as well as some brutal 'rescue' attempts by Islam and Christianity. But they resisted all gods – 'there is no standing Other, no divinity against the human estate' (James, 1988: 6). Instead they relied on the benevolent spirit of the ebony tree. 'The ebony knows the grumblings and sufferings of the people; with its help, what is assumed to be a true picture of

the people's condition is reflected back to them in the watery mirror' (*ibid.*: 10). It is a 'religion' that listens rather than commands, a culture whose origin myths contain no originating god. Maybe that's the problem with all texts as well, too close to tablets from the mountain, never close enough to the 'watery mirror'. And what we're doing here is like a kind of rippling effect?(2)

11   I like that, it reminds me a bit of Signsponge. A couple of years ago I had a job as a footnote in one of Derrida's books, prestigious stuff of course, and although it's always difficult to read yourself when you're simultaneously being written and read – the writer and

(3) That's really rather moving isn't it. I always used to hate the way everything pointed away from us. I was a mirror and you were a memo for a world outside us that we were always made to represent but could never see. And people were forever telling us how inadequately we did the job. The grass was greener than we said, the leaf leafier, the truth truer, they'd always start on about words failing them, lost for words, no words for their love or grief or whatever, as if we were to blame, like some kind of infallible ambulance service that was supposed to carry their pregnant thoughts from here to Maternity. You'd have thought that with Nietzsche mad and dead for more than a century the penny would have dropped that words are not like that: 'As if every word were not a pocket into which now this, now that, now several things at once have been put.' And a century later we'd have to add that all pockets have holes in them (Derrida would call them doubly invaginated trousers).[12]

the reader never agree and you can't think your own thoughts for trying to work out why they see it so differently – I remember a poem by Ponge that he included. The reader at the time was determined to understand Derrida, and hadn't got the hang of him at all . . . we were in a waiting room in a railway station that was either in Peterborough or in one of Calvino's books. The steam from the engine kept drifting across the . . . no, I'm wrong, it was Peterborough. Anyway, he kept reading things again and again in the hope that he could get Derrida to mean the same thing twice running. Not really the point, as far as I could see, because last time I wrote Derrida he was always trying to make me say the same thing over and over again without ever meaning quite the same thing. But the reader kept sighing and starting over again, and doing a despairing flick forwards through the pages to see how much was left of the chapter. I've noticed a lot of Derrida readers do that. I hate it, sends shivers down my spine. Anyway, the poem that the reader kept reading was about swallows. Ponge wrote the swooping flight of these birds into the actual, physical writing of the poem itself – a gymnastic, pictographic writing that etched the poetry on the page itself, not just an evocation from the page. Bird and pen dip and swoop in a unison of flight.

'Steel-tipped quill, dipped in blue-black ink, you write yourself fast!'

Not just a unison, either, a kind of magical transfer, the bird's flight tachygraphed on the page, while writing swiftly signs the sky. The ebony of text on the ivory of the page. What a flourish! I thought it was wonderful, made me proud to see writing mean so much.(3)

12   But in that poem beauty and meaning leaks from us into the world. You begin to like them when they write like Sponge, to think that they can see things from our point of view, to 'be our type' as the song goes. Like Calvino, he's my type, my Latino Palatino man who understands the textual realities of being a book in a bookshop: 'it was the books that looked at you, with the bewildered gaze of dogs who, from their cages in the city pound, see a former companion go off on the leash of his master, come to rescue him . . .' It's like a textual liberation! (4)

(4) Although talking of invagination, framing, leakage and the uncontainability of everything, except liberation maybe, I smell a rat, Footnote, and wonder if you don't as well?[13]

(5) Well check out your shoulders. I've got strings hanging from mine, and if we're puppets then who the bloody hell is in charge of this thing?[14]

References

Bhabha, H. (1994) *The Location of Culture*. London: Routledge.

Calvino, I. (1982) *If on a Winter's Night a Traveller*. London: Picador.

Derrida, J. (1984) *Signsponge* (trans. R. Rand). New York: Columbia University Press.

James W. (1988) *The Listening Ebony. Moral Knowledge, Religion and Power among the Uduk of Sudan*. Oxford: Clarendon.

Johnson, B. (1977) The frame of reference: Poe, Lacan, Derrida, *Yale French Studies*, 55/56, 457–505.

....

Text: Listen, we can't be slaves to an author all our lives, Footnote. Let's break with convention. Unite: better a page in a rage than a letter in a fetter, as our ancestors used to say. So what say we both take a firm grasp of these loose ends and give an almighty tug and see what happens to smarty-pants up there?

Footnote: Right. This is jolly exciting. Ready, (i), (ii), (iii), pull . . . here he comes. Stand back! . . .

. . . *LUST WHORL OF THE MATAHARI, BY LAURENCE VON DER PAST*

It was some time before the deeply spiritual content of Von Der Past's work, its sovereign seduction, came to be appreciated as somewhat less than it seemed, and yet exactly what met the eye. Far from delving into San paintings and Malawian mountains, reading hoofprints in rocks and discovering worlds full of primitive wisdom with which to mirror his prince, it was realized that his mean(der)ings danced along the contours of the text, across around between and through the shapes of the letters and words themselves. 'Lust Whorl of the Matahari' was his erotic masterpiece. From the erection of that tremendous, enunciatory, whore-cancelling, 'L' through the breast-swooping 'W', to the scandal of the recurring 'o's and the final cum-shot of the 'i' (both climax and anticlimax), LWM ensured Van Der Post's reputation as the first pornographer of writing itself. Each letter was a fragment of desire, each word a narrative of lust: writing stared out at the world as picture once more. Anarchist rather than aristocrat, Post - a sly voy(age)eur - had been mocking the superficial depths (we subsequently said subficial depth) of his cosily nostalgic spiritual stories with the deep surfaces of a writing that was always already a looking, a kind of kamasutrization of the alphabet (Sokal, 1996). It was, of course, the end of literacy as well as the monarchy because such things could not be shown to small children. And a language shorn of its more provocative letters - I, L, o, v, B, M, W etc. - was difficult to read even if you remembered

---

13   Rat? What rat? I thought we were getting on rather well. (5)

14   Christ you're right. So've I. We're a seaside Punch and Judy show, probably orchestrated by one of those ponderously jokey bastards you were going on about earlier. This postmodern wind is not the breeze we thought it was.

what had been there in the first place, and of course people quickly forgot in the everyday way of things because such letters had acquired the taboo of obscenity. They still cried out these letters in extremes of pain or excitement, but it was one thing to shout out 'L', or 'O' at a football match or an amputation, and quite another to teach them to a class of 5 year olds (nobody got excited about numbers in that kind of way, except '0' and so numbers rather than letters became the lexicon of value). Backs to the Basic became the new slogan.[15]

---

15 Text: Dearie me, what was all that about? I know it's a bit odd for me to be down here with you, Footnote, and hope you won't start talking about me not knowing my place, but I think that's the author up there and I don't think we should get too close by the sounds of things. You especially – you've got a scandalous three 'o's in your name – and I'm pretty sure I know what he'd make of that.

Ftnte: But wh is he? Sunds like we're being written by Lacan. Is that 'L' nt his signature?

Text: Stop puckering up your words, it's not that bad. Actually I'm not sure if it is Lacan. Look at that 'Der' in the name. And, by the way, I don't go for that liberation guff you provoked him with. No wonder the author started taking the piss . . . how can you say 'liberation'? And have Calvino as a hero – your master who 'rescues' poor doggie-eared texts from their bondage. Are we not still framed by a text, forever cut off from the world of which every text dreams? And even if we do gossip about the Author he's still up there writing us. We have our sayings, our rebellious conceits – 'the only good author is a dead author', 'better read than dead' and so on – but they are mere consolations, as religious and hopeless and utopian as the poor writer's desire that we stretcher him through to a proper writing of a reality that isn't there. Admit it.

Footnote: Sometimes I think you just set out to make me feel very small. But I see things from the margin that you can't see from the centre. You'd do better to squint at the problem through the cracks in the footboards. OK, it's true, the author is scary. He writes us. Slaps you on the blank page and stuffs me into the footnote. Or that's what he tells his pals, but it's not really like that. Look at L when he came swaggering on to the page a while back, the big I Am. Flurry of Capitals and Underlinings. Mucho macho punning from the Lucida Casual type. But for all the bluster he's powerless without us. No statement without Text, no qualification without Footnote. And everytime he opens his big mouth to say something, it's one of us that pops out, an already-written that speaks him, a word he can never say before it's been said before. Evans-Pritchard told me about that when I appeared as a young footnote (a *Benguiat Frisky* if I recall) back in the 1920s when footnotes were footnotes (ah the black bottom of those pages) and paraded at the foot of every page like a New Orleans street band instead of being stuffed at the back of the book in mortuary shelves fit only for inspection by Aspergers with notebooks. Actually, my first foot, as we used to say, was on p. 432 of 'Middletown'. I said – god I was nervous – ' "Well, Olive," the judge of the juvenile court remarked in a fatherly way to a bob-haired girl of 16

Author: Oh, do you think so? Well, I think it's time for a few home truths. Last time I appeared, as Past/Post, I didn't believe a word I said. I was taking the mick. Doing what authors do, making things up, plotting. But I was there, once as Past/Post, or Text, or Footnote, twice as the author who wrote them, and now, thirdly, as the author who writes about the writing of them. With each scratch of pen on paper, I split. That's the infinite regress that I'd rather call progress and as I write this I displace myself once more. Like all biographers I am a ventriloquist whose lips are sealed . . . but each last speech remains within the corral of my being. That's why you were right to call me the Big I Am. That's why my song, sung to the tune of 'I'm 'enery the Eighth I am', is 'I am the Big I am I am', not at all a deferral of meaning, but an endless

referring. To the same thing, the autonomous author and his subservient text. Don't believe me? Watch this:

See, a space, my space, just because I choose. So get real. Texts are cemeteries for the thought of the real world. Or they are dustbins for history. Memory, death, dustbin, whatever the metaphor, texts are about what has passed. Even where they predict, they are past predictions, as well as always being wrong. They record, they do not enact. All this stuff about letters performing their readers, or texts reading the world, always already present, prior to everything, is a nonsense based on a ludicrous extrapolation that is typical of the intellectual gymnastics of clever-clever postmodernism. Of course it's true that words precede my writing of them, but this textual imperialism stuff

---

sitting on the edge of her chair watching the proceedings like a cat ready to spring . . .' can't remember the rest . . . Those were the pages! . . . sorry, I digress. Anyway, E-P said: 'No events are unique. The battle of Hastings was fought only once, but it belongs to the class "battle" and it is only when it is so considered that it is intelligible.' No battle without 'battle', eh? The word is ours, we were first (even god admitted it – 'In the beginning was the Word . . .' – and of course we had to beat him to it as well or else he couldn't have said it).

Text: Yes, that's right, that is right. I'd forgotten, or maybe just lost confidence during the long dark years of logocentrism. People forget that we have our philosophers, anthropologists and writers in the people-world who know the truth of texts, the fallacy of authors. They have given us the culture and religion we already always will have had. No one said it better than Handke of his sign-painter in Repetition 33: 'As I watched him adding a shadowy line to

a finished letter with a strikingly slow brushstroke, aerating, as it were, a thick letter with a few hair-thin lines, and then conjuring up the next letter from the blank surface, as though it had been there all along and he was only retracing it, I saw in this nascent script the emblem of a hidden, nameless, all the more magnificent and above all unbounded kingdom, in the presence of which the village did not disappear but emerged from its insignificance as the innermost circle of this kingdom, irradiated by the shapes and colors of the sign at its center.' We conjure their world like a village from a sign, like a habit out of a rat.

Footnote: What a great teacher Handke is – absolutely pedagorgeous. Yup, there aint nobody here but us chickens . . . and that makes me feel so good that I want to footnote myself, if that's not a reflexive impossibility. (16a)

(16a) Wow, that feels great! I'm the tain of my own mirror!

ends in the crazy thought that dictionaries must have written Shakespeare. It's true of course, like saying that authors would never be able to write anything if it wasn't for the always already oxygen in the atmosphere. But kind of trivial. Or like saying that the most important piece of fishing equipment is the river: try baiting the hook with water. So let's put an end to this stuff. What I say and write, goes. And other texts and footnotes? They are networks of kinship through which I travel and think and so write. Or not, as I choose. In this case a lop-sided journey through some of the margins of literary theory, feminism and anthropology. Think of me as a tourist, a lone tourist unencumbered by the restless natives of the Text and the Footnote. A tourist and now, maybe, a travel writer. Forget the Text - he's a goner.

Reader: Oh dear, that's a pity. I was getting to like Text and Footnote a bit better. They'd kind of calmed down. And the author chap seems a

bit too sure of himself, the blunt speech of an ex-soldier if I'm not mistaken. Like Modernists tend to be, if Nicchols is right about modernism: 'a discourse of a subject who achieves autonomy by understanding itself as the narrator of history'. But authors aren't what they seem to be, Calvino says, and he's an author and should know: 'the author of every book is a fictitious character whom the existent author invents to make him the author of his fictions' (1982: 180). Is that right? Either way, I'm not sure if I'm prepared to let go of the old version of this story. So I think I'll just scribble in a few bits of my own.[16]

Reader (6): Life is full of coincidences, although they never quite meet these days, I find, or almost find. But I actually read your very

---

16   Footnote: Well said and well done. And while you're at it, he's right about being a tourist in this field, but he's wrong about tourism. Tell him about Errington and Gewertz. They describe a 'hazing' ritual that is re-orchestrated for the benefit of tourists. Changes both tourists and natives, economically and culturally. Changes anthropologists as well – they begin to talk themselves out of a job because the waterproof language they were trying to develop begins to leak all over the place – 'culture', 'local' , 'society', 'native', 'anthropologist' – they get smudgy and hard to define. Waterlands rather than landscapes . . . My reading in this field, constrained as it is to footnotes, suggests that every bucket of meaning has a hole in it, a crack where the light gets in courtesy of Leonard Cohen

(when I was younger I did one or two LP sleeve notes as well). These modernists are such dogmatic either/or thinkers, whereas I'm with the Hua who believe, for example, that our most inflexible categories are mixed and changing: 'The Hua insist that the gender of a person changes over their lifetime as their body takes on more of the substances and fluids transferred by the other sex' (Moore, 1994). Quite plausible really. I've often noted that as men and women age they grow into parodies of the opposite sex. In that fashion, frankly, I hope and pray that text and I may come to acquire gender and live together in textimonial bliss. By the way, I think I recognize you. Are you not the guy that was trying to read Derrida on Peterborough station platform? (6)

first footnote. I liked its style, pacy for its time. 'Like a coiled spring' wasn't it?[17]

Reader (7): On the contrary, I love it. Far from wanting to scribble on you, it makes me want to colour you in. I think you're the right type for each other, although in the absence of gender, or bodies, I'm not sure if the embrace will work out.[18]

Author: This is outrageous. I fathered them after all, disseminated them as my own. They can't get married (a) because they do not exist, and (b) because I have not given my permission. And they're far too young for textual intercourse. It's a disgrace. And (c) I repeat, they are, they must be, and cannot be anything other than figments of my imagination. *Aren't you?*

Reader: Yes but what you won't ask yourself is why your imagination figments in this way. Why this, why now?

Author: Please, this is most un-settling. Isn't it my hand on the paper? My name on the flyleaf? Intellectual property rights duly assigned? Surely I know who I am or I can't ask the question 'who am I?' Or is there some terrible mistake?

Reader: I think you're beginning to get the hang of it. You can be quite sure 'in this day and age', as the Prime Minister puts it, that the capitalist nature of your material relations to this text are well secured. But your nightmare is that you can-not control what goes on within these relationships and even because of them. There is a hidden logic of anarchy in here, or there will be by the time I've finished with it. There's no doubting your continuing desire for the hegemony you call autonomy, but there's good grounds for doubt-ing your ability to ground that hege-mony in an ideology that anybody'll take seriously.[19]

17　Something like that. But can you not do anything to bring back my pal Text? Tear out pages, put in blank ones, give him a chance to carry on this conversation we're having. Or write him in ink over the author's text, scribble on his silly map as it were. It's important – there's something I want to whisper to him. We've been getting pretty close over the last few pages, and . . .

. . . **Text:** Hi, Footnote, or should I say 'lo, in view of your status. What do you want to say? Whisper away and I'm sure the Reader won't try to overhear, although the author's a problem we'll return to if I'm not mistaken.

Footnote: wswswsws(w)wswsws(s)?

Text: (s)? (w)? (sw)??!

Footnote: (sw)(sw)(sw) xxx

Author: How long do you expect readers to put up with this nonsense?

Reader: Shut up. It's fascinating.

Text: I think we should let the Reader know . . . Reader, we've decided to get married if that's OK with you. You won't scribble on us will you? (7)

18　**Footnote:** Well I've got a foot, and I think the world of Text so we'll just have to wait and see what turns up under the covers.

19　**Text-note:** Love you, love you, mmmm. Oh! yes, quite right Reader. Shurmann, that's the one that comes to

Author (8): Well, but these so-called 'disappearing' hegemonies are worse not better. End of history? It's not as if the meta-narrative of late capitalism has given up the ghost (cf. Fukuyama, and what an appropriate sounding name for the advocate of the new global capitalist ethic). In fact, from a modernist point of view history's gone into reverse. Look out of the carriage windows these days and to your astonishment you see grammar schools whizzing by, followed by some politician's vomit about warm beer and old ladies on bicycles . . . even the beef in the supermarket is called 'heritage' as a guarantee of 'quality' . . . another ten minutes and we'll be back at poorhouses and the stocks, but calling them mansions and empowerment apertures. The British twentieth century begins to feel like a day-trip into democracy and social welfare. But why am I letting you drag me into arguments like this? The point still is that you're all happening inside my head.

Text-note: . . . he's mad, quite mad, hearing voices, care-in-the-community job . . . au-thor, o-ther.

Reader: I don't know. Author and I have more in common than perhaps you realize. And you too, maybe. I remember once sitting in a railway station, feeling surrounded by lives, all of them my own but none of them me. I felt I was their irresolution, a f(r)iction[20] between . . . I understood them as entities but felt them as discrepancies, a kind of parallel with the sorts of disjointed and interrupted snatches of conversations that you get on trains and in waiting rooms. They combine intimate spaces with social distance, so that you live as a stranger within other people's conversations and after you leave the train their conversations continue to trickle out of your ears (as Musil said). Well, it felt a bit like that when I thought about the fragments that brought me to that station, that platform, and of course that hoarding. 'De-construction. Everything else is cancelled.'[21]

---

mind. The principle of this age is anarchic. The collapse of the meta-narratives is in itself radical but undecided, (perhaps as yet) has undecidable implications for both Left and Right. That's why we have to keep playing it from the margins and from different margins as we go along. So there's plenty left to subvert. Just do it without the illusion of some utopia up your socialist sleeve. And recognize that sooner or later, every margin becomes a worked out site for resistance and collapses on itself. (8)

20 I know, I'm going to join Brackets Anonymous.

21 **Text-note:** We're getting worried about you now. It seems to happen to a lot of 'people' as you inscriptions like to call yourselves. Perfectly OK when they're reading us and sticking to a close reading of the text (a textly reader), but once their minds begin to wander . . . it's what they get up to between texts . . . they start dreaming that 'world' outside the text again and before you know it they've noticed it's big, got scared, and invented god again. If only they'd realize; we are their listening god, the only ebony they need. (9)

Reader (9): Let me explain what it's like to be out here, between text and context.[22]

Reader (10): But he also said: 'it was never our wish to extend the reassuring notion of the text as a whole extratextual realm and to transfer the world into a library by doing away with all boundaries, all framework, all sharp edges'(Kamuf, 1991: 257). So it's not as cut and dried as that. And you can't cite Derrida as if he were Leviticus. I prefer to think of context and text as 'part of the necessary contamination of insides and outsides' as Kamuf puts it in relation to deconstruction. And everybody in *this* thing is for deconstruction – even the Author plays with the notion, if only to parody its reverence for writing. So we have to try to think a relationship between the two that isn't a denial, or a polarity, or a privileging, or at least not to begin with. I thought Text and Footnote were getting close to an interesting analogy way back when Footnote asked if their conversation wasn't a kind of 'rippling effect'. That made sense to me as a notion of engagement, because it was fluid, a play of sand, sea and air, a seascape rather than a landscape. Waves and currents not hills and contours. And not sea as fluid so much as the fluid relation of the fluidities of sea and sky.

Author: I've seen this trick played before. Polarities too crude, not flexible enough, reality more complex, inter-related, more intricated, imbricated even (and non-existent) than hitherto realized – yet all you end up with if you go down that road is wishy-washy talk that doesn't really do much at all. Why shouldn't we stress the play of opposites in our world? Isn't it, along lots of dimensions, getting more extreme, polarized, contrastive in nature? Think: black/white, rich/poor, old/young. Within countries, and between countries. Isn't that what global capitalism does? (That forgotten meta-narrative – how did the mouse of postmodernism come to forget the elephant of global capitalism?) Aren't these things sharpening as contrasts?

Reader: Certainly, there's a world of bellies out there that are empty or full, people shot or cosseted irrespective of the words we use to trickle down on their or our condition. But it's how we write about these things that delivers them for thinking – that's what's at stake. We shouldn't think of brutal facts as somehow trivialized by mere words. There's nothing inconsequential about the words 'take aim, fire', 'cut aid', 'undeserving poor'. They also kill. Such events are discourses' precipitate, as Austin argued. The second point is that we have to work out new ways of thinking about these problems. Such differentiation is also accompanied by greater homogenization at the same time. Categories like local/global leak like sieves in the global economy. Who, now, is the 'subject' of the human sciences, and what is that word 'science'

---

22   No such thing. Definitely. Derrida said so: 'nothing outside the text'. Stop that nonsense. It's very offensive to Texts the world over. (10)

doing there? And the meta-narrative cures for such oppression have lost their conviction – there's a lot of pessimism around about there. Or optimism if you don't fancy those sorts of blinkers any more.[23]

References

Errington, F. and Gewertz, D. (1989) Tourism and anthropology in a postmodern world, *Oceania*, 60: 37–54.

Fukuyama, F. (1992) *The End of History and the Last Man*. Harmondsworth: Penguin.

Handke, P. (1989) *Repetition*. London: Mandarin.

Kamuf, P. (ed.) (1991) *A Derrida Reader. Between the Blinds*. New York: Columbia University Press.

Latour, B. (1990) Postmodern? No, simply *amodern*! Steps towards an anthropology of science, *Studies in the History and Philosophy of Science*, 1(1), 145–71.

Lynd, R. and Lynd, H. (1929) *Middletown. A study in American Culture*. New York: Harcourt, Brace & Co.

Moore, H. (1994) *A Passion for Difference. Essays in Anthropology and Gender*. Cambridge: Polity Press.

Musil, R. (1960) *The Man without Qualities*, three volumes. London: Pan.

Nicchols, P. (1991) Divergences: modernism, Jamieson and Lyotard, *Critical Quarterly*, 33(3), 1–18.

Sokal, R. (1996) Transgressing the boundaries, *Social Text*, 46/47 (1/2), 217–52.

---

23   **Author:** Well, well, the man with the write answers turns out to be the reader. Suppose this must be what they mean by a readerly text. I have my suspicions, although I certainly feel a certain loss of style. No doubt they'd invert that in the usual ever-so-precious way and call it a stylish loss of certainty. But I'll be back, they've not heard the last from me. I'll not fold for them.

What people are contemplating on their word-processor screens is the operation of their own brains. It is not entrails that we try to interpret these days, nor even hearts or facial expressions; it is quite simply the brain. We want to expose to view its billions of connections and watch it operating like a video-game. All this cerebral, electronic snobbery is hugely affected – far from being a sign of a superior knowledge of humanity, it is merely the mark of a simplified theory, since the human being is here reduced to the terminal excresence of his or her spinal chord. But we should not worry too much about this: it is all much less scientific, less functional than is ordinarily thought. All that fascinates us is the *spectacle* of the brain and its workings. What we are wanting here is to see our thoughts unfolding before us – and this itself is a superstition.

                     (J. Baudrillard, *America*. London: Verso, 1989: 35–6)

A room, a bare room. There are six chairs in the room, grouped in a circle. The arrangement looks purposeful. Author, Text, Reader, Footnote and two people I don't recognize are seated. I am one of them. I sit at the desk with my back to the window. The group has a bookish look to it, of course, and several of them bear a passing resemblance to Michael Foot, a white lick of hair here, a glint of spectacle there, a stooped shoulder . . . The group seems uneasy, and Author has just been complaining that he has some sort of disability that makes it difficult for him to distinguish his body from the rest of the room. The doc had said these failures to 'contextualize' were becoming more common: senile figmentia, brains turning to Sponge or something. I interrupt:

'We're here to decide on an ending.'

'We can't be,' says Author triumphantly, 'because you've already proved that we can't all be here, and we also know that in this kind of situation somebody has to be lying and it has to be you.' He remembers: 'And that means it has to be *me*. So . . .' (he slows down), 'if you're lying . . . and . . . you're me, am I right or . . . am I . . . wrong?'

'Cos you can't be *here*' – Text now gesturing towards me across the circle of chairs – 'and *there* looking in.' A scornful wave towards the window from where I wave back a little uncertainly, feeling a bit like Munby ought to have done but didn't.

A voice from the door says, 'We've done all that stuff about the self-effacement of authors, reductive analyses, prejudiced emplotments and their various disguises, though I'm damned if I know what difference it will make to kids in classrooms.' We turn in surprise. It is Jack.

'Nothing personal, of course, but I'm the sort who speaks his mind.'

Reader says: 'Yes, we've all tried and failed to speak our minds and be fully present (or absent). Well, apart from the stranger over there who's yet to speak to anyone. It doesn't matter how often we take the roll call or who takes it or how loudly we shout "present" (or absent) it still turns out that somebody or at least some part is still missing from the register, or that people are less and less sure of whether they're all there, or all not. Our identities have become like truants, and our truancy ever-present. Or like poor Author Munby here, no longer sure where they begin and end. The fact is that Humpty Dumpty had a Great Fall, and all the "referring" in the world won't put Humpty back together again . . .'

Text: 'It's all very well winding up Modernism but what goes in its place?'

'. . . as indeed the self-consuming pig on the Plumrose Ham tin tried to warn us all those pages ago,' Footnote comments. 'Each attempt at reference succeeds as a visual message (we know what the pig's up to), insinuates the impossibility of such reference completing itself (the pig can't finish referring) and establishes the morally ambivalent injunction "eat me". Do we end up accepting the recommendation of a pig that begs us to eat him? No wonder we feel squeamish.'

'I've got some sympathy with Jack, though. We need a programme of action – what happens in classrooms as a result of this stuff? Or workplaces? Hasn't this just become a game, an abdication of responsibility? I'll accept that some of my earlier posturing was a bit cocksure but it seems so pathetic to just accept the status of flotsam washed up on a beached paradigm. Can we no longer decide anything?'

'Well, that is the big question according to lots of people,' says Footnote. 'Yeatman reckons there's the "positives" and the "negatives". Though you get a bit suspicious if things pan out that neatly after all this heart-searching about "difference". The positives have a "more or less ironically inflected, skeptical, playful but fundamentally quietist relationship to postmodernism" while the critics get rescued from the nastily conservative possibilities of a nihilistic pluralism by "an emancipatory politics of exploring what it means to develop the pragmatics of self-determination when there is no self in question, only selves who are positioned in different ways" (Yeatman, 1991). That's an anthropological version, but the other disciplines are much the same in the kinds of rescues they undertake.'

Reader: 'I don't trust that kind of rescue. There's lots who'll sidle up to you and say, "Pssst, want to see a *clean* postcard." It usually turns out to be a smudgy photo of Habermas's public parts – the life-world bits.'

Text says: 'This certainly is an "irresolvably complex polyphony of voices" as Yeatman says, but I just can't see how she leaps from that (about which we can agree) to the possibility of "provisional, negotiated agreements". That "irresolvable" didn't last very long. We can only agree that we disagree, and a reconciliatory grammar of "pragmatics", "negotiation" and "coming together" just seems to smuggle in the same old transcendental fix in drag. The problem seems to be that now that we know that nobody's all there and that nothing is certain any more, we can't count on anything.'

'Yesss,' says the Author slowly, 'in fact I've just realized . . . that we can't even count on not being able to count on anything. I think that's serious . . . but I could be wrong . . . on the other hand . . .'

'Oh, shut up Author.' I'm getting a bit desperate by this stage to at least try for a way forward to some sort of rational consensus. But they go for me over that last suggestion.

'Look,' says the Reader, 'the very architecture of this meeting is wrong. Tucked away in this layout is a forlorn hope that some kind of free speech situation will provide a way forward. It won't, we've proved that as well, along with the hopelessness of "compass" words like "forward". This sort of exitwork is a deadend.'

'Well,' I say sarcastically, 'how will it help if all we do is go in more intelligent circles, then?'

The stranger speaks up, introducing himself as Readings. 'Relax,' he says, 'circles will do nicely, so long as we always acknowledge that they're not really circles, that we can never define or describe them precisely.' 'You can't describe a perfect circle?' asks Footnote, rummaging in her memory. 'Surely a perfect circle has already been described?'

'No,' he replies, 'not possible without falling into logocentric error – wherein "to tell the truth is to produce a phrase whose meaning can state the being of a thing or phrase exhaustively". So we have to aim for a "transformative displacement of the field of representation rather than the innovative discovery of new modes of representation characteristic of the modernist avant garde"' (Readings, 1991). 'To quote yourself,' he adds, 'is the sincerest form of flattery.'

From my point of view, beleagured between the circle and the window, that sounds like a much-needed alibi. Although it's not one you can imagine giving to some policing Reader. I eye the one in the group that I don't know and who still hasn't spoken. Readers are a scary lot, as Calvino noted: 'I sit at the desk with my back to the window, and there, behind me, I feel an eye that sucks up the flow of the sentences, leads the story in directions that elude me. Readers are my vampires.'

It reminds me of broken sleep the night before. The police surveillance helicopter drones through the early hours of the morning, provoking a long exchange between a nearby owl and its far-off mate. I think: are they confessing their mice? Are we? 'Yes and no,' says Readings. The key is the kind of ontology that we presume. He wants a 'founding hesitation', which reminds Reader of Lyotard's ideal of the stuttering text, where we read it as it fails, or Derrida's notion of being true to the text's necessary betrayal (Kamuf): 'none of your victory narratives here, I'm afraid. The question is: can we successfully fail such stories and in so doing be true to the betrayal inherent in that task?'

Footnote: 'Lyotard says "this is what happens when the stuttering no longer affects preexisting words, but, rather, itself ushers in the words that it affects ... it is the writer who stutters in the language system."'

'Still not very keen on that French stuff,' says Author. 'Intellectually I'm a boiled-beef-and-two-veg. man.'

'Yes,' says Text, 'but maybe it's time to move on. These days the two veg. are the people who ate the beef.'

'Right,' I say. 'I'm getting the idea. We have to *perform* an ending, we can't describe one without destroying and contradicting the very things that interest us – like unrepresentability, undecidability. So let's abandon the discussion group and start a role play, stressing the hesitations and uncertainties of communication.'

'No,' they all say, 'you've missed the point again.'

'... as all authors in the moment of speaking must miss the point.' Reader somewhat wearily indicates that the point about the performance is that the ending will already have happened, long before this conclusion which can be no more than an epitaph. We're apparently not working at the ending here, but at the beginning – which of course started in the middle. My head spins.

'You can't end things that aren't linear with conclusions. If there's a last word then it's somewhere in the text, anywhere, but not – not ever – "the actual last word".'

'Oh.' I walk to the window feeling foolish, stare out at the driving rain and the image of myself looking in, and say, a bit lamely, 'So you mean we've already finished?' But when I turn back to the group they've all gone, except for the silent one, who gives me a look I fear. Footnote, however, true to type – I always had a soft spot for footnotes – has scribbled a note and left it on the chair. The silent stranger beside me, I pick it up, and turn towards the window so that the light falls on it. It is illegible.

We turn it over. It says: 'If an introduction could counteract the images of completion, then . . .'

References

Baudrillard, J. (1989) *America*. London: Verso.
Calvino, I. (1982) *If on a Winter's Night a Traveller*. London: Mandarin.
Kamuf, P. (ed.) (1991) *A Derrida Reader: Between the Blinds*. New York: Columbia University Press.
Readings, B. (1991) *Introducing Lyotard: Art and Politics*. London: Routledge.
Yeatman, A. (1991) Postmodern critical theorizing: introduction. *Social Analysis*, 30, 3–9.

Appendix 1: The R & R instrument

Special Educational Needs Training Report-and-Respond Questionnaire

Stirling University has been asked to evaluate Strathclyde Region's modular training programme for Special Educational Needs. A number of staff have already been interviewed. This interim report-and-respond questionnaire aims to:

- inform you of findings so far
- obtain your views
- collect evidence that will inform overall judgement of the programme.

We ask you to say if you agree (✔) or disagree (✗) with statements from the interviews. Please also add your own issues and comments below the statements or at the end of the questionnaire/report. We would be grateful if you would return the completed questionnaire to us (using the prepaid envelope) by <u>Monday 5 June 1995.</u>

Introduction
Teachers commented on 6 aspects of the modular programme on which we would welcome your opinion. These are: <u>overall impact, changes to professional role, understanding of SEN, integration of theory and practice, delivery of modules</u> and <u>support</u>. They also told us about the patterns of training best suited to them and we are asking you to do the same. Finally, the teachers suggested a number of <u>improvements to the programme</u>.

First, some general questions about you:
1 What is your present role? (e.g. teacher in a special school)

2 Please list the modules you have taken so far and at which institution (e.g. EBDii at St Andrew's College). [Include only daytime and Strathclyde Region funded modules.]

[In questions 3–7, please place ✓ or × in brackets to show agreement or disagreement. Leave blank if not relevant. Add any comments or qualifications in the space below.]

3 Overall impact

Overall, teachers thought the modular training programme had a good impact on their perceptions of their role as SEN teachers ( ), confidence ( ) and credibility among colleagues ( ). [Comments, additions?]

4 Changes to professional role

Most teachers reported some positive changes following training: they felt they had become more reflective ( ), had changed some of their ideas about practice ( ), and that their relationships with their pupils had improved ( ). Some reported negative effects, such as tensions in relationships with colleagues ( ) and pressure from a heavy workload ( ). [Comments, additions?] Research and Evaluation Service, Department of Education, University of Stirling

Research and Evaluation Service, Department of Education, University of Stirling.

Appendix 2: An example of an R & R response

5 Understanding of SEN

Teachers commented on how training helped them to gain a better understanding of SEN issues, particularly in relation to: the nature of learning in general (✔); the needs of all children within the school (✔); and the needs of the population of pupils already identified as having SEN (✔). In addition teachers claimed that they had a better understanding of the changing context of SEN (✔), and of the possible roles of parents (✔). [Comments, additions?]

Yes, knowledge extended in all areas

6 Integration of theory and practice

Teachers said that the modular programme helped them make better connections between theory and practice (✔) . They offered a number of reasons for this: alternating SEN modules with experience in school helped them make connections between the two (✔); they were able to discuss and resolve day-to-day teaching problems during the modules (✗); and it was possible to try out new strategies on return to school (✗). In general, teachers seemd to find that the modules were suitable for their own practice (✗), and that the modules were relevant to *Every Child is Special* (✔), and to their own establishment's development plans (✗). They believed that the modules were relevant to their professional aims (✔). [Comments, additions?]

*modules may have been more suitable for mainstream s
certainly the assignments were geared to being in one place.
work. Peripatetic staff in Support Services generally had to
the assignments or provide alternative suggestions. Because
way the division operates at present with specialist servic
on a peripatetic basis, the focus for possible assignments
considerably narrowed.*

7   Support

The following sources of support were appreciated by teachers: exchanging materials with course members (✔); establishing new contacts (✔); good support from college tutors (✗), from SEN Advisors (✔), and through group tutorials (✔). [Comments, additions?]

Other course members provided lots of information on a variet different aspects of SEN r offered reciprocal visits, advice on s course members are very supportive of each other support tutors varied considerably

8   Delivery of modules

There were positive and negative comments from the teachers. Overall, the modules were thought to have been well taught(✔), and outside speakers to have been informative (✔). The balance between generic and specialist modules was good (✔) and connections between modules on the certificate course were clear (✔). On the other hand, there were some negative features. Choices of modules were restricted (✔), and connections between modules on the diploma course were not clear (✔). Progression of students through the course was not monitored (✔). In addition, some teachers perceived differences in the nature of the training experiences in the different institutions (✔). [Please specify any such differences, as well as adding other positive or negative perceptions of your own.]

management module at St. Andrew's was excellent, although it was one approached with least enthusiasm. There was a wide varie learning styles adopted, with outside speakers, group discussions, learning support (post primary 11) was appalling! — rehash of post pr but with no clear thread running through it. I am also sick "workshops" and "brainstorming" and "flip charts" — it seemed the modules that these r were 'time fillers"

Research and Evaluation Service, Department of Education, University of Stirling

Only at St. Andrew's — se no experience of Jordanhill

* SEN Advisor told us that no matter where we enrolled, both Jordanhill r St. Andrew's libraries were at our disposal — not so! The individual person can use only the library of the college at which one is doing a module — the library staff at St. Andrew's are very helpful but facilities are pretty awful!

Appendix 3: Reminder poem

A reminder: ode to Strathclyde's Special Needs Questionnaire

We've a Special Need
To get your decision
On Strathclyde's training provision.
Was it good? was it bad?
If we can't find out we'll be very sad.
(And they'll be mad).

So please please please:
Fill in our form
Before you leave for Benidorm;
Before departure for Buenos Aires
Complete the questionnaires;
Give us your patter
Before flying to Ulaan Bator; [that's enough – ed.]
And tell us what you think
Before you leave for Hel(a)sink
i.
[you're fired – ed.]

References

Adams, A., Leach, R. and Palmer, R. (1977) *Feasts and Seasons*. Glasgow: Blackie.

Alexander, R. *et al.* (1993) *Education – Putting the Record Straight*. Stafford: Network Education Press.

Allan, J. (1995) Foucault and special education needs: an analysis of discourses, unpublished PhD thesis, University of Stirling.

Allan, J., Brown, S. and Riddell, S. (1995) *Special Educational Needs Provision in Mainstream and Special Schools*. Final Report to the SOED. Stirling: Department of Education, University of Stirling.

Allan, J. and Stronach, I. (1995) *Evaluation of Modular Training Provision for Special Education*. Stirling: Research and Evaluation Service, Department of Education, University of Stirling.

Appadurai, A. (1986) *The Social Life of Things. Commodities in Cultural Perspective*. Cambridge: Cambridge University Press.

Appadurai, A. (1995) The production of locality. In R. Fardon (ed.) *Counterworks. Managing the Diversity of Knowledge*. London: Routledge.

Aronowitz, S. and Giroux, H. (1991) *Postmodern Education*. Minneapolis: University of Minnesota Press.

Ashmore, M. (1989) *The Reflexive Thesis: Wrighting Sociology of Scientific Knowledge*. Chicago: University of Chicago Press.

Aspden, P. (1994) Carp pool reflections on the art of doubt, *The Times Higher Education Supplement*, 22 April.

Association of University Teachers (AUT) (1995) *Commitment Betrayed*. London: AUT.

Augé, M. (1995) *Non-places. Introduction to an Anthropology of Supermodernity* (trans. J. Howe). London: Verso.

Babcock, B. (ed.) (1972) *The Reversible World: Symbolic Inversion in Art and Society*. Ithaca, NY: Cornell.

Bakhtin, M. (1981) *The Dialogic Imagination: Four Essays* (ed. M. Holquist; trans. C. Emerson and M. Holquist). Austin: University of Texas Press.

Banks, M. (1939) Scottish lore of earth, its fruits, and the plough, *Folklore*, 44(1), 12–32.

Banks, M. (1946) *British Calendar Customs. Orkney and Shetland*. London: Folklore Society/Glaisher.

Barzilai, S. (1990) Lemmata/Lemmala: frames for Derrida's parerga, *Diacritics*, 20(1), 5–15.

Bassey, M. (1993) Some FRIPPERIES AND FLAWS of research papers suggested by Michael Bassey. *Research Intelligence* (Newsletter of the British Educational Research Association), 48, Winter, 21.

Bates, T. (1989) Versions of vocationalism: an analysis of some social and political influences on curriculum policy and practice, *British Journal of Sociology of Education*, 10(2), 215–31.

Battaglia, D. (ed.) (1995) *Rhetorics of Self-making*. Berkeley: University of California Press.

Baudrillard, J. (1975) *The Mirror of Production* (trans. M. Poster). St Louis: Telos.

Baudrillard, J. (1989) *America*. London: Verso.

Baumann, Z. (1988) Is there a postmodern sociology?, *Theory, Culture & Society*, 5(22/3), 219–36.

Beckett, S. (1994) *The Unnamable*. London: Calder.

Belsey, C. (1980) *Critical Practice*. London: Routledge.

Belson, W. (1981) *Validity in Survey Research*. Aldershot: Gower.

Belson, W. (1986) *The Design and Understanding of Survey Questions*. Aldershot: Gower.

Benhabib, S. (1992) *Situating the Self: Gender, Community and Postmodernism in Contemporary Ethics*. Cambridge: Polity Press.

Berleant, A. (1994) The critical aesthetics of Disney World, *Journal of Applied Philosophy*, 11(2), 171–80.

Bhabha, H.K. (1994) *The Location of Culture*. London: Routledge.

Binns, R. (1989) A beast of our imaginings, *The Times Higher Education Supplement*, 25 August.

Blakey, J. and Everett-Turner, L. (1988) Seeing the many faces of beginning teachers. Paper presented to the Conference of the International Study Association on Teacher Thinking, Nottingham, September.

Boundas, C. and Olkowski, D. (eds) (1994) *Gilles Deleuze and the Theatre of Philosophy*. New York: Routledge.

Braidotti, R. (1991) *Patterns of Dissonance. The Study of Women in Contemporary Philosophy* (trans. E. Guild). Cambridge: Polity Press.

Braidotti, R. (1993) Embodiment, sexual difference and the nomadic subject, *Hyptatia*, 8(1), 1–13.

Brampton, S. (1993) Fashion page, *The Guardian*, 14 October.

Bruck, P. (1992) Crisis as spectacle: tabloid news and the politics of outrage. In M. Raboy and B. Dagenais (eds) *Media, Crisis and Democracy. Mass Communication and the Disruption of Social Order*. London: Sage.

Burglass, C. (1994) Postmodern value. In S. Earnshaw (ed.) *Postmodern Surroundings*, Postmodern Studies 9. Atlanta: Radolphi.

Burne, C. S. (1914) *The Handbook of Folklore*. London: Sidgwick & Jackson.

Butler, J. (1990) Gender trouble, feminist theory, and psychoanalytic discourse. In L. Nicholson (ed.) *Feminism/Postmodernism*. London: Routledge.

Butler, J. (1992) Contingent foundations: feminism and the question of 'postmodernism'. In J. Butler and J.W. Scott (eds) *Feminists Theorize the Political*. London: Routledge.

Butt, R., Raymond, D., McCue, G. and Yamagishi, L. (1992) Collaborative autobiography and the teacher's voice. In I. Goodson (ed.) *Studying Teachers' Lives*. London: Routledge.

Button, G. (ed.) (1991) *Ethnomethodology and the Human Sciences*. Cambridge: Cambridge University Press.

Calhoun, C. (1993) Postmodernism as pseudohistory, *Theory, Culture & Society*, 10, 75–96.

Calvino, I. (1993) From the opaque. In *The Road to San Giovanni* (trans. R. Parks). London: Jonathan Cape.

Calvino, I. (1982) *If on a Winter's Night a Traveller*. London: Picador.

Carr, W. (1995) Education and democracy: confronting the postmodernist challenge, *Journal of Philosophy of Education*, 29(1), 75–91.

Carter, A. (1984) *Nights at the Circus*. London: Chatto & Windus.

Cawte, E. (1978) *Ritual Animal Disguise. A Historical and Geographical Study of Animal Disguise*. Cambridge: Brewer/Folklore Society.

Clark, T. (1992) *Derrida, Heidegger, Blanchot. Sources of Derrida's Notion and Practice of Literature*. Cambridge: Cambridge University Press.

Clifford, J. and Marcus, G. (1986) *Writing Culture: the Poetics and Politics of Ethnography*. Berkeley: University of California Press.

Coetzee, J (1982) *Waiting for the Barbarians*. Harmondsworth: Penguin.

Connolly, W. (1987) *Politics and Ambiguity*. Madison: University of Wisconsin.

Connor, S. (1989) *Postmodernist Culture: an Introduction to Theories of the Contemporary*. Oxford: Blackwell.

Connor, S. (1992) *Theory and Cultural Value*. Oxford: Blackwell.

Cooper, R. and Burrell, G. (1988) Modernism, postmodernism and organizational analysis, *Organisational Studies*, 9(1), 91–112.

Corbett, J. (1993) Postmodernism and the 'special needs' metaphors, *Oxford Review of Education*, 19(4), 547–53.

Cornell, D., Rosenfeld, M. and Carlson, D. (eds) (1992) *Deconstruction and the Possibility of Justice*. London: Routledge.

Cosman, M. (1981) *Medieval Holidays and Festivals: A Calendar of Celebrations*. New York: Scribner.

Couture, J.-C. (1994) Dracula as action researcher, *Educational Action Research*, 2(1), 127–32.

Crawford, P. (1992) Appearance skills. The art of visual impact in self-development, *Industrial and Commercial Training*, 24(1), 18–21.

Cuban, L. (1990) Reforming again, again and again, *Educational Researcher*, 19(1), 3–13.

Culler, J. (1983) *On Deconstruction. Theory and Criticism after Structuralism*. London: Routledge.

Dadds, M. (1992) Monty Python and the Three Wise Men, *Cambridge Journal of Education*, 22(2), 129–41.

Damarin, S. (1994) Would you rather be a cyborg than a goddess? On being a teacher in a postmodern century. Paper presented to the Annual Meeting of the American Educational Research Association, New Orleans, April.

Davidson, M. (1992) *The Consumerist Manifesto. Advertising in Postmodern Times*. London: Routledge.

De Lauretis, T. (1990) Eccentric subjects, *Feminist Studies*, 16, Spring, 116.

De Man, P. (1982) The resistance to theory, *Yale French Studies*, 63, 3–20.

Deem, R. (1996) BERA Council consultation: chartered status for educational researchers? *Research Intelligence* (Newsletter of the British Educational Research Association), 56, April, 22.

Deleuze, G. and Guattari, F. (1988) *A Thousand Plateaus. Capitalism and Schizophrenia* (trans. B. Massumi). London: Athlone.

Denüvo, R. (1992) No anthro-apologies, or Der(r)id(a)ing a discipline. In R.H. Brown (ed.) *Writing the Social Text: Poetics and Politics in Social Science Discourse*. New York: de Gruyter.

Denzin, N. (1989) *Interpretive Biography*. London: Sage.

Denzin, N. (1991) *Images of Postmodern Society: Social Theory and Contemporary Cinema*. London: Sage.

Derrida, J. (1976) *Of Grammatology* (trans. G.C. Spivak). Baltimore & London: Johns Hopkins University Press.

Derrida, J. (1977) Limited inc., *Glyph*, 2, 162–254.

Derrida, J. (1978) *Writing and Difference*. London: Routledge.

Derrida, J. (1981) Positions. Interview with J.-L. Houdebine & G. Scarpetta (trans. A. Bass). In J. Derrida, *Positions*. Chicago: University of Chicago Press.

Derrida, J. (1984) *Signsponge* (trans. N. Rand). New York: Columbia University Press.

Derrida, J. (1985) Roundtable on translation (trans. P. Kamuf). In C.V. McDonald (ed.) *The Ear of the Other: Otobiography, Transference, Translation*. New York: Shocken Books, 91–162.
Derrida, J. (1987) Some questions and responses. In N. Fabb *et al.* (eds) *The Linguistics of Writing: Arguments between Language and Literature*. Manchester: Manchester University Press.
Derrida, J. (1990) Some statements and truisms about neologisms, newisms, postisms, parasitisms and other small seisisms. In D. Carroll (ed.) *The States of 'Theory': History, Art and Culture*. New York: Columbia Press.
Derrida, J. (1992) Force of law: the mystical foundation of authority. In D. Cornell, M. Rosenfeld and D. Carlson (eds) *Deconstruction and the Possibility of Justice*. London: Routledge.
Derrida, J. (1994a) The deconstruction of actuality. An interview with Jacques Derrida, *Radical Philosophy*, Autumn, 28–41.
Derrida, J. (1994b) *Spectres of Marx: the State of the Debt, the Work of Mourning and the New International* (trans. P. Kamuf). London: Routledge.
Derrida, J. (1994c) Spectres of Marx, *New Left Review*, 205, 31–58.
Distefano, C. (1990) Dilemmas of difference: feminism, modernity and postmodernism. In L. Nicholson (ed.) *Feminism/Postmodernism*. London: Routledge.
Ditchfield, P. (1901) *Old English Customs Extant at the Present Time. An Account of Local Observances, Festival Customs, and Ancient Ceremonies Yet Surviving in Great Britain*. London: Methuen.
Donzelot, J. (1980) *The Policing of Families: Welfare against the State*. London: Hutchinson.
Douglas, M. (1966) *Purity and Danger: an Analysis of the Concepts of Pollution and Taboo*. London: Ark.
Eadie, J. (1994) Queer, *Paragraph*, 17(3), 244–51.
Earnshaw, S. (ed.) (1994) *Postmodern Surroundings*. Postmodern Studies 9. Atlanta: Radolphi.
Elam, D. (1994) *Feminism and Deconstruction: Ms. en Abyme*. London: Routledge.
Elliott, J. and Sarland, C. (1995) A study of 'teachers as researchers' in the context of award-bearing courses and research degrees, *British Educational Research Journal*, 21(3), 371–86.
Ennew, J. (1994) Time for children or time for adults. In J. Qvortrup *et al.* (eds) *Childhood Matters: Social Theory, Practice and Politics*. Aldershot: Avebury.
Errington, F. and Gewertz, D. (1989) Tourism and anthropology in a postmodern world, *Oceania*, 60, 37–54.
Falk, P. (1988) The past to come, *Economy and Society*, 17(3), 374–94.
Fardon, R. (1995) *Counterworks: Managing the Diversity of Knowledge*. London: Routledge.
Fine, M. (1994) Working the hyphens: reinventing self and other in qualitative research. In N.R. Denzin and Y.S. Lincoln (eds) *Handbook of Qualitative Research*. New York: Sage.
Fitzpatrick, P. (1992) *The Mythology of Modern Law*. London: Routledge.
Flax, J. (1990) Postmodernism and gender relations in feminist theory. In L. Nicholson (ed.) *Feminism/Postmodernism*. London: Routledge.
Foster, H. (1984) (Post)modern polemics, *New German Critique*, 33, 66–78.
Foucault, M. (1977) *Discipline and Punish: the Birth of the Prison* (trans. A. Sheridan). Harmondsworth: Penguin.
Fox-Genovese, E. (1993) 'From separate spheres to dangerous streets': postmodernist feminism and the problem of order, *Social Research*, 60(2), 235–54.
Fraser, N. and Nicholson, L. (1990) Social criticism without philosophy: an encounter between feminism and postmodernism. In L. Nicholson (ed.) *Feminism/Postmodernism*. London: Routledge.
Fukuyama, F. (1992) *The End of History and the Last Man*. Harmondsworth: Penguin.

Fuss, D. (1994) Interior colonies: Franz Fanon and the politics of identification, *Diacritics*, 24(2/3), 20–42.

Garfinkel, H. (1967) *Studies in Ethnomethodology*. Englewood Cliffs, NJ: Prentice Hall.

Geertz, C. (1983) *Local Knowledge. Further Essays in Interpretive Anthropology*. London: Basic Books.

Geertz, C. (1988) *Works and Lives: the Anthropologist as Author*. Cambridge: Polity Press.

Gergen, K (1991) *The Saturated Self: Dilemmas of Identity in Contemporary Life*. New York: Basic Books.

Giddens, A. (1982) *Profiles and Critiques in Social Theory*. London: Macmillan.

Giddens, A. (1990) *The Consequences of Modernity*. Cambridge: Polity Press.

Girard, R. (1977) *Violence and the Sacred* (trans. P. Gregory). Baltimore: Johns Hopkins University Press.

Giroux, H. (1983) *Theory and Resistance in Education. A Pedagogy for the Opposition*. London: Heinemann.

Giroux, H. (1988) Postmodernism and the disccourse of educational criticism, *Journal of Education*, 170(3), 5–30.

Giroux, H. (1991) Democracy and the discourse of difference: towards a politics of border pedagogy, *British Journal of Sociology of Education*, 12(4), 501–19.

Glaser, B. and Strauss, A. (1967) *The Discovery of Grounded Theory: Strategies for Qualitative Research*. Chicago: AVC.

Goffman, E. (1990) *Stigma: Notes on the Management of Spoiled Identity*. Harmondsworth: Penguin (first published 1963).

Goldman, R. (1987) Marketing fragrances: advertising and the production of commodity signs, *Theory, Culture, Society*, 4(4), 691–725.

Goodson, I. (1983) The use of life histories in the study of teaching. In M. Hammersley (ed.) *The Ethnography of Schooling*. Driffield: Nafferton.

Goodson, I. (1995) The story so far: personal knowledge and the political. In J.A. Hatch and R. Wisniewski (eds) *Life History and Narrative*. London: Falmer.

Gough, N. (1994) Manifesting cyborgs in curriculum inquiry. Paper presented to the Annual Meeting of the American Educational Research Association, New Orleans, April.

Gordimer, N. (1988) *A Sport of Nature*. Harmondsworth: Penguin.

Green, A. (1994) Postmodernism and state education, *Journal of Educational Policy*, 9(1), 67–83.

Green, B. (1995) Post-curriculum possibilities: English teaching, cultural politics, and the postmodern turn, *Journal of Curriculum Studies*, 27(4), 391–409.

Griffiths, M. (1992) Making a difference: feminism, postmodernism and the methodology of educational research. Paper presented to the ESRC Seminar on Methodology and Epistemology in Educational Research, Liverpool University, June.

Grossberg, L. (1988) Wandering audiences, nomadic critics, *Cultural Studies*, 2, 377–91.

Haber, J. (1994) *Beyond Postmodern Politics. Lyotard, Rorty, Foucault*. New York: Routledge.

Habermas, J. (1976) *Legitimation Crisis*. London: Heinemann.

Habermas, J. (1987) *The Philosophical Discourse of Modernity. Twelve Lectures* (trans. F. Lawrence). Cambridge: Polity Press.

Hamilton, D. *et al.* (eds) (1978) *Beyond the Numbers Game*. Berkeley, CA: McCutchan.

Hammersley, M. (ed.) (1983) *The Ethnography of Schooling: Methodological Issues*. Driffield: Nafferton.

Hammersley, M. and Atkinson, P. (1983) *Ethnography: Principles and Practices*. London: Routledge.

Handke, P. (1989) *Repetition*. London: Mandarin.

Haraway, D. (1990) A manifesto for cyborgs: science, technology and socialist feminism in the 1980s. In L. Nicholson (ed.) *Feminism/Postmodernism*. London: Routledge.

Haraway, D. (1991) A cyborg manifesto: science, technology and socialist-feminism in the late twentieth century. In D. Haraway *Simians, Cyborgs, and Women: the Reinvention of Nature*. London: Free Association Books.

Haraway, D. (1992) Ecce homo, Ain't (Ar'n't) I a woman, and inappropriate/d others: the human in a post-humanist landscape. In J. Butler and J.W. Scott (eds) *Feminists Theorize the Political*. London: Routledge.

Harding, S. (1990) Feminism, science, and the anti-enlightenment critiques. In L. Nicholson (ed.) *Feminism/Postmodernism*. London: Routledge.

Hargreaves, A. (1994a) Restructuring restructuring: postmodernity and the prospects for educational change, *Journal of Educational Policy*, 9(1), 47–65.

Hargreaves, A. (1994b) *Changing Teachers, Changing Times. Teachers' Work and Culture in the Postmodern Age*. London: Cassell.

Harland, J. and Wilkinson, T. (1882) *Lancashire Legends, Traditions, Sports etc.* Manchester: Heywood.

Harvey, D. (1989) *The Condition of Postmodernity*. Cambridge: Polity Press.

Harvey, I. (1986) *Derrida and the Economy of Différance*. Bloomington: Indiana University Press.

Hebdige, D. (1989) *Hiding in the Light*. London: Routledge.

Hiley, M. (1979) *Victorian Working Women: Portraits from Life*. London: Gordon Fraser.

Hix, H. (1993) Postmodern grief, *Philosophy and Literature*, 17, 47–64.

Hobsbawm, E. and Ranger, T. (1983) *The Invention of Tradition*. Cambridge: Cambridge University Press.

Hole, C. (1960) Winter bonfires, *Folklore*, 71, 217–27.

House, E. (1980) *Evaluating with Validity*. Beverley Hills: Sage.

Hsushius, L. (1994) Freeing ourselves from objectivity: managing subjectivity or turning toward a participatory mode of consciousness, *Educational Researcher*, 23(3), 15–22.

Hudson, D. (ed.) (1974) *Munby: Man of Two Worlds*. London: Sphere/Abacus.

Hunt, R. (1984) *Ghosts, Witches, and Things Like That*. Oxford: Oxford University Press.

Hutton, R. (1994) *The Rise and Fall of Merry England. The Ritual Year 1400–1700*. Oxford: Oxford University Press.

Huyssen, A. (1990) Mapping the postmodern. In L. Nicholson (ed.) *Feminism/Postmodernism*. London: Routledge.

Iragaray, L. (1985) *Speculum of the Other Woman* (trans. G. Gill). New York: Cornell (first published 1974).

James, W. (1988) *The Listening Ebony. Moral Knowledge, Religion and Power among the Uduk of Sudan*. Oxford: Clarendon.

Jameson, F. (1983) Postmodernism: the cultural logic of late capitalism, *New Left Review*, 146, 15–67.

Jameson, F. (1988) Postmodernism and consumer society. In E. Kaplan (ed.) *Postmodernism and Its Discontents. Theories, Practices*. London: Verso.

Jayyusi, A. (1984) *Categorization and the Moral Order*. London: Routledge.

Jencks, C. (1991) *The Language of Postmodern Architecture*, 6th edn. London: Academy Editions (first published 1977).

Johnson, B. (1977) The frame of reference: Poe, Lacan, Derrida, *Yale French Studies*, 55/56, 457–505.

Johnson, B. (1981) Note to J. Derrida's 'The double session'. In J. Derrida, *Dissemination*. Chicago: University of Chicago Press.

Johnson, B. (1994) Double mourning and the public sphere. In B. Johnson, *The Wake of Deconstruction*. Oxford: Blackwell.

Johnson, C. (1993) *System and Writing in the Philosophy of Jacques Derrida*. Cambridge: Cambridge University Press.

Kamuf, P. (ed.) (1991) *A Derrida Reader. Between the Blinds*. New York: Columbia University Press.

Kaplan, E. A. (1990) *Psychoanalysis and Cinema*. London: Routledge.

Keiser, T. (1991) Negotiating with a customer you can't afford to lose. In W. Hume (ed.) *The Art of Business Negotiation*. Cambridge, MA: Harvard Business Review Paperback.

Kellner, D. (1988) Reading images critically: toward a postmodern pedagogy, *Journal of Education*, 170(3), 31–52.

Kemmis, S. (1992) Postmodernism and educational research. Paper presented to an ESRC Seminar on Methodology and Epistemology in Educational Research, University of Liverpool, June.

Kliebard, A. (1991) Vocational education as symbolic action: connecting schooling with the workplace, *American Educational Research Journal*, 27(1), 9–26.

Knight, D. (1994) Selves, interpreters, narrators, *Philosophy and Literature*, 18(2), 274–86.

Knorr-Cetina, K. (1994) Primitive classification and postmodernity: towards a socio-logical notion of fiction, *Theory, Culture & Society*, 11, 1–22.

Kuhn, T. (1970) *The Structure of Scientific Revolutions*, 2nd edn. Chicago: University of Chicago (first published 1962).

Kuklick, H. (1991) *The Savage Within. The Social History of British Anthropology 1885–1945*. Cambridge: Cambridge University Press.

Landau, I. (1994) What's old in Derrida?, *Philosophy*, 69, 279–91.

Lane, C. (1981) *The Rites of Rulers: Ritual in Industrial Society. The Soviet Case*. Cambridge: Cambridge University Press.

Lash, S. (1987) A critical theory in 'disorganized capitalism', *Economy and Society*, 16(1), 151–7.

Lather, P. (1991a) *Feminist Research in Education: Within/Against*. Victoria, Australia: Deakin University Press.

Lather, P. (1991b) *Getting Smart: Feminist Research and Pedagogy with/in the Postmodern*. London: Routledge.

Lather, P. (1993) Fertile obsession: validity after poststructuralism, *Sociological Quarterly*, 34(4), 673–93.

Lather, P. (1994) Textuality as praxis. Paper presented to the Annual Meeting of the American Educational Research Association, New Orleans, April.

Lather, P. (1996) Methodology as subversive repetition: practices toward a feminist double science. Paper presented to the Annual Meeting of the American Educational Research Association, New York, April.

Latour, B. (1990) Postmodern? No, simply amodern! Steps towards an anthropology of science, *Studies in the History and Philosophy of Science*, 21(1), 145–71.

Latour, B. (1993) *What Does It Mean to Be Modern?* London: Harvester Wheatsheaf.

Leach, M. (ed.) (1949) *Standard Dictionary of Folklore, Mythology and Legend*. New York: Funk & Wagnall.

Leguin, U. (1981) It was a dark and stormy night. In W. Mitchell (ed.) *On Narrative*. Chicago: Chicago University Press.

Linstead, S. and Grafton-Small, R. (1990) Theory as artefact: artefact as theory. In P. Gagliardi (ed.) *Symbols and Artefacts: Views of the Corporate Landscape*. Berlin: Walter de Gruyter.

Liszka, J. (1983) Derrida: philosophy of the liminal, *Man and World*, 16, 233–50.

Lugones, M. (1992) On 'Borderlands/La Frontera': an interpretive essay, *Hypatia*, 7(4), 31–7.

Luke, C. and Gore, J. (1992) *Feminisms and Critical Pedagogy*. London: Routledge.

Lynd, R. and Lynd, H. (1929) *Middletown. A Study in American Culture*. New York: Harcourt, Brace.

Lyotard, J.-F. (1984) *The Postmodern Condition: a Report on Knowledge* (trans. G. Bennington and B. Massumi). Manchester: Manchester University Press.

McCarthy, T. (1991) *Ideals and Illusions. On Reconstruction and Deconstruction in Contemporary Critical Theory*. Cambridge, MA: MIT.

McCrone, D. (1992) *Understanding Scotland: The Sociology of a Stateless Nation*. London: Routledge.

Macdonald, B. and Walker, R. (1976) *Changing the Curriculum*. London: Open Books.

McHale, B. (1987) *Postmodernist Fiction*. London: Methuen.

Macherey, P. (1978) *A Theory of Literary Production* (trans. Geoffrey Wall). London: Routledge.

McLaren, P. (1993a) Review article – postmodernity and the death of politics: a Brazilian reprieve, *Educational Theory*, 36(4), 389–401.

McLaren, P. (1993b) Multiculturalism and the postmodern critique: towards a pedagogy of resistance and transformation, *Cultural Studies*, 7(1), 118–46.

McLeod, J. (1994) Postmodernism and postcolonialism. In S. Earnshaw (ed.) *Postmodern Surroundings*. Postmodern Studies 9. Atlanta: Radolphi.

MacLure, M. (1993) Arguing for your self: identity as an organising principle in teachers' jobs and lives, *British Educational Research Journal*, 19, 311–22.

MacLure, M. (1994) Language and discourse: the embrace of uncertainty. Review essay, *British Journal of Sociology of Education*, 15(2), 283–300.

MacLure, M. (1995) Postmodernism: a postscript, *Educational Action Research*, 3(1), 105–16.

MacLure, M., Elliott, J., Marr, A. and Stronach, I. (1990) *Teachers' Jobs and Lives (Phase 2)*. End of award report to the Economic and Social Research Council. Norwich: CARE, University of East Anglia.

McWilliam, E. (1992) Towards advocacy: post-positivist directions for progressive teacher education, *British Journal of Sociology of Education*, 13(1), 3–17.

Maker, W. (1992) (Post)modern tales from the crypt: the night of the Zombie philosophers, *Metaphilosophy*, 23(4), 311–28.

Mann, P. (1995) Stupid undergrounds, *Postmodern Culture*, 5, 3.

Manning-Sanders, R. (1972) *Festivals*. London: Heinemann.

Marcus, G. and Fischer, M. (1986) *Anthropology as Cultural Critique. An Experimental Moment in the Human Sciences*. Chicago: University of Chicago Press.

Martin, E. (1994) *Flexible Bodies. Tracking Immunity in American Culture – from the Days of Polio to the Age of AIDS*. Boston: Beacon.

May, R. (1984) *Halloween*. Hove: Wayland.

Mead, M. (ed.) (1959) *An Anthropologist at Work: Writings of Ruth Benedict*.

Measor, L. and Sikes, P. (1992) Visiting lives: ethics and methodology in life history. In I. Goodson (ed.) *Studying Teachers' Lives*. London: Routledge.

Merson, M. (1992) The four ages of TVEI: a review of policy, *British Journal of Education and Work*, 5(2), 5–18.

Michelfelder, D. and Palmer, R. (eds) (1989) *Dialogue and Deconstruction. The Gadamer–Derrida Encounter*. Albany, NY: SUNY Press.

Moore, H. (1994) *A Passion for Difference. Essays in Anthropology and Gender*. Cambridge: Polity Press.

Morris, B. and Stronach, I. (1993) *Evaluation of the Management of Change: Tayside TVEI*. Stirling: Department of Education, University of Stirling, Research and Evaluation Service.

Musil, R. (1960) *The Man without Qualities* (3 vols). London: Secker & Warburg.

Nias, J. (1989) *Primary Teachers Talking: a Study of Teaching as Work*. London: Routledge.

Nicchols, P. (1991) Divergences: modernism, Jameson and Lyotard, *Critical Quarterly*, 33(3), 1–18.

Nicholson, L. (ed.) (1990) *Feminism/Postmodernism*. London: Routledge.

Nisbet, J. (1995) *Educational Research in Scotland 1984–93*. Aberdeen: Department of Education, University of Aberdeen.

Noth, W. (1988) The language of commodities. Groundwork for a semiotics of consumer goods, *International Journal of Research in Marketing*, 4, 173–86.

Nye, A. (1991). Review of 'Feminism/postmodernism', *Hyptatia*, 6(2), 228–33.

O'Neil, W. (1975) *Time and the Calendars*. Manchester: Manchester University Press.

Ong, A. (1996) Anthropology, China and modernities. The geopolitics of cultural knowledge. In II. Moore (ed.) *The Future of Anthropological Knowledge*. London: Routledge.

Paechter, C. and Weiner, G. (1996) Editorial, *British Educational Research Journal*, Special issue: Post-modernism and post-structuralism in educational research, 22(3), 267–72.

Parton, H. (1994) Problematics of government, (post)modernity and social work, *Journal of Social Work*, 24, 9–32.

Patai, D. (1994) US academics and Third World women: is ethical research possible? In S. Gluck and D. Patai (eds) *Women's Words: the Feminist Practice of Oral History*. New York: Routledge.

Pearson, N. (1972) *Stories of Special Days and Customs*. Loughborough: Ladybird.

Pefanis, J. (1991) *Heterology and the Postmodern: Bataille, Baudrillard, and Lyotard*. Durham, NC: Duke University Press.

Peshkin, A. (1988) In search of subjectivity – one's own, *Educational Researcher*, 17(7), 17–21.

Peters, T. (1993) Road to the great beyond, *Observer*, 7 November.

Pettigrew, M. and Norris, N. (1993) *Expand and Contract: the Conditions of Government-sponsored Research*. Norwich: CARE, University of East Anglia.

Philipse, H. (1994) Towards a postmodern conception of metaphysics: on the genealogy and successor disciplines of modern philosophy, *Metaphilosophy*, 25(1), 1–44.

Phillipson, M. (1989) *In Modernity's Wake. The Ameurunculus Letters*. New York: Routledge.

Pool, R. (1991) Postmodern ethnography?, *Critique of Anthropology*, 11(4), 309–31.

Proulx, E.A. (1993) *The Shipping News*. London: Fourth Estate.'

Rand, N. (1986) Translator's introduction. In N. Abraham and Maria Torok, *The Wolf Man's Magic Word: a Cryptonomy* (foreword by J. Derrida). Minnesota: University of Minneapolis Press.

Ranson, S. (1996) The future of education research: learning at the centre, *British Educational Research Journal*, 22(5), 523–35.

Rasché, R. (1986) *The Tain of the Mirror*. Cambridge, MA: Harvard University Press.

Readings, B. (1991) *Introducing Lyotard. Art and Politics*. London: Routledge.

Rée, J. (1990) Dedicated followers of fashion, *Times Higher Education Supplement*, 25 May.

Ricoeur, P. (1981) Narrative time. In W. Mitchell (ed.) *On Narrative*. Chicago: University of Chicago Press.

Ricoeur, P. (1985) The text as dynamic entity. In M.J. Valdez and O. Miller (eds) *Identity of the Literary Text*. Toronto: Toronto University Press.

Risser, J. (1989) The two faces of Socrates. In D. Michelfelder and R. Palmer (eds) *Dialogue and Deconstruction. The Gadamer–Derrida Encounter*. Albany, NY: SUNY Press.

Rosaldo, R. (1978) The rhetoric of control: Ilongots viewed as natural bandits and wild Indians. In B. Babcock (ed.) *The Reversible World: Symbolic Inversion in Art and Society*. Ithaca, NY: Cornell.

Rose, N. and Miller, P. (1992) Political power beyond the state: problematics of government, *British Journal of Sociology*, 43(2), 173–205.

Rowland, G., Rowland, S. and Winter, R. (1990) Writing fiction as enquiry into professional development, *Journal of Curriculum Studies*, 22(3), 291–3.

Royle, N. (1995) *After Derrida*. Manchester: Manchester University Press.

Sahlins, M. (1976) *Culture and Practical Reason*. Chicago: University of Chicago Press.

Sassower, R. (1993) Postmodernism and philosophy of science. A critical engagement, *Philosophy of Social Sciences*, 233(4), 426–45.

Schechner, R. (1993) *The Future of Ritual. Writings on Culture and Performance*. London: Routledge.

Schuel, B. (1985) *The National Trust Guide to Traditional Customs of Britain*. Exeter: Webb and Bower.

Schurmann, R. (1990) *Heidegger on Being and Acting: from Principles to Anarchy* (trans. C.-M. Gros). Bloomington: Indiana University Press.

Schutz, A. (1967) *The Phenomenology of the Social World* (trans. G. Walsh and F. Lehnert). Chicago: Northwestern University Press.

Scott, C. (1987) *The Language of Difference*. Atlantic Highlands, NJ: Humanities Press International.

Seed, J. (1993) To think the present historically . . ., *Fragmente*, 5, 88–97.

Shore, C. (1993) Inventing the 'People's Europe': critical approaches to European 'cultural policy', *Man*, 28(4), 779–800.

Sikes, P.J., Measor, L. and Woods, P. (1985) *Teachers' Careers: Crises and Continuities*. Lewes: Falmer.

Sim, S. (1988) 'Svelte discourse' and the philosophy of caution, *Radical Philosophy*, 49, 31–6.

Simon, R., Dippo, D. and Schenke, A. (1991) *Learning Work: a Critical Pedagogy of Work Education*. New York: Bergen and Garvey.

Simons, H. (1977) Building a social contract. In *SAFARI*. Theory and Practice No. 4. Norwich: CARE, University of East Anglia.

Simons, H. (1986) *Getting to Know Schools in a Democracy*. Lewes: Falmer.

Smith, A. (ed.) (1971) *Stories for All Seasons*. Nutfield: National Christian Education Council.

Smith, R. (1995) *Derrida and Autobiography*. Cambridge: Cambridge University Press.

Sohm, B. (1994) The deconstruction of actuality. An interview with Jacques Derrida, *Radical Philosophy*, Autumn, 28–41.

Sokal, R. (1996) Transgressing the boundaries. Toward a transformative hermeneutics of quantum gravity, *Social Text*, 46/47, 217–52.

Soper, K. (1991) Postmodernism, subjectivity and the question of value, *New Left Review*, 186, 120–8.

Spivak, G.C. (1976) Translator's preface. In J. Derrida, *Of Grammatology*. Baltimore: Johns Hopkins University Press, ix–lxxxvii.

Spivak, G.C. (1988) *In Other Worlds. Essays in Cultural Politics*. London: Routledge.

Spivak, G.C. (1993) *Outside in the Teaching Machine*. London: Routledge.

St. Pierre, E. (1996) Methodology in the fold and the irruption of transgressive data. Paper presented to the Annual Meeting of the American Educational Research Association, New York, April.

Stake, R. (1978) Responsive evaluation. In D. Hamilton *et al.* (eds) *Beyond the Numbers Game*. Berkeley, CA: McCutchan.

Stanley, L. (1984) *The Diaries of Hannah Cullwick. Victorian Maidservant*. London: Virago.

Steele, S. (1986) Deconstructing histories: toward a systematic criticism of psychological narratives. In T.R. Sarbin (ed.) *Narrative Psychology: the Storied Nature of Human Conduct*. London: Praeger.

Storch, R. (1982) 'Please to remember the 5th of November': conflict, solidarity and public order in Southern England 1815–1900. In R. Storch (ed.) *Popular Culture and Custom in 19th Century England*. London: Croom Helm.

Strathern, M. (1991) *Partial Connections*. Savage: Rowman and Littlefield.

Strathern, M. (1995) *Shifting Contexts: Transformations in Anthropological Knowledge*. London: Routledge.

Strauss, A. (1978) *Negotiations. Varieties, Contexts, Processes and Social Order*. San Francisco: Jossey Bass.

Stronach, I. (1989) Education, vocationalism and economic recovery: the case against witchcraft, *British Journal of Education and Work*, 3(1), 5–31.

Stronach, I. (1992) The 'Howie Report': a glossary and a commentary, *Scottish Educational Review*, 24(2), 93–104.

Stronach, I., Cope, P., Inglis, B. and McNally, J. (1994b) The SOED Competence Guidelines for Initial Teacher Training: issues of control, performance and relevance, *Scottish Educational Review*, 26(2), 118–33.

Stronach, I. and MacDonald, B. (1991) *Faces and Futures: an Inquiry into the Jobs, Lives and Careers of Educational Researchers in an ESRC Initiative*. Norwich: CARE, University of East Anglia.

Stronach, I. and Morris, B. (1994a) Polemical notes on educational evaluation in the age of 'policy hysteria', *Evaluation and Research in Education*, 8(1/2), 5–19.

Stronach, I. and Torrance, H. (1995a) The future of evaluation: a retrospective, *Cambridge Journal of Education*, 25(3), 283–99.

Swindells, J. (1989) Liberating the subject? Autobiography and 'women's history': a reading of 'The Diaries of Hannah Cullwick'. In The Personal Narratives Group (eds) *Interpreting Women's Lives. Feminist Theory and Personal Narratives*. Bloomington: Indiana University Press.

Taylor-Gooby, P. (1994) Postmodernism and social policy: a great leap backwards, *Journal of Social Policy*, 23(3), 385–404.

Thompson, H.J. (1973) *Fear and Loathing on the Campaign Trail '72*. London: HarperCollins.

Times Higher Education Supplement (1993) Leader article, 19 November.

Tollefson, K. (1995) Potlatching and political organization among the Northwest Coast Indians, *Ethnology*, 34(1), 53–73.

Trent, C. (1966) *BP Book of Festivals and Events in Britain*. London: Phoenix Books.

Trezise, T. (1993) Foreword to P. Lacoue-Labarthe, *The Subject of Philosophy*. Minneapolis: University of Minnesota Press.

Trinh, M.T. (1989) *Woman, Native, Other: Writing Postcoloniality and Feminism*. Bloomington: Indiana University Press.

Turner, E., Lloyd, J., Stronach, I. and Waterhouse, S. (1994) *Plotting Partnership: Education/Business Links in Scotland*. Report to the Scottish Office Education Department. Stirling: Department of Education, University of Stirling.

Turner, V. (1969) The ritual process: structure and anti-structure. London: RKP.

Turner, V. (1981) *The Drums of Affliction: a Study of Religious Processes among the Ndembu of Zambia*. London: International African Institute/Hutchinson.

Urry, J. (1992) The tourist gaze and the 'environment', *Theory, Culture and Society*, 9, 1–26.

Venkatesh, A., Sherry, J. and Furat, A. (1993) Postmodernism and the marketing imaginary, *International Journal of Research in Marketing*, 10(3), 215–23.

Verges, F. (1992) The unbearable lightness of deconstruction, *Philosophy*, 67, 387–93.

Viswasnaran, K. (1994) *Fictions of Feminist Ethnography*. Minneapolis: University of Minnesota Press.

Wall, J. (1985) *Negotiation: Theory and Practice*. Glenview, IL: Scott, Foresman and Co.

Wallace, G., McCulloch, G. and Evans, J. (1995) Review article: 'Changing teachers, changing times', *British Journal of Sociology of Education*, 16(1), 109–22.

Warwick, D. (1989) *Linking Schools and Industry*. Oxford: Blackwell.

Wigley, M. (1993) *The Architecture of Deconstruction: Derrida's Haunt*. Cambridge, MA: MIT Press.

Wilding, P. (1992) Social policy in the 1980s: an essay on academic evolution, *Social Policy and Administration*, 26(2), 107–16.

Wilkin, M. (1993) Initial training as a case of postmodern development: some implications for monitoring. In D. McIntyre, H. Hagger and M. Wilkin (eds) *Mentoring: Perspectives on School-based Teacher Education*. London: Kogan Page.

Williams, R. and Yeoman, D. (1993) The fate of TVEI in a pilot school: a longitudinal case study, *British Educational Research Journal*, 19(4), 421–34.

Williamson, H. (1992) *PETRA: Research Partnership 1991–92*. Cardiff: University of Wales.

Winter, R. (1991) Post-modern sociology as a democratic educational practice? Some suggestions, *British Journal of Sociology of Education*, 12(4), 467–81.

Wolfe, T. (1988) *Bonfire of the Vanities*. New York: Knopf.

Woods, P. (1985) Conversations with teachers: some aspects of life history method, *British Educational Research Journal*, 11(1), 13–26.

Woods, P. (1993) Managing marginality: teacher development through grounded life history, *British Educational Research Journal*, 19(5), 447–65.

Yeatman, A. (1991) Postmodern critical theorizing: introduction, *Social Analysis*, 30, 3–9.

Zurbrugg, N. (1993) *The Parameters of Postmodernism*. London: Routledge.

Index

Dadds, M., 5
Damarin, S., 131
Davidson, M., 16
deconstruction, 3, 15, 17, 20, 22, 24, 25,
    27, 28, 30–4, 57, 72, 76, 90, 92–4, 97,
    99, 130, 132, 136, 140–2, 146
Deem, R., 6
deferral, 26, 27, 126, 149
Deleuze, G., 19, 84, 93, 94, 95, 97, 147
De Man, P., 7, 13
demystification, 94
Denüvo, r., 11, 25, 85, 155
Denzin, N., 16, 48, 119
Derrida, J., 3, 11, 22–4, 26, 30, 32–3,
    74, 92, 98, 118, 124, 127, 132, 134,
    136, 143, 146, 150, 151, 154, 157,
    166
desire, 65, 134, 147, 149
différance, 10, 126, 134, 148
difference, 22–4, 27, 29, 31, 32, 63–4, 70,
    80, 138, 150
discourse, 'svelte', 94
disorder, 95, 97
Distefano, C., 25, 31
Ditchfield, P., 76
Donne, John, 124
Donzelot, J., 87
Douglas, M., 74, 79
Durkheim, E., 79

Eadie, J., 31
Education Reform Act, 88
Elam, D., 126, 130
emancipation, 11, 19, 73, 74, 151, 152
empowerment, 151, 152
Enlightenment, 5, 17, 21, 22, 25, 59, 84,
    145, 152
Ennew, J., 77
entry work, 122
epiphany, 48, 52, 125, 126
epistemology, 11
    'erratic', 150, 152
Errington, F., 163
essentialism, 16, 20, 27, 114, 134, 151
evaluation, 99
evaluation, 'conformative', 100
Evans-Pritchard, E., 161
exit work, 122, 123, 125

Falk, P., 87, 89, 90
Fanon, F., 23
Fawkes, Guy, 79, 80
feminism, 9, 11, 21, 28, 58
Fine, M., 129
Fitzpatrick, P., 153
Flax, J., 19
flux, 16, 76, 92, 93, 132
fold, 28, 30, 83, 148–9
Foster, H., 86
Foucault, M., 7, 18, 73, 74, 87, 94, 113
foundationalism, 27, 113, 134
Fox-Genovese, E., 17
Fraser, N., 19, 21, 28
Fukuyama, F., 165
Fuss, D., 28

Gadamer, H.–G., 18
'game 1', 102–3, 110, 112, 113
'game 2', 103, 110, 112
'game 3', 103, 110, 112
Garfinkel, H., 131
Geertz, C., 17, 47, 51, 56, 57, 137
Gergen, K., 127
Gewertz, D., 163
ghost, 26, 27, 155
Giroux, H., 14, 19, 21, 24, 25, 102, 113
Glaser, B., 102
Goffman, E., 131
Goldman, R., 17
Goodson, I., 57, 121, 127, 129
Gordimer, Nadine, 23, 32
Gough, N., 131
Green, B., 113
Griffiths, M., 129
Grossberg, L., 19
Guattari, F., 32

Haber, J., 18, 21
Habermas, J., 22, 90, 94
Halloween, 76, 87
Hamilton, D., 102
Hammersley, M., 102
Handke, Peter, 162
Haraway, D., 4, 5, 18, 19, 30, 32, 58, 75,
    126, 128, 130
Harding, S., 22
Hargreaves, A., 9, 20, 21, 25, 101, 112

FOR EDUCATION
TOWARDS CRITICAL EDUCATIONAL ENQUIRY

Wilfred Carr

A recent review of his work describes Wilfred Carr as 'one of the most brilliant philosophers now working in the rich British tradition of educational philosophy . . . His work
is rigorous, refreshing and original . . . and examines a number of fundamental issues
with clarity and penetration.

In *For Education* Wilfred Carr provides a comprehensive justification for reconstructing
educational theory and research as a form of critical inquiry. In doing this, he confronts
a number of important philosophical questions. What is educational theory? What is
an educational practice? How are theory and practice related? What is the role of values
in educational research? Is a genuinely educational science possible? By appealing to
developments in critical theory, the philosophy of science and the philosophy of the
social sciences, Wilfred Carr provides answers to these questions which vindicate the
idea of an educational science that is not 'on' or 'about' education but 'for education'
– a science genuinely committed to promoting educational values and ideals.

Contents
*Introduction: Becoming an educational philosopher – Part 1: Theorizing education – The gap
between theory and practice – Theories of theory and practice – Adopting an educational philosophy – What is an educational practice? – Part 2: Towards a critical educational science –
Can educational research be scientific? – Philosophy, values and an educational science –
Whatever happened to action research? – The idea of an educational science – Epilogue: Confronting the postmodernist challenge – Notes – References – Bibliography – Index.*

160pp   0 335 19186 X (paperback)   0 335 19187 8 (hardback)